Tim Wallace-Murphy studied medicine at University College, Dublin and then qualified as a psychologist. He is now an author, lecturer and historian, and has spent over thirty years following his personal spiritual path. He is co-author of three bestsellers: *The Mark of The Beast*, *Rex Deus: The True Mystery of Rennes-le-Château* and *Rosslyn: Guardian of the Secrets of the Holy Grail*. This last book provided invaluable source material to Dan Brown for his bestselling novel, *The Da Vinci Code*. He lives in Devon.

Also by Tim Wallace-Murphy

The Mark of the Beast (with Trevor Ravenscroft)
The Illustrated Guidebook to Rosslyn Chapel
The Templar Legacy and the Masonic Inheritance within Rosslyn Chapel
Rosslyn: Guardian of the Secrets of the Holy Grail (with Marilyn
  Hopkins)
Rex Deus: The True Mystery of Rennes-le-Château (with Marilyn
  Hopkins and Graham Simmans)
Templars in America: From the Crusades to the New World
  (with Marilyn Hopkins)
Custodians of Truth: The Continuance of Rex Deus (with Marilyn
  Hopkins)

CRACKING THE SYMBOL CODE

REVEALING THE SECRET HERETICAL MESSAGES
WITHIN CHURCH AND RENAISSANCE ART

Tim Wallace-Murphy

WATKINS PUBLISHING

LONDON

First published in the UK in 2005

This edition published in 2006 by
Watkins Publishing, Sixth Floor, Castle House,
75–76 Wells Street, London W1T 3QH

1 3 5 7 9 10 8 6 4 2

Designed and typeset by Jerry Goldie Graphic Design

Printed and bound in Great Britain

British Library Cataloguing-in-Publication data available

ISBN-10: 1-84293-207-1
ISBN-13: 9-781842-932070
www.watkinspublishing.com

Contents

The publisher would like to thank the following people, museums, and photographic libraries for permission to reproduce their material. Every care has been taken to trace copyright holders. However, if we have omitted anyone we apologize and will, if informed, make corrections to any future edition.

List of Plates

Text Illustrations

This work is respectfully dedicated to
a treasured spiritual brother, the renowned Provençal scholar
Guy Jourdan,
Le Mage de Bargemon.

Acknowledgements

While responsibility for this book rests entirely with the author, I gratefully acknowledge the encouragement and insight I have gained over many years of research from: Alexandre Angelitti of Paris; Gerard Bacquet of Auxi le Château; Yves Bacquet of Bargemon, Provence; Stuart Beattie of the Rosslyn Chapel Trust; Richard Beaumont of Staverton, Devon; Dr Marco Bellani of Varese; Dr Anglo Benevento of Varese; Laurence Bloom of London; Robert Brydon of Edinburgh; Richard Buades of Marseilles; Nicole Dawe of Okehampton; Baroness Edni di Pauli of London; William and Heather Elmhirst of Dartington; Dr Reshad Field of the Chalice Foundation; Jean-Michel Garnier of Chartres; Michael Halsey of Auchterarder; Professor Biorn Ivemark of Gramazie; Patrick Keane of Paignton; Georges Keiss of the Centre d'Etudes et de Recherches Templière, Campagne-sur-Aude; J. Z. Knight of the Ramtha School of Enlightenment; Elizabeth Lane of Concord; Robert Lomas of Bradford; Michael Monkton of Buckingham; Dr Hugh Montgomery of Somerset; James Mackay Munro of Penicuick; David Nelson of Lorgues-en-Provence; Andrew Pattison of Edinburgh; Alan Pearson of Rennes-les-Bains; David Pykett of Burton-on-Trent; Amy Ralston of Staverton, Devon; Victor Rosati of Totnes; Pat Sibille of Aberdeen; Niven Sinclair of London; Nicolo and Eleanora Zeno of Venice; and, those who are sadly no longer with us but from whom I have learned so much: William Anderson; Andy Boracci; Anthony Tancred; Frederic Lionel; Trevor Ravenscroft and Michael Bentine. Last, but certainly not least, Duncan Baird, Michael Mann, John Baldock, Penny Stopa and Gillian Holmes, all of Watkins Publishers.

Introduction

The phenomenal sales of Dan Brown's thriller, *The Da Vinci Code*, and the success of Umberto Eco's *Foucault's Pendulum* are a demonstrable sign of the public's growing fascination with the idea that heretical thought has been secretly encoded within religious art. Despite the fictional nature of both *The Da Vinci Code* and *Foucault's Pendulum,* the truth about 'Hidden Symbolism' is far more fascinating than any fiction.

This work is an explanation of the history and importance of symbolism in mankind's long and tortuous exploration of the fascinating world of the spirit: one that focuses heavily on the development of Christian symbolism and then, within that, delineates why and how 'heretical' ideas were kept hidden from the prying eyes of a repressive hierarchy. It demonstrates some of the indicators that will alert astute seekers to the presence of hidden symbolism before introducing them to some of the many layers of meaning conveyed by this truly arcane art form. Direct experience of the mystical effects of sacred symbolism opens up not only the hidden world of the medieval 'heretics' but also the inner world of the viewer leading to transformative experiences that are hand-tailored to the needs and understanding of the individual.

Any study of works such as this should be followed, as soon as possible, by personal on-site visits to view such symbols *in situ*, for sacred symbols need to be experienced rather than explained. What a true symbol expresses is ultimately intangible; it conveys a mystery that can only be felt and cannot be adequately expressed in words. Such a symbol is the mysterious meeting-point between the material and the spiritual, the conscious and the unconscious that will act, at one and the same time, both as a signpost and as a transformative catalyst on the quest for spiritual enlightenment – the true objective of the search for the Holy Grail.

SECTION 1

In the Beginning

The field of symbolism is one that spans the entire history of man, for sacred symbolism pervades and charts almost the entire history of mankind from distant Palaeolithic times to the present. The earliest archaeological artefacts pertaining to man are human bones and primitive stone tools, and even these simple relics seem to possess a spiritual aspect that was noted by Jacob Bronowski in his description of the Taung baby, the primordial infant from which, he claims, the whole adventure of man began. He wrote: 'The human baby, the human being, is a mosaic of animal and angel.'[1] Thus inadvertently putting his finger on one essential difference between man and other animals.

Not surprisingly, mankind's demonstrable spiritual dimension was made manifest in his ability to record spiritual aspirations, knowledge and beliefs in symbolic terms. We have apparently always felt conscious of something strange about ourselves that transcends the day-to-day struggle to survive or the ever-present fear of the unknown – an innate sense that there is another spiritual world that pervades, informs and controls the phenomenal, visible world in which we live. Furthermore, according to Sir Kenneth Clark, mankind has always felt the need to develop these spiritual 'qualities of thought and feeling so that they might approach, as nearly as possible, to an ideal of perfection ... and he has managed to satisfy this need in various ways – through myths, through dance and song, through systems of philosophy and through the order that he has imposed on the visible world.'[2]

John Baldock, an English authority on Christian symbolism, echoed this when he wrote: 'The symbolic meaning contained in the word or image may be presented in any one of a number of forms: legend, myth, allegory, metaphor or analogy. All of these draw on a reality originating, to a variable extent, in this world to express another reality.'[3] The 'other reality' is, of course, spiritual reality. The English writer Colin Wilson claimed that: 'The higher the form of life, the deeper its capacity for registering meaning.'[4] Wilson then went on to describe the key to all poetic and mystical or spiritual experience, which he called Faculty X, and defined this natural ability as 'the latent power that all human beings possess *to reach beyond the present*.'[5] The true significance of this innate capacity has only been recognised by about five per cent of any given population, those whom Wilson describes as 'the Few'. The individuals who became shamans, priests, witch doctors, witches and mediums; natural leaders who, knowing they possessed spiritual powers, sought means to enhance them and put them to use for the benefit of the communities within which they moved.

The mystery investigated by 'the Few' and the absolute necessity of describing its reality in symbolic terms was given form by Nicolas Berdyaeff in the following terms: 'The whole meaning, importance and value of life are determined by the mystery behind it, by an infinity which cannot be rationalised, but can only be expressed in myths and symbols.'

CHAPTER 1

The Birth and Development of Sacred Symbolism

'The French speleologist Norbert Casteret found the underground caves at Montespan exciting to explore; but this was nothing to his excitement when he found the walls covered with paintings of lions and horses and realised that he had stumbled upon the art of prehistoric cave men.'

Colin Wilson[1]

One of the most startling discoveries of the nineteenth century was that of paintings, made by Palaeolithic man, of a variety of animals, found on the walls of caves in Spain and southwest France. When first discovered they were estimated to be over twenty thousand years old. They were not painted in easily accessible places open to any form of natural light, but on the walls of dark chambers situated deep underground and very difficult to access. Great care went into their preparation, and preliminary sketches and outline drawings for paintings that were never completed have been found. Obviously done by the light of some primitive torch, they are not only remarkably accurate depictions of a hunter's prey, but are painted in parts of the cave that scientific examinations have shown to be the places of maximum resonance within the cave complex.

Sadly, in order to protect them for the future, public access to these remarkable and intriguing works has had to be forbidden. The condensation produced by human breath in any quantity is enough to destroy the vulnerable pigments used in their creation. So, for most of us today, our only point of contact with these puzzling creations of our distant ancestors is through photographs, line drawings and the scholarly speculations that have ensued since their discovery.

According to the scientist Jacob Bronowski, the cave paintings were simply a record of the subjects that dominated the minds of the men who painted them. Hunters who were understandably obsessed by their prey, the animals whose meat fed the tribe and whose skins clothed them.[2] Described by many other scholars as the earliest examples of primitive man's art, speculation about their deeper purpose began almost immediately after they had been found. Even the hard-headed rationalist Bronowski was moved to suggest that they represented some form of primitive magic, an idea supported by Colin Wilson who suggested that the nearest modern parallel lay with the magical art of the Kalahari Bushmen.

Having proposed an idea that may well contain a degree of truth, Bronowski followed that up with an even more pertinent line of enquiry when he wrote: 'In itself, magic is a word that explains nothing. It says that man believed he had power, but what power? We still want to know what the power was that the hunter believed they got from the paintings.'[3]

The renowned scientist then veered sharply away from this concept that could have led to an insightful and credible answer. He went on to suggest that the paintings were simply a form of wish-fulfilment, just a statement of a desire for a successful outcome of future hunting expeditions. The real answer that he missed, or chose to ignore, was to be found

Figure 1

in another set of cave paintings in the caves of Les Trois Frères in the Ariège. Paintings of men dressed as animals, depictions of men clad in Shaman's costumes. (see figure 1)

The Intrinsic Spiritual Nature of the Paintings

Our Palaeolithic ancestors were nomadic hunter-gatherers who lived in harmony with nature. They had learned where and how to hunt; which fruits and seeds to gather at different times of the year; how to utilise natural materials, such as stone, flint, bone and animal skins to maximise their chance of survival. They knew how to discern the places of geographical sanctity, where to worship the spirits and, under the tutelage of 'the Few', the natural leaders and shamans among them, how to enhance their innate spiritual powers. When they fell ill they used natural plants as remedies and then used others, the ones we would classify as psychedelic, to stimulate their visionary capacities. They had learnt the mood-altering potential of certain sounds and where to chant them to maximum effect as well as what images to create in order to both portray and augment their spiritual vision.

The historian of religious development, Mircea Eliade, wrote that: 'It is impossible to imagine a period in which man did not have dreams and waking reveries and did not enter into "trance" – a loss of consciousness that was interpreted as the soul's travelling into the beyond'.[4]

Shamans believed that the phenomenal world we live in rested upon another reality, the invisible, spiritual world. Archaeological evidence allied to observed behaviour among present-day hunter-gatherer societies indicate that each Shaman, or tribal leader, knew the sacred places where this visionary experience could most readily take place, be it a cave, spring or mountaintop.[5] Therefore these Palaeolithic cave paintings are the earliest sacred symbols yet discovered.

Neolithic Sacred Sites

As our Stone-Age ancestors left us with no written records, trying to make any realistic and detailed assessment of their sense of the sacred or their 'religious' practices is virtually impossible. However, certain aspects of their belief system, its truly cosmic nature and its vital importance to early man can be reasonably estimated by a rational analysis of the many Neolithic sacred sites throughout the world. Let us examine some of those that adorn the European landscape – not for any reasons of pro-European bias, but simply because they have been the most closely studied and well documented and are familiar, to one extent or another, to readers throughout the world.

Thousands of megalithic structures of varying size and purpose, all of great antiquity, punctuate the landscape of western Europe. Dolmens, long barrows, stone circles, solar temples and solitary megaliths point heavenwards in mute testimony to antique and puzzling systems of belief and ritual that predate the art of writing by a thousand years or more. Unused for any religious or sacred purpose for many millennia, these sites are still imbued with a mystical power that is tangible today by even the most sceptical and rational modern visitor.

The purpose of some of these structures is patently obvious for many of them, long barrows and dolmens, are burial places, such as Newgrange for example with much of its interior decorated with spiral designs (see figure 2). And there are many sites that are obviously highly complex temples, such as Stonehenge and Avebury. However, the exact purpose and meaning of many others remains an insoluble mystery. It is plain to see that their location was deliberate as geological analysis of the stones at Stonehenge, for example, disclose that the rocks used were quarried many miles away in Wales and transported with unbelievable difficulty across land and sea to their present location. The people who erected these puzzling monuments were subsistence-level tribesmen who devoted enormous expenditures of effort and time to build them, so these sacred monuments were of supreme importance to their builders.

The precise location of these sites poses at least two intriguing problems. Firstly, the vast majority of them seem to be aligned with either

Figure 2

constellations of the stars or with planetary bodies. This gives rise to the unanswerable questions of both 'Why?' and 'How?' This precision of alignment demonstrates beyond all doubt that our so-called primitive ancestors possessed levels of astronomical knowledge that we can only wonder at. Secondly, they are all located at places of demonstrable telluric power that can be shown by the ancient art of dowsing. According to Plato, the ancients were simple people, who did not question nature, but accepted things as they were. Thus if a certain place had a mystical appeal, or a discernible magical effect such as a demonstrable healing power, they would simply use it without question. Two questions then arise. Did our ancestors find these sites because of their inherent ability to detect telluric powers? Secondly, was the conjunction of sacred usage and telluric power simply a coincidence?

The English author and dowser Paul Devereux calls these sites 'places of geographical sanctity', the later Romans named the mysterious power found at such places the *genius loci,* or the spirit of the place. A spirit that is still tangible at many Neolithic sites today. Indeed many sensitive people report a subtle but distinct shift in consciousness that occurs when visiting sites such as Stonehenge, Avebury, Silbury Hill or Newgrange. Therefore the question that naturally arises is this: 'Does such a shift in consciousness arise as a result of the *genius loci,* the telluric power of such places, or as a result of the symbolic effect of the structure itself? Or, indeed, is it some strange combination of at least those two factors among possible and, as yet, indefinable, others?

Silbury Hill

The structures themselves are symbolic, despite the fact that we have lost the mystical key that could reveal their full significance. Take Silbury Hill, for example, insofar as we can establish at the present time, it is not aligned with any stellar body and its relationship to the complex Neolithic standing stones at nearby Avebury remains a mystery. Its internal structure has been excavated with results that reveal strange parallels with a much later monument to be found in Egypt. Excavations conducted jointly by the Department of the Environment and the University of South Wales reveal that Silbury Hill is entirely man-made and was constructed in three stages.

The first stage was the creation of a mound, or inner core, that measured 120 feet across. This was later doubled in size; chalk being removed to do this from a ditch some twenty feet in depth. This double mound was then covered by a third stage that the archaeologists described as a vast engineering feat that they estimate took more than four million man-hours of work to complete. A huge ditch was dug to provide the chalk that was then used to create a limestone, seven-stepped, terraced structure with retaining walls. This terraced, pyramidal structure was then covered in earth and turf to create Silbury Hill as we know it today. Outwardly an almost conical mound; inwardly an artificially constructed, seven-stepped limestone structure that almost exactly replicates the external design of the much later and much larger seven-stepped pyramid of Zoser in Egypt.

No one can explain why this internal seven-stepped core was constructed and then covered in earth, so the purpose that lay behind the complex inner form of Silbury Hill remains a mystery to this day. Nor is there any more clarity about the precise function of the adjoining Neolithic complex of Avebury.

Archaeological Insights into Early Religious Practices

One of the first investigators of Avebury was William Stukely who, in 1743, described the site as a Winged Serpent Temple. He claimed that the design was one of an alchemical symbol of sacred energy, created by priests to sanctify the surrounding countryside. Another possibility is that the entire Avebury complex, including Silbury Hill, is a Neolithic celebration of the Earth Goddess. A massively landscaped hymn of praise to the fertility of 'Mother Earth'. This would certainly be in line with the majority of the sacred symbols from that era and later that have come to light in archaeological excavations throughout Europe and the Near East.

Archaeology has shown that about twenty thousand years ago, at approximately the same time the cave walls were painted at Altimera, Lescaux, Montespan and in the Ariège, images of a goddess began to appear right across Europe from the Pyrenees to Lake Baikal in Siberia. Statues have been found carved in bone, stone and ivory; small figurines of round, motherly figures, heavily pregnant, many with signs scratched on them consisting of lines, triangles, circles, zigzags, leaves and spirals.[6]

Insofar as it can be established, Homo sapiens began to multiply fruitfully in Europe after the end of the last Ice Age and, when the glaciers that had previously covered much of Europe began to melt and retreat, some men followed the herds eastwards while others stayed in the fertile valleys of the Dordogne, the Vézère and the Ariège. It was at this time that the statuettes of the goddess were carved and the paintings made on the walls of the caves in these limestone regions. The statues are usually small, naked and obviously pregnant; it is as if all the femininity within them was concentrated on the mysteries of pregnancy and birth. Many were coloured with red ochre, the vivid reminder of life-giving blood. A large number taper to a point as though they were made to be to fixed in the ground for some, unknown, ritual purpose.[7]

One outstanding statue of this 'Earth Mother' type of goddess was found at Laussel in the Dordogne not far from Lascaux. She has been chiselled out of the limestone with flint tools and holds in her right hand a bison's horn, shaped like a crescent moon. On the moon are thirteen notches, held to represent the thirteen days of the waxing moon and the thirteen lunar months of the year. Her left hand points to her pregnant belly.[8] The internationally renowned authority on mythology, Professor Joseph Campbell made a vivid connection between the phases of the moon and the mystery of birth when he wrote:

'The phases of the moon were the same for Old Stone Age man as they are for us; so also were the processes of the womb. It may therefore be that the initial observation that gave birth in the mind of man to a mythology of one mystery informing earthly and celestial things was the recognition of an accord between these two 'time-factored' orders: the celestial order of the waxing moon and the earthly order of the womb.'[9]

It is easy to classify this type of carved figure, as so many museums are prone to do, as a 'Statue of a Woman' or, equally dismissively, as 'fertility symbols', which to a certain extent they undoubtedly are. The narrowness of both these descriptions simply misses the point. As those meticulous scholars Baring and Cashford point out, there is something far more spiritual at work here in that the whole mystery of birth not merely shows how life comes into being, but also demonstrates the unmanifest becoming manifest; how the spiritual and invisible informs and then becomes the material and the tangible. That is why they are classified as goddesses – sacred images enshrining the life-giving, nourishing and mysterious principle of the regeneration of life itself.

The Palaeolithic age flowed on into the Neolithic and that, in its turn, moved on again until mankind took the greatest stride of all, one where, by means of the cultivation of plants, settled living became possible giving rise to the foundation of cities and the beginnings of civilization as we now call it. With this massive leap forward came the invention that totally transformed human life as well as our capacity to understand not merely the past but also our own continuing evolution as thinking, sentient, social beings, namely the invention of writing.

Early Historical Records

With written records we can now learn directly from our ancestors how they lived and organised themselves into ordered, hierarchical societies and begin to gain some semblance of understanding as to their spiritual and religious beliefs and aspirations. We find at this time, with the rise of Babylonian and early Egyptian civilizations, that it is not only the social systems of man that have undergone an increasing degree of complexification, but also their religious beliefs. Religion developed rituals, practices and beliefs that were recorded and thus can be compared with those of other cultures and civilizations. The surprising result, for many devout Christians at least, is that a high degree of continuity with certain present-day beliefs, ritual and symbolism, soon becomes apparent. As Baring and Cashford have written:

> 'From the labyrinthine passages of the Palaeolithic caves to the labyrinth inscribed on the floor of Chartres Cathedral there is a distance of twenty-five millennia in linear time, but an identity of symbolic image nullifies the passage of centuries. The flying birds in the burial sites at Mal'ta reach forward to … the doves of the Sumerian Goddess Inanna, the Egyptian Isis, the Greek Aphrodite and the Dove of the Holy Spirit.'[10]

Thus with the rise of the civilizations of Babylonia, Sumer and Egypt, we find not only written records disclosing social organisation, law and regulation, but also representations carved in stone and inscribed on clay tablets depicting gods and goddesses as well as symbols of highly charged spiritual significance such as those of the Tree of Life and that of the Serpent representing the divine gift of Wisdom or sacred gnosis.

The Coming of Polytheism

The rise of civilization heralded the end of the monopoly of the great Goddess, the Earth Mother, who was now joined in her celestial power by gods, all of whom were deemed to be related to her in one manner or another; either as her consort, suitor or her son. All the new emerging centres of civilization developing at different sites and times, revered a body of knowledge indicating the 'divine' origin of the gifts of agriculture that had allowed civilization to begin in the first instance. This process did not stop with the civilizations of Babylonia, Sumer, Akkad or Egypt; it is common to all peoples and cultures.

There are many mythologies that speak of a divine origin for agriculture and handicrafts.[11] Professor Joseph Campbell wrote about those of the North American Indians and the Polynesian peoples of the Pacific that claimed, quite clearly, to have received agricultural knowledge as a God-given gift. While there is absolutely no evidence for any cultural contact between these races there is, nonetheless, a degree of unanimity between their mythologies that is truly startling. This is in harmony with the traditions of all the ancient civilizations that also speak reverently of a divine origin for their practical skills.

The Persian prophet Zoroaster, the founder of Zoroastrianism, claimed that he had been taught the art of agriculture by the sun god, Ahuro Mazdao. The Egyptian god Osiris, the judge in the underworld, who is also described as both the brother and consort of Isis the goddess of fertility, is credited with having taught the ancient Egyptians the art of growing corn; the Greek god of wine and fertility, Dionysus, travelled all over Greece and the islands to impart knowledge of the vine. Similar divine origins were claimed for the principles of law that allowed man to found civilization, for example, the Old Testament prophet Moses who led his people from bondage to freedom, received the Tablets of the Law from Jehovah on Mount Sinai; Khammurabi, King of Babylon, who collated the laws of both his people and the Sumerians, was believed to have been personally instructed by the god Shamash; Numa Pompilius, the second legendary King of Rome was instructed by the goddess Egaria to establish nearly all the ancient Roman religious institutions and rituals.[12]

The Descent of Consciousness

The multi-faceted problems of the accurate interpretation of the history of our early ancestors are compounded by our own previous reluctance, or unwillingness, to concede that man himself is an integral part of the evolutionary process. A process that is not simply a biological one but is also one of intellect and consciousness. The Jesuit anthropologist and theologian, Pierre Teilhard de Chardin, described this process of the gradual evolution of the mind and of mental properties as one whose ongoing evolution, the incremental and cumulative results of the development of intellect and thinking, provide the keys to our understanding, not only of the past development of human culture, but also of what is to come in the future.

The psychologist, Julian Jaynes, claimed that in Neolithic times human consciousness was united with the divine to such an extent that early man responded to divine commands that he 'heard' in a similar manner to the way in which a schizophrenic hears voices. Jaynes described the evolution of consciousness as a descent of consciousness from this state of divine union that proceeded step by step until we achieved our present level of independent, complex scientific thinking.[13] This descent of consciousness, traces of which can be found in the divergence between 'Right and Left Brain Function' is something that also exerts an influence on the understanding of sacred symbolism. However, as I mentioned earlier, there are certain problems that have to be overcome if we are to gain a true appreciation of our ancestor's spiritual beliefs.

We all have great difficulty in stripping our minds of the many accretions of belief that have accumulated over the millennia and that inevitably distort our understanding of many of the concepts and symbolic representations that originate in the distant pre-Christian past. Take for example, one symbol that we have already mentioned – the serpent that in Babylonian and Sumerian culture was a symbolic representation of Wisdom or the divine gift of sacred knowledge or gnosis. Intertwined serpents of wisdom form the hieroglyph of the god Ningizzida in ancient Sumerian culture and also form the caduceus of Hermes (see figure 3), the Greek Messenger of the gods. A serpent also winds itself around the staff of the Greek representation of Asclepius, the god of healing.[14]

Two thousand years of Christian culture have made an almost indelible imprint on both our consciousness and appreciation so that to the vast majority

Figure 3

of people today, the serpent is representative of either the devil or of original sin. Such meanings as these have to be firmly set aside if we are to harvest the real fruits of ancient knowledge and beliefs. There are also certain startling parallels of meaning and usage that occur that do not sit easily on the consciousness of those who mistakenly believe that Christianity is a unique religion, one without precedent.

One such can be found in the list of titles given to the goddess Inanna in Sumeria 3500 BCE. She is called at various times, Virgin Queen of Heaven; Light of the World; Morning Star; Evening Star; Forgiver of Sins; terms of amazing familiarity to Roman Catholics who daily recite a litany of the Blessed Virgin Mary using precisely those phrases. Inanna's symbolic images were, like those associated with the Virgin Mary today, the crescent moon and the morning and evening star that we call Venus.[15]

Similar phraseology and symbolic representation were used for a later Sumerian goddess, Ishtar, whose temples were decorated with five pointed stars and rosettes. Ishtar had a son who died annually and descended into the underworld each autumn only to resurrect to a verdant new life each springtime. Tammuz, known as 'The Son of the Widow', a term that resonated down the millennia from the era of ancient Sumeria, through Pharaonic Egypt and is still of immense symbolic significance to the worldwide brotherhood of Freemasonry today. Tammuz is the among the first lasting concepts we have of a sacrificial dying and resurrecting god; one who came to represent a vital aspect of most spiritual paths, namely death to the things of the temporal world and rebirth to the realities of the spiritual world, an essential part of any pathway of initiation.

Thus, in the records preserved in the clay tablets of Sumeria and Babylonia we have spiritual concepts that have truly stood the test of time, all expressed in symbolic form, which continued to exert their mystical effect in the worlds of ancient Egypt, in biblical Judaism and that were adopted, in one form or another, by Christianity in all its many forms.

CHAPTER 2

The Legacy of Ancient Egyptian Gnosis

T he great civilization of ancient Egypt has left us with a massive databank of written records and an architectural and archaeo-logical heritage of supreme importance to all three of the world's great monotheistic religions, namely Judaism, Christianity and Islam. Yet, Egyptian civilization seems to have sprung into being almost fully formed without any developmental period that can be discerned in either of the written or the archaeological records, abundant though they are. The Pyramid Texts, which are the oldest record of esoteric knowledge yet discovered, make repeated references to *Tep Zepi*, the so-called 'First Time', which was the legendary time of Osiris when Egypt was supposedly ruled directly by the gods in human form who gave the Egyptians the blessed gift of sacred knowledge as well as a complex, profound and uncannily accurate knowledge of astronomy.

Two significant questions arise from this: firstly, how did this highly sophisticated level of astronomical knowledge arise in the prehistoric Egypt? Secondly, when was the First Time and where did it take place?

The author, John Anthony West, provides one possible answer to the first question:

> 'Every aspect of Egyptian knowledge seems to have been
> complete at the very beginning. The sciences, artistic and
> architectural techniques and the hieroglyphic system show

virtually no signs of 'development'; indeed many of the
achievements of the earliest dynasties were never surpassed or
even equalled later on. . . . The answer to the mystery is, of
course, obvious, but because it is repellent to the prevailing cast
of modern thinking, it is seldom seriously considered.
Egyptian civilization was not a development, it was a legacy.'[1]
[my emphasis]

If these complex levels of knowledge were a legacy, then whose legacy
were they? The absence of any evidence of a developmental period within
Egyptian history leads inevitably to the conclusion that this knowledge
was either acquired and developed elsewhere, or that it arose from a
much earlier and as yet undiscovered civilization that flourished
somewhere within Egypt itself.

The latter idea is not as crazy as it may sound at first hearing, for there
are vast areas of Egypt buried by the sands of the desert or rendered
incapable of excavation by the sprawling suburbs of Cairo and other
cities. Nonetheless, the most plausible theory that has been advanced to
explain the origin of these highly sophisticated levels of knowledge is the
so-called 'dynastic race theory' first proposed by William Matthew
Flinders Petrie, one-time Professor of Egyptology at University College,
London, and now revered as the father of modern Egyptology.

Archaeological Clues to the Origins of Egyptian Culture

Flinders Petrie and James Quibell made excavations at Nakada in 1893/4
that examined over 2,000 graves of the pre-dynastic period. The pottery
and artefacts found during these investigations were from two distinct
periods, which Petrie designated as Nakada I and Nakada II.[2] In the
graves of the Nakada II period, Petrie found pottery fragments of a
distinctly Mesopotamian character,[3] yet in all other excavations of Nile
valley sites prior to this era, artefacts of foreign manufacture were
virtually non-existent.[4] Petrie also recorded discoveries of lapis lazuli in
the Nakada II tombs, the only instance of finds of this exotic and precious

stone in any sites of the pre-dynastic period. Yet this stone was highly prized and sought after in Mesopotamia long before the time of the Nakada II interments in the Nile Valley.

These were not the only signs of a sudden appearance of Mesopotamian cultural influence in Egypt at this time, for depictions of the pear-shaped mace, the increasing use of the cylinder seal, the sudden appearance of remarkable brick architecture and hieroglyphic writing are all claimed to be evidence of the Mesopotamian origin of this apparently inexplicable cultural transformation.[5] The English Egyptologist, Douglas Derry, one of Flinders Petrie's pupils, was quite specific about the origins of this great leap forward when he wrote in 1956:

> 'It is also very suggestive of the presence of a dominant race,
> perhaps relatively few in numbers but greatly exceeding the
> original inhabitants in intelligence; a race which brought into
> Egypt the knowledge of building in stone, of sculpture,
> painting, reliefs and above all writing; hence the enormous
> jump from the primitive pre-dynastic Egyptian to the advanced
> civilization of the Old Empire (the Old Kingdom).'[6]

The Dutch Egyptologist and orientalist Henry Frankfort, describes the appearance of the cylinder seal in pre-dynastic Egypt as, 'the strongest evidence of contact between Mesopotamia and Egypt'.[7] However, the sudden appearance of a large body of evidence of cross-cultural contact between Mesopotamia and Egypt, important though it may be, does little or nothing to explain the route by which such influences and artefacts arrived in the Nile Valley.

Arthur Weighall, the senior inspector of antiquities for the Egyptian government from 1905 until 1914, explored the desert region of Wadi Abbad in the eastern desert in March 1908. This wadi, which leads from the Nile Valley town of Edfu towards the Red Sea port of Mersa Alam, contains the temple of Kanais dedicated to the god Amun-Re and built by Seti I (19th dynasty, c. 932 BCE), the father of Ramses the Great. Weighall found and recorded graffiti carved in the rocks of the wadi depicting strange high-prowed boats. He published his drawings the following year.[8]

Early in 1936, Hans Winkler, the German ethnologist and explorer, investigated the nearby Wadi Hammamat and found another series of rock drawings similar to those found earlier by Weighall. When he published his findings[9] he suggested that these drawings were of seafarers who, as part of a military expedition, had landed on the west coast of the Red Sea and crossed the desert en route to the Nile Valley.[10] The English Egyptologist David Rohl investigated both of these wadis and then extended his search into Wadi Barramiya in 1997. In Wadi Barramiya Rohl found more drawings of the high-prowed boats and proposed the hypothesis that there was a direct connection between the people whose voyage was recorded in all three wadis and the Nakada II graves excavated by Petrie.[11]

The Followers of Horus

Rohl's investigations were part of his quest seeking evidence for the *Shemsa-Hor*, the followers of Horus, which he suggests were the immediate ancestors of the early pharaohs.[12] The earliest surviving references to the followers of Horus can be found within the Pyramid Texts[13] and these are the first references to a manner of transmission of sacred knowledge that has lasted from that time right down to the present day.

The follower's of Horus were a succession of priestly initiates who preserved, enhanced and transmitted an extraordinary body of knowledge from master to pupil down through the generations. According to sacred Egyptian legend, this knowledge first arose in the mysterious 'time of the Neteru' – the fabled era when the gods ruled Egypt immediately prior to the time of the earliest Pharaohs. These initiates were not Pharaohs but immensely powerful and enlightened individuals, members of 'the Few' who had been carefully selected by an elite academy that established itself at the sacred site of Heliopolis-Giza in the era of Egyptian prehistory.[14]

Georges Goyon, the one time Egyptologist to King Farouk, claimed that, 'Giza was chosen by the priest-astronomers because of certain religious and scientific factors'.[15] Sadly he did not elaborate on what those factors may have been.

Ancient Egyptian Astronomers

The scholars of the classical world, with first-hand experience of the knowledge of the ancient Egyptians, were amazed and incredibly impressed with the level of sacred knowledge and wisdom shown by the Heliopolitan and Memphite priests. The ancient Greeks had an immense respect for the astronomical knowledge of the Egyptians[16] and Aristotle recorded his view of Egyptian astronomers when he wrote of them: '...observations have been kept for many years past, and from whom much of our evidence about particular stars is derived.'[17] As late as the fifth century CE, the neoplatonist Proclus Diodachus wrote: 'Let those, who believe in observations, cause the stars to move around the poles of the zodiac by one degree in one hundred years towards the east, as Ptolemy and Hipparchus did before him know . . . that the Egyptians had already taught Plato about the movement of the fixed stars . . .'[18]

The modern authors and Egyptologists Robert Bauval and Graham Hancock record that, 'the Heliopolitan priests were high initiates in the mysteries of the heavens and their dominant occupation was the observation and recording of the various motions of the sun and the moon, the planets and the stars'.[19] Another English author, John Anthony West, paraphrased the views of France's leading twentieth-century spiritual scholar of Egyptology, Schwaller de Lubicz, when he recorded that Egyptian science, medicine, mathematics and astronomy were of an exponentially higher order of refinement and sophistication than modern scholars will generally acknowledge and that the whole of Egyptian civilization was based upon a complete and precise understanding of universal laws.[20] According to Schwaller de Lubicz, it was by the inspired use of mythology, symbolic imagery and the geometric proportion of their architecture, that the Egyptians were able to encapsulate their knowledge of the basic pattern structures of the universe.[21]

Gnosis

The sophisticated and incredibly high levels of sacred knowledge, or gnosis, preserved and enhanced by the priesthood were passed down through successive generations from master to pupil by the process of initiation into the Temple mysteries. They were not used for personal gain by the priestly and royal initiates, for while rank and royal birth undoubtedly carried enormous levels of privilege, sacred knowledge of subjects such as astronomy, agriculture, architecture, building, medicine, mathematics, navigation and metallurgy was used for the benefit of the entire community served by the priests, the Pharaohs and the aristocracy.

Sustained by divinely inspired gnosis and protected by the deserts that surrounded it, Egyptian civilization developed a degree of sophistication, stability and complexity that has yet to be equalled, much less exceeded. A vast body of esoteric knowledge was recorded within the Pyramid Texts, the Edfu Texts and the *Book of the Dead* as well as being encoded on temple walls and elsewhere. The dualism that lay at the heart of Egyptian sacred knowledge was recorded by Bauval and Hancock when they wrote: 'The language of all these texts is exotic, laden with the dualistic thinking that lay at the heart of Egyptian society and that may have been the engine of its greatest achievements.'[22] The Edfu Texts in particular refer repeatedly to the 'wisdom of the Sages' and constantly emphasise that, to the Egyptian elite, their most valued gift was knowledge.[23]

According to Schwaller de Lubicz, the ancient Egyptians had their own unique and effective way of understanding the universe and man's place within it, in a completely different knowledge system from that revered by modern man.[24] This sacred 'way of knowing' could not be adequately transmitted by the normal vehicle of language but could only be taught or shown in myth and symbolism.[25] Robert and Deborah Lawlor, who translated much of Schwaller de Lubicz's work into English, state that symbolism was used as the principal means of recording and transmitting a precise supra-rational knowledge and intuitive vision which, according to Schwaller, was a major aspect of ancient science.[26]

Schwaller began his own important work on symbols and symbolism, by stating that there are always two distinct and different ways of inter-preting Egyptian religious texts – the exoteric and the esoteric. The exoteric meaning is the standard explanation, which can be arrived at by interpretation of the hieroglyphic records or by the study of the appro-priate textbooks on religion and history. This 'standard' version also serves as a vehicle for the deeper, hidden, or esoteric meaning, which Schwaller described as the *symbolique* interpretation.[27] While this form of esoteric knowledge has usually been ignored or is long forgotten, its symbolic remnants have been transmitted, in one form or another, down through all the great monotheistic religions of Judaism, Christianity and Islam that sprang from Egyptian roots.[28]

La Symbolique

Symbols and hieroglyphs evoke far more complex responses within even the modern viewer, than can ever be achieved by words, be they transla-tions or explanations, no matter how beautifully or clearly they are written. They evoke a richer response based upon a far deeper and spiritual integration of body, mind and spirit than modern psychology can ever grasp. Those who have studied the sculptures, paintings or stained glass created by medieval craftsmen or who have immersed themselves in Egyptology will know of this from their own experience. Two French mystical writers, Pauwels and Bergier, commented on exactly this aspect of ancient symbolism and of the insight of the initiates who used it:

> 'They . . . wrote in stone their hermetic message. Signs,
> incomprehensible to men whose consciousness had not
> undergone transmutations . . . These men were not secretive
> because they loved secrecy, but simply because their discoveries
> about the Laws of Energy, of matter and of the mind had been
> made in another state of consciousness and so could not be
> communicated directly.'[29]

The ancient Egyptian initiates were not the only ones to use symbols in this manner; symbolism is an effective and instinctive form of communication, one that has been used for millennia by sages and initiates of all the world's great religious traditions. Not only did the ancient Egyptians tend to restrict their use of symbolism to matters of religion and knowledge, which at that time were synonymous, or, at the very least, regarded as different aspects of the same reality, but also used it to reinforce the divine origin, power and lineal descent of the pharaohs. Depictions of the Pharaohs traditionally showed them wearing the double crown of both Upper and Lower Egypt. Clearly defined on the front of this formal headdress, as well as on their death masks, were the twin symbols of the heads of a falcon and cobra.

The Pharaoh's incarnation as the living embodiment of Horus was indicated symbolically by the falcon's head, while the head of the cobra carried two linked, but different, symbolic interpretations; one as the seat of wisdom and the other indicating his divine ancestry. Other religious symbols also told of the descent of divine wisdom to the royal family and priestly initiates; symbols that were transformed in later times to create a similar reinforcement of the claim to the divine origin of medieval kings.

Egyptian Sacred Symbolism

Egyptian temples were plentifully adorned with symbols and hieroglyphs celebrating the wisdom, power and worldly achievements of the pharaohs who endowed them. Huge obelisks, all richly decorated and surmounted by a *ben-ben* stone, were erected in pairs flanking the avenue approaching most temples. The *ben-ben* stone, or pyramidal top on each obelisk represented the resting place of the phoenix, the legendary bird that arises from its own ashes in a ritually symbolic representation of spiritual death and rebirth.

In the time of Tuthmosis III (1476–1422 BCE) this form of symbolism was transformed to one that reverberates in one form or another through Egyptian religion and biblical Judaism and, through the worldwide brotherhood of Freemasonry, right down to the present day. In an open courtyard in front of the main temple at Karnak the tradi-

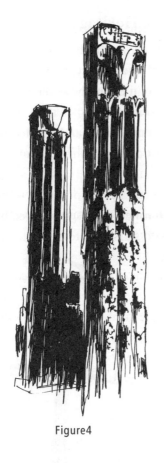

Figure 4

tional symbolism of the obelisks was transformed into two free-standing pillars. These are purely symbolic, as they perform no architectural function whatsoever. The English Egyptologist, David Rohl, asserts that they are representative of the two kingdoms of Egypt[30] and describes the carvings on them (see figure 4) in the following terms: 'The pillar on the south side has three tall stems ending in an elaborately stylised flower with partly pendant petioles. If one were to trace its outline and transfer the design to the coat of arms of the French monarchy you would immediately recognise the "Fleur-de-Lys".'[31] Lilies were not native to Egypt at that time and could only be cultivated there with considerable difficulty. They were cultivated by royal order and used for their mood-altering qualities when ingested. They remained the sole property of the Pharaohs and became the pattern for another form of symbolic representation of the royal lineage. As sacred gnosis was imparted to the initiates as they underwent states of altered consciousness, the lilies also became symbols of wisdom, as did the pillars themselves. Over time they also became inseparably associated with ancestral descent from the royal house of Egypt and, from that time forward two freestanding pillars came to represent the twin royal attributes of the divine gifts of strength and wisdom, irrespective of the culture of religious beliefs of the builders.

Our Egyptian Symbolic Heritage

In a brief work such as this, we can only list some of the vast array of symbols that formed such an integral part of ancient Egyptian religious life. There were so many that they were beyond count, however certain symbols of those fascinating times have not only come down to us in the archaeological record, but have been used, transformed and adapted by later religions and thereby are still in common use throughout the Western world today.

For many people, the most important purely Egyptian symbol is the life-affirming ankh (see figure 5), an equal-armed cross surmounted by an oval. From Babylon came the five-pointed stars used to decorate the temples of Ishtar and Inanna, and that are found in abundance throughout the buildings and tombs of ancient Egypt. Then there is the all-seeing 'Eye of Horus', a representation of the eye that Horus lost in his battle with Seth; the eye that was re-assembled by Thoth. This protective and all-seeing eye of the god was painted on the prows of Egyptian ships (see figure 6) and also used on protective amulets. Today it is commonplace, enshrined within a triangle, depicted on dollar bills and still used in mainstream Christian symbolism. The cult of motherhood and wisdom was communicated by a variety of symbols of the goddess Isis and the Horus child, with the child either seated on the mothers lap or being suckled (see figure 7), an obvious ancestor of later Roman Catholic depictions of the Madonna and Child – truly there is nothing new under the sun.

We have mentioned serpents conveying

Figure 5

Figure 6

Figure 7

the concept of divine descent or sacred gnosis; the fleur-de-lys, yet
another symbolic representation of divine and kingly descent, but a direct
link to Neolithic practices can be found in Egypt's architectural heritage.
The King's Chamber in the Great Pyramid is deliberately constructed to
maximise resonance – it rings like a bell when anyone walks across its

floor – temples were also constructed to enhance resonance and many modern scholars claim that they were designed to be energised by sound. These practices, as we have mentioned above, were common in the caves of Lascaux and Altimera, in the tombs of Newgrange and Maes Howe and are a foretaste of what was to come in Christian Europe during the medieval era. Certain gods had the heads of animals, and certain animals were believed to be endowed with divine duties and gifts, such as Upuaut, or the desert fox, which was described as 'the opener of the ways'. Certain principles that became an integral part of later religious systems were clearly established in Egyptian times, such as the judgement of the soul in the court of Osiris according to tenets that are the obvious basis for the Ten Commandments of the Judaeo/ Christian tradition.

The vast array of symbolic representations of many gods, or *Neters*, has led to much confusion in the modern mind. The nearest parallel we have to this pantheon today is most probably that which exists in the Hindu religion where all these apparently 'different gods' are, in truth, expressions of the multitude of aspects of one god, and one god alone. Schwaller de Lubicz described the situation in ancient Egypt in the following terms:

> 'Study of the texts shows, in fact, that since the Ancient Empire, there is an affirmation of faith in a one and only God, eternal and nameless; the *Neter of Neters*, boundless and incomprehensible. Parallel to this vision, there exists a pantheon composed of a considerable number of *Neters* or principles ... These *Neters* belong to several "theological systems" taught in different, well-defined locations.'[32]

Thus, despite the apparent plethora of gods and goddesses, or *Neters*, they are all expressions of different aspects of one God. Therefore ancient Egypt may well prove to be the demonstrable country of origin for monotheism.

The Opener of the Ways

In the winter of 1879, an Arab workman standing near the pyramid of Unas at Saqqara spotted a desert fox silhouetted against the light of the rising sun. The animal was behaving rather oddly. It moved, stopped and looked at the workman as if inviting his observer to follow, then moved again before disappearing into a crevice in the north face of the pyramid. Scenting loot, the workman followed and after a difficult crawl through a tunnel-like passage, found himself in a large chamber within the pyramid.[33] When he lit his torch, to his amazement, he found that the walls of the chamber were covered with turquoise and gold hieroglyphic inscriptions.[34] Later, similar inscriptions were found in other pyramids and they are known by the collective name of the Pyramid Texts,[35] and consist of over 4,000 lines of hymns and formulae.

The first scholar to see them *in situ* was Professor Gaston Maspero, the director of the Egyptian Antiquities Service. Like the desert fox which had led the workman to his 'treasure', the Pyramid Texts themselves now began to play a long and tortuous role in the 'opening of the ways', for their eventual translation led to a profound understanding not only of the spiritual beliefs at the time of Unas, but also of the great depth that sacred knowledge or gnosis had attained in remote antiquity when the texts were actually composed.

Professor Maspero claimed that most were the written version of a far older tradition dating back to Egypt's prehistoric past,[36] predating events described in the Book of Exodus by at least two millennia, and the writing of the New Testament by nearly 3,400 years.[37] Professor I E S Edwards of the British Museum stated unequivocally that, 'The Pyramid Texts were certainly not inventions of the Vth or VIth dynasties, but had originated in extreme antiquity; it is hardly surprising, therefore, that they sometimes contain allusions to conditions which no longer prevailed at the time of Unas . . .'[38]

Thus two of Egyptology's greatest authorities state unequivocally that the Pyramid Texts are the oldest collection of religious writings ever discovered. Yet, despite their importance, it was not until 1969 that

Raymond Faulkner, Professor of ancient Egyptian language at University College London, published what is now accepted by most scholars as the truly authoritative translation and concluded that, 'the Pyramid Texts constitute the oldest corpus of Egyptian religious and funerary literature now extant'.[39] Therefore, the hieroglyphics decorated with turquoise and gold found within the pyramids at Saqqara are demonstrably the earliest collection of sacred knowledge, or 'esoteric wisdom' yet to be found. Thus ancient Egyptian symbolism is all embracing, not only exerting its influence throughout history down to the modern era, but also reaching back to the very dawn of time. Egyptian religious thought also influences us today in ways well known to scholars, but almost unrecognised by most ordinary, deeply religious people throughout the world – it was both the ethnic and the sole spiritual source for Judaism, the precursor of both Christianity and Islam.

SECTION 2

The Bible, Egyptian Origins of Judaism and Two Conflicting Views of Jesus

Millions of devout followers from all three great monotheistic faiths believe fervently that the Bible is not merely the most inspirational book ever written, but that it is, more or less, a valid historical record that traces the origins of their faith. Be they Jew, Christian or Muslim, they are seemingly unaware of the true Egyptian origin of Judaism and completely ignorant of the fact that there are at least two conflicting accounts of the life of Jesus. Yet their faiths, devout but historically flawed, have given rise not only to mass devotion but also to seemingly perpetual conflict. But when analysed with any degree of dispassion, the similarities between their beliefs far outweigh the differences that are apparent between their various practices. They all spring from the same roots and, in different forms of literary symbolism, preach the same essential message of peace, brotherhood and harmony, principles that, at first glance, are hard to discern when one studies the record of their relationships over the last two millennia.

CHAPTER 3

The Bible and the Israelites

I t is widely recognised that the laws of Judaism strictly forbid the use of 'graven images'. From this it would be easy to assume that their use of symbolism was non-existent – yet nothing could be further from the truth. There was a startling degree of continuity of symbolic usage uniting Egyptian and early Israelite practice that is of supreme relevance to the development of later Christian iconography. Indeed, the use of literary symbolism, in the form of allegory and parables was the main vehicle for the communication of spiritual insight used by the writers of the books we call the Bible.

There are traditionally at least four levels of interpretation that can be applied to any biblical text, just as there are several levels of meaning encoded within visual symbols. These different levels of meaning seem, at first sight, to be separate from one another, but they are not. They are all simultaneously present, at one and the same time, each one contained 'within' another. Our first contact with the symbol is a purely external one that may, on the surface at least, have no apparent symbolic or inner significance.[1]

At the second level we go beyond this as our experience of the literary symbol expands, opening us up to non-sensory perceptions of the text, as we begin to free it from the limitations of time and space. At the third level we need to proceed with extreme caution lest we impose our own individual and personal meaning on the symbol as our innate sensitivity to its deeper significance has been 'activated', stimulating our mind, if it remains open, so that the symbol can begin to 'act' through it and link itself spiritually with what is being symbolised, thus bringing this particular symbol into the realm of our own personal experience. In this way, the symbol acquires personal relevance for us and we now begin to achieve a heightened awareness of ourselves and develop a transcendental and intimate relationship with the rest of creation. Yet, there is a potential danger here, for as we become more spiritually aware of the tremendous energy flowing through all of creation, we may become tempted to turn this heightened awareness into purely 'personalised' or 'egocentric' experience, instead of taking from it what we need in order to progress to a higher level.[2]

That perceptive English writer, John Baldock described the fourth, meditative level in the following terms:

> 'At the fourth, anagogical level … the importance that may have been attached to the physical nature or material form of the symbol melts away making way for a new form of understanding. … the symbol itself dissolves as what it symbolises flows uninterrupted through the observer's mind. Our personal vision gives way to a … new vision that expands beyond the comprehension of the rational mind; instead of thinking it is as though thought passes through us. This is the level at which true contemplation or meditation takes place.'[3]

Therefore, biblical symbolism can be taken firstly at the literal level wherein the text can be understood as a record of simple fact or verbal instruction. At the second, or allegorical level, each element in the text can be perceived as standing for something else. The third or moral level is where the text can yield a meaning of particular relevance to the reader's own situation and can be described as the personal level. The fourth, or highest is the anagogical or mystical level. To be capable of interpreting scripture at the highest level demonstrates the acquired capacity to open oneself up to all the infinite meanings that the words may have for you, meanings that ultimately may well transcend the comprehension of any 'normal' individual.

Any serious study of the Bible will always be coloured by the religious background of the individual student. For example, for many devout Christians, their approach to the Bible may be unwittingly distorted by a firmly held belief that this collection of scriptural books is 'the inerrant word of God'. A belief that completely ignores the fact that it was written by fallible human beings, all imbued by complex motives encompassing both political and spiritual elements and that, furthermore, in many instances, they were describing events that took place many centuries, sometimes millennia, before they actually wrote the text.

The true miracle of the Bible rests in the fact that, notwithstanding its flawed and distorted historical basis, its spiritual impact is profound. Thus we have to treat it in the same manner we treat myth and legend and ask not is it historically true, but in what manner is it spiritually true? For, despite all its apparent historical imperfections, the Holy Scriptures remain the most important spiritual work in the history of mankind.

The Writing of the Bible?

The Bible as we now know it, began to take shape during the Babylonian exile of the people of Israel in the sixth century BCE. The Jewish scribes and priests of that era knew that without a temple or a country of their own, they faced the probability of imminent extinction as a people through absorption by their conquerors. To counter this tendency, they turned towards God. They had the Torah and some other sacred writings, and around these early forms of scripture they created a form of Judaism, stripped of all territorial limitations and founded strictly upon piety and learning, religion and study.[4] The adversity of exile was turned to advantage in a manner that not only completely changed Jewish religious practice and ensured the survival of the people of Israel for all time, but also transformed the world.

Out of their primitive sacred writings and traditions, they created the literary and spiritual masterpiece that we call the Old Testament. The basis for this inspiring work was 'The Law', some legends of their past, the Book of Deuteronomy – discovered just before the fall of Jerusalem – their oral and mystical traditions, sayings of the prophets and a passionate sense of spiritual purpose. They projected their vision not only to the future, but also retrospectively within the newly created and carefully embroidered accounts of the past. From this we are led to the inevitable, if somewhat surprising, deduction that many of the pivotal figures of biblical history, such as Saul, David, Solomon,[5] Elijah and Joshua had lived and died without the benefit of the Scriptures to guide them. What had guided and influenced these kings, judges and prophets of earlier centuries was the mystical and initiatory heritage of Egypt which was now incorporated in the emerging Scriptures taking written form in Babylon.

It took over four centuries for the work to be completed and by the second century BCE, the Hebrew Bible consisted of three major parts: The *Torah* or Pentateuch, The *Neviim* or Prophets and The *Ketuvim* or Sayings. With the exception of parts of Daniel, Ezra and Jeremiah, which were written in Aramaic, the rest was written in Hebrew.[6]

Both the Dead Sea Scrolls scholar John Allegro, and the biblical scholar Professor Morton Smith contend that Jews brought a volatile brand of esoteric religion back with them from Babylon that was mixed with the more sedate biblical religion we recognise today.[7] Whatever the truth of that assertion, however, the Scriptures reveal that the Jews treasured their own, earlier mystical and initiatory religious traditions and clearly recorded their importance in the new Scriptures composed in exile. The mystical insights of the prophets were extolled repeatedly, the role of the priest-kings, such as David and Solomon, as the embodiment of enlightenment, was revered, and the initiatory concept of ascending degrees of holiness was seen to pervade all aspects of Jewish life. Despite the strange political circumstances under which the Scriptures were written, which certainly skewed their contents in a perceptible way, certain aspects of the origins of the founders of the people of Israel nonetheless escaped the censors and can lead us to revise our ideas of both the ethnic origins of the People of Israel and the true foundations of their monotheism.

The Egyptian Origins of Abraham and Sarah?

The Scriptures claim that the patriarch and prophet Abraham was born in the city of Ur, which may be a simple matter of camouflage created by Israeli scribes to disguise the patriarch's true origins. The account in Genesis does disclose certain facts about Abraham and his family that clearly demonstrate that he was a highborn Egyptian. Abraham is quoted as describing his wife: '. . . and yet indeed she is my sister; she is the daughter of my father, but not the daughter of my mother; and she became my wife.'[8] This incestuous marriage to his own sister has hardly been commented upon, yet it is of supreme importance, for such marriages between siblings were restricted to the members of the Egyptian royal family. Therefore the question arises: was Abraham a member of the Pharonic family? It is almost certain that he was and, furthermore, this may explain why the twelfth-century rabbinical scholar Rabbi Solomon Isaacs wrote that, 'you should know that the family of Abraham was of a high line',[9] contradicting the notion that Abraham was a nomadic shepherd and confirming his true social status.

The patriarch's original name, Abram,[10] translates as 'exalted father', which is one of the ritual names regularly used by the kings of Egypt. This may be accurately translated as Ab – ra – 'am, which in Egyptian, means 'the father of the House of Ra'. There is also the strange matter of a complete change of names for both Abram and Sarai, his wife, which is also recorded in the Scriptures,[11] and this reinforces the notion of Abraham's Egyptian origin.[12] Abraham is referred to as 'a father of many nations' in Genesis.[13] His wife's new name, Sarah, is the Egyptian term for princess. Genesis also records that Sarah's handmaiden Hagar was not merely an Egyptian but a relatively highborn one at that, being the daughter of the Pharaoh by one of his concubines.[14] Furthermore, the patriarch's son, Ishmael took an Egyptian wife.[15]

The bizarre liaison between Sarah and the unnamed Pharaoh,

recorded in the scriptures,[16] gave rise to much scholarly speculation in both Judaism and Islam. Both the Babylonian Talmud[17] and the Koran [18] raise grave doubts about the paternity of Abraham's son Isaac, and imply that the Pharaoh was the boy's real father, not the Jewish patriarch. So in the 'divinely inspired word of God's' account of the foundation of the Jewish people there are two important questions to be answered: firstly, was Abraham from Ur of the Chaldees, or was he an Egyptian? Secondly, do the people of Israel descend from the patriarch Abraham or the Pharaoh?

These controversial ideas, while they seem to contradict religious teaching based upon the Scriptures, are founded on clear and unequivocal statements in the book of Genesis and are reinforced by the words of Melchizedek, the King of Righteousness: 'Blessed be Abram, the most high of God, possessor of heaven and earth.'[19] Both Melchizedek, the priest-king of Jerusalem, and Abraham, the father of the people of Israel, repeatedly use exactly the same telling phrase to describe the deity, *the Most High God*,[20] a description that, not surprisingly in the light of my earlier comments, happens to be one of the commonest terms used in the Egyptian records for the supreme god of the pantheon.

The meeting between Abraham and the Pharaoh signals the beginning of an ongoing cross-fertilization of spiritual ideas and experiences that took place between the 'people of Israel' and the land of Egypt leading ultimately to the foundation of the Jewish religion. Several leading scholars of international repute, including Sigmund Freud[21] and Ernst Sellin,[22] have written prolifically about the overwhelming significance of Egyptian thought on early Judaism. It is also significant to note that Abraham adopted for himself and all his descendants the Egyptian custom of circumcision, ostensibly at the command of Almighty God himself.[23] Circumcision, a most unusual practice elsewhere had, significantly, been mandatory among the Egyptian royal family, hereditary priesthood and nobility since 4000 BCE.[24]

One of the most important episodes in the story of Abraham is the recounting of the patriarch's obedience to God's request that the prophet's son Isaac should be sacrificed as a burnt offering on Mount Moriah.[25] Yet, as Abraham prepared to slaughter his son, the Lord God of Israel sent an angel to stop this terrible sacrifice. God, having seen Abraham's total obedience to his demands, was not prepared to see the shedding of innocent blood. As a reward for his loyalty, Abraham received the following promise: '... and in thy seed shall all the nations of the earth be blessed because thou hast obeyed my voice.'[26] From that time onward, throughout the history of the Jewish people, human sacrifice of any kind, particularly the sacrifice of one's children, was held to be an abomination in the eyes of the Lord.

Who was Moses?

The story of the infant Moses being found in the bulrushes by Pharaoh's daughter and his adoption by the Egyptian royal family[27] is the starting point for the series of events that culminated in the Exodus of the so-called 'people of Israel' from Egypt. Implicit in this fascinating fable is the previously unquestioned assumption that by this time the people of Israel were an identifiable and distinct ethnic group, a monotheistic nation who had long since entered into a covenant, or *berit*, with the God of Abraham. This belief is deeply entrenched in the public consciousness of the followers of Judaism, Christianity and Islam and all who grew up in cultures under the influence of these great religions. Yet, according to scholars of impeccable and international repute, nothing could be further from the truth.

Sigmund Freud, who was not only the father of psychoanalysis but also a biblical scholar of considerable stature, wrote that he could find no trace of the term Hebrew prior to the Babylonian exile.[28] Then, as I have described earlier, the Scriptures were first transcribed from oral legend into written form. Thus, the events described in Exodus and Kings were not given authoritative written form until over seven centuries after they took place.

The modern Israeli biblical scholars, Messod and Roger Sabbah, wrote a book, *The Secrets of the Exodus*, which describes in great detail the true

Egyptian origins of the Hebrew people. They assert categorically that there is no proof of the Hebrews' existence as a nation or tribe at the time of Moses in the manner described in the scriptures.[29] They also pose the following uncomfortable question: 'How could a people so impregnated with such a major part of the wisdom of Egypt disappear from the (Egyptian) historical record so mysteriously? More than 200 years of research in the deserts, tombs and temples have shown nothing!'[30]

For those who believe in the historicity of the Bible, the uncomfortable fact is that, despite the voluminous and detailed scriptural descriptions of the prolonged sojourn of the people of Israel in Egypt, no identifiable trace of these people can be found in the comprehensive and voluminous Egyptian historical records. Indeed, the term Hebrew as an indication of race is not found in any source other than the Bible, prior to the Jewish exile in Babylon. Furthermore, there is only one independent early reference to the people of Israel before that. The fact that a nation or tribe called Israel had been established by 1207 BCE is confirmed by a stele recording their conquest by Pharaoh Mernephtah that reads: 'Israel is laid waste, his seed is not . . .' Thus the first independent verification of the existence of the people of Israel does not occur until nearly two centuries after the latest date given for the Exodus from Egypt.[31]

Pharaoh or Foundling?

When we study the circumstances of the Exodus from Egypt, the evidence for the Egyptian ethnic and religious foundations of biblical Judaism becomes overwhelming. Prior to the late eighteenth and early nineteenth centuries, the biblical accounts had been believed to be accurate historical accounts of very real events. With the beginnings of critical biblical scholarship at that time, this conception began to undergo a radical and cumulative change. By the early part of the twentieth century a renowned Jewish biblical scholar, Dr Karl Abraham, published an article claiming that the Pharaoh Akenhaten may have been the biblical character known as Moses.[32]

This disturbing idea received a degree of confirmation when Sigmund

Freud published his final work *Moses and Monotheism* just before the Second World War. Freud demonstrated that the story of Moses' birth, as recounted in the Old Testament, was based upon an amalgamation of the earlier mythology of Sargon (2800 BCE) and Egyptian legends of the birth of the Horus, for both characters had been hidden in a reed bed to avoid their murder. Freud claimed that the story of Moses' humble origins was a deliberate fabrication composed during the exile in Babylon in order to disguise the fact that this leading 'Jewish' prophet was, in truth, a member of the Egyptian royal family. He showed conclusively that the name Moses itself was simply a derivative of the common Egyptian name of *Mos* or child.

Karl Abraham and Freud were certainly not the first authorities to claim that Moses was born an Egyptian, for the same assertion had been made repeatedly by several, far earlier writers including Manetho, the Egyptian historian and high priest of the third century BCE; by the first-century BCE Jewish historian Philo of Alexandria; by Flavius Josephus the Jewish historian of the first century CE, and by Justin Martyr, an early father of the Christian Church who lived in the second century CE.

Freud and Dr Abraham were later followed by Robert Feather the modern English writer, who claimed that: 'Detailed analysis of the Torah, the Talmud and Midrash led me to the conclusion that Moses was not only born and raised as an Egyptian, but was, in fact, a Prince of Egypt – a son of the Royal House of Pharaoh.'[33]

In the controversy over the dating of the Exodus, a number of scholars such as Dr Karl Abraham, Sigmund Freud and the popular English writer Maurice Cotterell,[34] have agreed that it was in the era of Akenhaten. Freud concluded that the historical character who later became known as the prophet Moses was an official in the entourage of Akenhaten, called Tuthmosis, who some Egyptologists claim was thatPharaoh's older brother.[35] These conclusions were expanded and reinforced by the perceptive Islamic scholar Ahmed Osman whose considerable forensic skill was deployed to prove, almost beyond all reasonable doubt, that the most likely candidate who could be identified as Moses was not Freud's choice, Tuthmosis, but Dr Abraham's original suggestion, the Pharaoh Akenhaten himself.[36] The same Pharaoh who had attempted to bring a degree of honesty and unity to Egyptian religion by abolishing the apparent panoply of the gods and replacing all previous religious practice with the 'heresy' of monotheism. His insistence on the sole worship of the sun god Aten, brutally consigned the worship of Amun to the past, thereby bringing economic and religious chaos in its train. These traumatic circumstances provoked prolonged civil unrest and the deposition of Akenhaten who seemed to disappear from the records without trace.

Atenism or Judaism?

Freud described the startling similarities between Atenism, the religion of Akenhaten, and Judaism. He stated that Moses had simply transmitted his own religion of Atenism virtually unchanged to the new people of Israel. At the risk of upsetting a vast swathe of his fellow Jews, Freud claimed that the prayer so beloved of the Jews, *Schema Yisrael Adonai Elohenu Adonai Echod* (Hear, O Israel, the Lord thy God is One God), was not a new and unique, post-Exodus Jewish invocation, but an exact copy of an Atenist prayer.

He claimed that, in translation, the Hebrew letter 'd' is a transliteration of the Egyptian 't', and, in similar manner, 'e' becomes 'o', thus this prayer when transcribed into Egyptian reads: 'Hear, O Israel, our god Aten is the only god.'[37] More than two millennia before Freud published *Moses and Monotheism*, the priest and chronicler Manetho had noted that Moses had discharged priestly duties in Egypt.[38] Akenhaten most certainly did just that as the supreme high priest in his newly built temple to the Aten at Amarna.

One Egyptian traditional religious practice was adopted under the leadership of Moses. The creation of the hereditary priesthood based upon the tribe of Levi was an extension of the Egyptian priests, a hereditary cast who were the guardians of sacred knowledge. Thus the foundation of the Levitic hereditary priestly tribe simply extended the rank, rights and privileges of the Atenist priesthood to their Levitic successors in exile. A new 'Jewish' hereditary priesthood who continued the onward transmission of sacred wisdom, from master to pupil and on down through the generations, much as before. Another example of a distinctly Egyptian origin for one of the central aspects of Judaism can be found when we examine the basis for all Jewish Law.

The Ten Commandments

The Law of Moses is founded firmly upon the Ten Commandments. But where did they originate? According to the Bible, Moses received the Commandments from Almighty God on Mount Sinai. There are two different versions of the Ten Commandments in the Scriptures and one found in Deuteronomy reads as follows:

> 'I am the Lord thy God, which brought thee out of the land of
> Egypt, from the house of bondage. Thou shalt have no other
> gods before me. Thou shalt not make thee any graven image, or
> any likeness of any thing that is in heaven above, or that is in
> the earth beneath, or that is in the waters beneath the earth.
> Thou shalt not bow down thyself unto them, nor serve them:
> **for I the Lord thy God am a jealous God**, visiting the iniquity
> of the fathers upon the children unto the third and fourth
> generation of them that hate me.' [39] [My emphasis]

This again links early Judaism to Atenism, for, according to Professor Flinders Petrie, the major difference between Aten and all other Egyptian gods, was that Aten was not the supreme god in a pantheon, but the one and only god. Petrie also claimed that: 'The **Aten was the only instance of a jealous God in Egypt**, and this worship was exclusive of all others, and claims universality.' [40] [My emphasis]

The modern Israeli scholars, Messod and Roger Sabbah, stress that Atenism abolished all the images and idols of other gods and proposed the revolutionary concept of one god: abstract, invisible, transcendental, omnipotent and all knowing. This unique, yet supposedly 'new' concept, was of a god that was deemed to be the creator of the universe in a manner that was in complete accord with ancient Egyptian belief.[41]

The injunctions against the use of graven images given in Deuteronomy's version of the Ten Commandments replicate those in the Atenist code. The Egyptian *Book of the Dead* lists the principles attested to by souls being assessed by the court of Osiris[42] after death, namely:

> 'I have done no falsehood against men,
> I have not impoverished (robbed) my associates,
> I have not killed.'[43]

In the Exodus account of the Ten Commandments, we can read a similar version:

> 'Thou shalt not kill.
> Thou shalt not steal.
> Thou shalt not bear witness against thy neighbour.' [44]

As Judaism has traditionally claimed that the Ten Commandments were a divine revelation made uniquely to the chosen people, this comparison strengthens the hypothesis that Judaism is an evolution from the religion of Akenhaten. Comparing psalm 104 in the Old Testament and Akenhaten's Hymn to the Aten, again conclusively indicates the links between these two religions:

> 'O Lord, how manifold are thy works!
> in wisdom hast thou made them all:
> the earth is full of thy riches.' [45]

Allowing for translation issues, a suspiciously similar passage is found in Akenhaten's Hymn to the Aten:

> 'How manifold are all your works,
> They are hidden from before us,
> O sole god, whose powers no other possesses
> You did create the earth
> According to your desire.' [46]

The Similarity of Sacred Terminology

The word for ark or casket is remarkably similar in both Egyptian and Hebrew. Indeed, the nineteenth-century specialist in Semitic languages, Antoine Fabre d'Olivet, wrote: 'I regard the idiom of Hebrew sensed in the Sepher [the scriptural rolls of the Torah] as a transplanted branch of the Egyptian language.'[47] The Ark, ritually employed as a symbolic form of transport for the god Aten in ceremonies at Amarna, was used by the Jews of the Exodus to carry items associated with divine revelation, such as the tablets of stone inscribed with the Ten Commandments. With the occupation of the Promised Land, the Ark was housed in Shiloh within a sanctuary staffed by priests of the House of Eli. The Scriptures record that these priests traced their consecration back to Egypt.

Further evidence of Egyptian religious practices found within Judaism also include the ten *Sephirot*, or attributes of God, found in the Kabbala or mystical wisdom tradition: crown, wisdom, intelligence, mercy, power, beauty, victorious, glorious, foundation and royalty. These, according to the Sabbah brothers, were originally listed as attributes of the Pharaohs.[48] Akenhaten sacrificed animals at Amarna and Moses' manner of sacrifice was identical. Armana was described as the Holy City and it is written that Akenhaten abandoned the sacred land of Karnak for *the Holy Land* of Akhetaten or Amarna. The 'Holy Land' is a telling phrase for both Jews and Christians.[49] The ancient Egyptians ritually inscribed sacred texts above the entrances of their temples, a habit that is replicated today by the Jewish people where such texts known as *mezzuzot* can still be found high up near the doors of orthodox homes.[50]

The fact that early post-Exodus Judaism was, both ethnically and spiritually, Egyptian in origin has been recognised by scholars for years yet, sadly, has not impinged itself upon public consciousness in the world at large. Now, when the world of Islam sees itself as persecuted by the Christian West as well as by the state of Israel, it is perhaps time that the devout in all three great faiths recognised the common, Egyptian foundations of their religions and learned to behave as brothers rather than antagonists.

Symbolic Continuation

These direct correlations between Egyptian religious usage, ritual and practice and those adopted by Moses and his followers are not merely proofs of the ethnic and religious origins of the Jews, but are symbolic of them. Other examples of the continued usage of Egyptian symbolism in Judaic practice abound. They include the symbolism of the freestanding twin pillars uniting mankind and God that marked the entrance to the temple of Karnak. In the book of Exodus this symbolism was vibrantly transformed from their original architectural form into a literary one that celebrated and dramatised the sacred nature of the Exodus. The biblical account tells us that as Moses led his people out of Egypt:

'The Lord went before them by day in a pillar of cloud to lead them along the way, and by night in a pillar of fire to give them light, that they might travel by day and night; the pillar of cloud by day and the pillar of fire by night did not depart from the people.'[51]

This vivid symbolism was also used to signify the presence of God in the Tabernacle:

'When Moses entered the tent, the pillar of cloud would descend and stand at the door of the tent, and the Lord would speak with Moses. And when all the people saw the pillar of cloud standing at the door of the tent, all the people would rise up and worship, every man at his tent door. Thus the Lord used to speak to Moses face to face, as a man speaks to his friend.'[52]

Later, the psalmists state that God spoke to them in a pillar of cloud,[53] a form of literary symbolism that underwent a further transformation and took on a new meaning, namely the fount of revelation or the very seat of Wisdom herself.[54] Again forging a strong continuing bond between the Egyptian gratitude for the gift of divine wisdom and the continuing importance of the wisdom tradition of the early Jews who regarded 'Wisdom' as an almost separate divine entity from the Lord God of Israel.

In the Apocrypha it is said of God: 'In the high places did I fix my abode, and my throne was in a pillar of cloud.'[55]

The ancient gift of gnosis, or sacred wisdom, was just as important to the 'new' hereditary priesthood instituted by Moses as it was to their Egyptian predecessors. The Dead Sea Scrolls scholar, John Allegro, claimed that the author of 'The Wisdom of Solomon' identified Wisdom with the pillars:[56] 'She became unto them a covering in the daytime and a flame of stars through the night.'[57] The Book of Proverbs describes Wisdom as God's helper in the act of creation: 'She built her house, she has set up her seven pillars (of Wisdom).'[58] Wisdom is also described as 'the consort of God', a strange term that poses immense problems for those who describe early Judaism as truly monotheistic and deny its earlier Egyptian origins. Centuries later as Judaistic beliefs were regularised, the interpretation of this term changed and Wisdom was described as a creation of God.[59]

The design of Solomon's Temple, as described in Kings, conformed closely to earlier Egyptian, Canaanite and Syrian models.[60] The entire edifice consisted of three square areas of increasing holiness in the initiatory tradition, culminating in a relatively small cube-shaped room known as the 'Most Holy Place' or the 'Holy of Holies' that became the resting place of the Ark of the Covenant.[61] Despite the injunction against graven images, the temple contained carved cherubim ten cubits high,[62] as well as depictions of palms and flowers, again recalling Egyptian custom. True to the ancient Egyptian tradition, standing before the temple were two freestanding pillars thirty-five cubits high, called Joachin and Boaz.[63]

> 'God gave Solomon wisdom and very great insight and a
> breadth of understanding as measureless as the sand on the
> seashore. Solomon's wisdom was greater than the wisdom of all
> the men of the East, and greater than all the wisdom of
> Egypt.'[64]

Thus the Holy Scriptures themselves relate Solomon's wisdom to that of

Egypt and also recount that King Solomon prayed for wisdom.[65] The importance accorded to the divine gift of sacred wisdom was elaborated in depth by the apocryphal book, 'The Wisdom of Solomon'. One later father of the early Christian Church, Eusebius, Bishop of Caesarea, cited the Jewish philosopher Aristobulus (c. 160 BCE) in support of the biblical accounts of the importance of wisdom to King Solomon: 'One of our ancestors, Solomon, [the reputed author of the biblical book of Proverbs] said more clearly and better that wisdom existed before heaven and earth, which agrees with what has been said [by Greek philosophers].'[66]

The ancient wisdom tradition thus passed in an unbroken chain from ancient Egypt into the belief system that was to sustain the 'Chosen' people of Israel and it was firmly embedded in the Scriptures composed with such inspirational effect during the Babylonian exile. The new Scriptures incorporated the Law and the sacred wisdom tradition within a matrix of stories of the prophets, some mythology and swathes of rather imaginative versions of history. The books of Exodus, Leviticus and Deuteronomy listed a number of obligatory laws based firmly on the Ten Commandments and that was now elaborated into complex and scripturally sanctioned legislation that comprised the 613 command-ments or *mitzvot* of the Pentateuch.[67]

Thus, by the codification and writing of the Scriptures, Judaism became transformed into a highly legalistic code that affected every aspect of an individual's behaviour. The emphasis was now on 'doing Torah' or keeping the Law; behaving with righteousness towards one's fellow man. Of increasing importance as an example of this ideal behaviour, was the concept of 'the Zaddik' or 'the Righteous One' who was also described as a 'Pillar' in the mystical tradition of the Kabbala.[68] Furthermore, according to the prophet Ezekiel, 'the Righteous One' will not suffer for someone else's sin. He will not die. It is: 'The man who has sinned who is the one who must die. A son is not to suffer for the sins of his father, nor a father for the sins of his son.'[69]

In the Sepher–al Zohar it is written that Noah was a righteous one of whom it was said: '"The Righteous One is the Foundation of the World," and the Earth is established thereon, for this is the Pillar that upholds the world.' So Noah was also called the Pillar in the sense of 'Righteous… and the embodiment of the world's Covenant of Peace'.[70] Thus Judaism became increasingly focused on doing Torah and behaving according to God's will, with only the guilty being punished for sin.

CHAPTER 4

Two Conflicting Accounts of The Life and Ministry of Jesus

ost people living in Europe, the Americas or any Christian community in the world today, grew up as children entranced by the magic of the Gospel stories. As a result, Christianity has exerted a profound influence on the development of Western culture and profoundly touched the lives of millions of people. This religion has left its indelible imprint on the landscape with architectural gems such as the cathedrals of Canterbury, Chartres and Notre Dame de Paris; with the basilica of St Peter's in Rome and with a multitude of parish churches of great charm dotted across the globe. Its musical heritage brought us the beauty of Gregorian chant, plainsong, oratorios and sung masses that continue to uplift and inspire us. In addition, the theologians, mystics and poets of earlier centuries have made an incalculable contribution to intellectual life.

Yet despite being a religion based upon the teaching of 'the Prince of Peace', Christianity has left in its wake repression, institutionalised terror, the Inquisition, centuries marred by war and brutality and two thousand years of institutionalised anti-Semitism, creating a sustained political climate that ultimately culminated in the Holocaust. How can this be? Let us look again at the Gospel story of Jesus, then compare that with what is known of the 'other' Jesus, the Jesus of history, and seek to discover the cause of such barbarity.

The Gospel Accounts of the Life of Jesus

Christians believe that they have a reasonable understanding of conditions in biblical Israel at the time of Jesus for the Gospels speak of a peaceful, pastoral land inhabited by the Jews who, according to the Gospel, were comprised of two religious groups, namely the Sadducees and the Pharisees with the occasional mention of Samaritans thrown in for good measure. This was the era of King Herod, a cruel and vicious Idumaean and not a Jew, who had been imposed upon the Jews by his allies and masters, the Roman Empire.

It was in the later days of Herod's rule that the child who later became known as 'Jesus of Nazareth' was born to The Virgin Mary and a carpenter called Joseph. The Gospel of St Luke tells us that Joseph and Mary, who was in the last stages of her pregnancy, had to travel from Nazareth to Bethlehem to comply with the demands of a Roman census.[1] The Gospels also tell us that Joseph was not the father of Jesus, but that God was, for Mary had conceived of the Holy Spirit.[2] Thus the infant Jesus, despite being born in the same way as millions of others, albeit in a cave used as a stable,[3] was far from being an average child, he was God incarnate. God made man. Furthermore, according to the Church, Mary remained a perpetual Virgin and bore no further children.

To mark this momentous birth, wise men, initiates of the Persian Order of Magi, followed a star until it hung over Bethlehem and brought gifts of gold, incense and myrrh as presents for the divine child.[4] Soon after this an angel gave warning that King Herod wanted to kill the child who was destined to be 'the King of the Jews'.[5] Indeed the king issued a proclamation that every newly born male child in Bethlehem was to be killed, the so-called 'slaughter of the innocents'[6] and, to save Jesus' life, the family had to flee to Egypt for safety.[7] Later they returned to the family's normal home in Nazareth and the Gospels recount how, as a young twelve-year-old boy, Jesus confounded the priests and teachers at the Temple in Jerusalem with his wisdom.[8]

Virtually nothing is told of Jesus' late childhood or adolescence. Indeed, by the time the story continues, he is a full-grown man and a religious teacher in company with his cousin John the Baptist, whose only function seems to be to mark out the way for the preacher from Nazareth. John is baptising people to cleanse them from sin and baptises Jesus whereupon a dove descends from heaven and God himself marks the occasion by proclaiming that: 'This is my Son, whom I love; with him I am well pleased.'[9]

Each of the Gospels give an account of the teachings of Jesus as well as a magical rendition of the many miracles he performed and detail his wandering ministry throughout the land. The three Synoptic Gospels of Matthew, Mark and Luke record the many occasions that Jesus used the phrase that became one of the central precepts of Christianity: 'Love thy neighbour as thyself.'[10] This instruction, which borders on the force of a commandment, is so important that it is found many times in the New Testament[11] and is as vital and relevant today as it was then. The Gospels also describe the many disputes Jesus had with the Pharisees as these learned men all try to lead Jesus into admissions of blasphemy. Indeed, in the Gospels the Pharisees get a very bad press.

Some of Jesus' followers are named and one of them Peter, is appointed to lead them after the death of Jesus with the words:

> 'And I tell you that thou art Peter, and on this rock I will build my church, And the gates of Hades will not overcome it. I will give you the keys of the Kingdom of heaven; whatever you bind on earth will be bound in heaven, And whatever you loose on earth will be loosed in heaven.'[12]

Later, Jesus' triumphal entry into Jerusalem is described in all four Gospels which tell how he was hailed ecstatically by the people in a manner befitting the 'King of the Jews' before chasing the money-changers out of the Temple, causing a near riot as he did so.[13] During his last supper with his disciples, so beautifully painted centuries later by Leonardo da Vinci, Jesus institutes the sacred ritual of communion:

'While they were eating, Jesus took bread, gave thanks and
broke it and gave it to his disciples, saying, "Take and eat, this is
my body." Then he took the cup, gave thanks and offered it to
them, saying, "Drink from it all of you. This is my blood of the
covenant, which is poured out for many for the forgiveness of
sins."' [14]

The dramatic Gospel stories then tell us how, shortly after the last supper,
Jesus was arrested by the Temple guard and brought to a night-time trial
in front of the supreme religious court in the land, the Sanhedrin.[15] He
was sent by this assembly of priests to stand trial before the Roman
Procurator, Pontius Pilate, who instinctively recognised that Jesus was an
innocent man. Pilate offered the assembled crowd an opportunity to free
Jesus under an amnesty, but the Gospels recount that the Jews bayed
insistently for his blood and so, reluctantly, and placing blame for Jesus'
execution firmly on the Jews, Pilate simply washed his hands of the whole
affair and Jesus was sentenced to be crucified.[16] Then, after three days, he
rose from the dead. Church teaching tells us that Jesus, who was God, and
therefore free from sin, was an innocent man who died in restitution for
our sins and that because of his redemptive sacrifice, we shall all inherit
eternal life.

This beautiful and inspiring story became the basis for Christianity
throughout the centuries that have elapsed since that cruel sacrificial
ritual took place at Golgotha. The belief system that has grown up
around it has been elaborated over time by Holy Mother the Church. In
its early years the Church, as the guardian of divinely revealed truth,
decided that Jesus, being God and the only child of a virgin who was born
without the stain of original sin, never had lustful thoughts, stayed
celibate without any difficulty and never married. His function in life was
to announce a 'New Covenant' with God, teach us how to live by it and
then experience the horrors of the sacrificial death by crucifixion at
Golgotha in order to redeem us from sin.

Western culture in all its facets coalesced around this haunting, cruel,
yet inspiring story of redemption. Promulgated as a series of verifiable

historical facts with a distinct and powerful spiritual core, the Church claimed that the teachings of Jesus were unique and the foundation of 'the True Faith'. The new priesthood of the Christian religion erected a temporal power base of great wealth and enormous political influence upon these foundations, and claimed absolute authority over all who lived under its sway, be they peasants, priests, nobles, kings or emperors.

However, in the last couple of centuries, the Gospel stories and the vast edifice of dogma and belief that flowed from them, have not merely been openly questioned, but are often described as Christian mythology, condemned as primitive superstition or derided as the 'opium of the masses'. In the last sixty years, documents have come to light that reinforce a growing scepticism about both the nature and the truth of the Gospel accounts. Scrolls of ancient and impeccable provenance, which, especially when studied in conjunction with the work of historians who were contemporary with Jesus, tell us a very different story indeed.

Biblical Israel in the Time of Jesus

The Gospels do not exist in some intellectual or historical vacuum for there are a wide variety of authentic histories and commentaries that predate the New Testament and many others, including various gospels and spiritually inspired scrolls that are contemporaneous with the composition of the Gospel stories. From these we learn that the Jewish state of Judea became a puppet state of Rome in 63 BCE as a result of Rome's intervention in a civil war between the Pharisees and the Jewish rulers, Hyrcanus and Aristobulus.[17] The Idumaean Herod the Great seized the throne in 43 BCE and had his rule confirmed by Rome four years later. According to the Greek geographer Strabo, Herod was, 'So superior to his predecessors, particularly in intercourse with Romans and in his administration of the affairs of state, that he received the title of King'.[18]

At first, Herod was a brave and resourceful king, a prolific builder, an efficient administrator and able politician who brought order to those he ruled. As an Idumaean who wore his Judaism lightly, he not only rebuilt the Jerusalem Temple, but also built several temples to pagan gods: three were dedicated to Roma and Augustus;[19] one to Ba'al at Sia; he also funded temple building at Berytus and Tyre[20] and helped to restore the temple of Pythian Apollo in Rhodes.[21]

King Herod is one of the best-documented characters in that era and it is a matter of record that he behaved murderously towards any members of his family that he perceived as a threat to his power.[22] The Emperor Augustus said of this type of behaviour: 'I would rather be Herod's pig than his son.'[23] In the last years of his life he developed even more cruel and violent habits that destroyed his reputation for all time, with the brutal execution of Rabbi Mathias and his devout students for pulling down the sacrilegious Eagle with which Herod had polluted the temple.[24] The New Testament account of his 'slaughter of the innocents'[25] maligns him, however. Doubt about this story first arises with the startling differences between the various accounts of the birth of Jesus in the Four Gospels. The failure of the Jewish historian Josephus to make any mention of this noteworthy event in his exhaustive litany of Herod's cruelty, gives us cause to question it further. In addition, the fact that there is no mention of it whatsoever in the Talmudic literature of the period, leads to one clear-cut and inevitable conclusion – it simply did not happen, it is a complete fabrication.

However, as with many other seeming inaccuracies within the scriptures, the report of this event carries a message of deep spiritual import. Symbolically interpreted this passage conveys the ever-present conflict between earthly power and ambition on the one hand, and aspirations towards spiritual enlightenment on the other. It also speaks movingly of the constant battle faced by devout people of all faiths – that of subduing personal ego and seeking spiritual submission to the will of God.

The Many Sects within Second Temple Judaism

The idea that the Jewish people were composed of two sects, the Pharisees and the Sadducees is both highly inaccurate and deliberately misleading. The Jewish historian Flavius Josephus describes four main sects, among many others, that operated within Judaism in first century Judea: the Esssens, the Sadducees, the Pharisees and those of the 'fourth philosophy'.[26]

The Essens, now more commonly called the Essenes, were the spiritual and lineal descendants of the Zadokite priests of the ma'madot, the hereditary families of the high-priesthood, who had withdrawn into the wilderness as a protest against the defilement of the temple by Antiochus, and the appointment of non-Zadokite high priests by the Maccabeans.[27] They held their goods in common, lived austere lives, maintained ritual purity, believed that the soul was immortal and, as their principal precept, maintained a fanatical insistence on 'doing Torah' – living life in strict accordance with the law of God. Josephus described them in the following terms: 'They exceed all other men that addict themselves to virtue, and this in righteousness …' [28]

The Sadducees were mainly drawn from the property-owning class and preached cooperation with Rome. While they did not believe in the immortality of the soul, nonetheless they insisted that the Law had to be followed precisely as it was written, permitting no deviation from it whatsoever.[29] The modern historian of the Jews, Isadore Epstein summarised the differences in attitude between the Sadducees and Pharisees to their Roman overlords, when he wrote:

> 'The Pharisees desired that all the affairs of the State should be governed on strict Torah lines, with no concern for any other consideration. The Sadducees, on the other hand, maintained that whilst it was well to recognize the Torah as the basic constitution of the State, it was impossible to carry on a Government, which, under changed conditions, necessarily demanded close relations with heathen powers without making political expediency and economic interest the final arbiter of things.'[30]

Bearing in mind the Gospel's innate antagonism to the Pharisees, it is interesting to note that Epstein believes that the Pharisees were the only party suitable to deal with the needs of the times. They were liberal in their attempt to interpret 'the Law' and its associated traditions and tried to modify its meaning and observance to make it relevant to the lives of ordinary people and this earned them considerable popular support. In all these beliefs, the Sadducees vehemently opposed them. Therefore, far from being the meddlesome troublemakers described in the Gospels, the Pharisees provided an inspired response to the dictatorial, anachronistic, legalism of the Sadducees as well as a necessary counterbalance to the innate subservience to Rome that this ultra-conservative, powerful, priestly and propertied class represented.[31]

Josephus also mentions 'the fourth philosophy' among the Jews, a sect that he describes as having 'an inviolable attachment to liberty which causes the nation to go mad with this distemper and makes them revolt against the Romans'.[32] These were composed of the Zealots and the Sicarii who campaigned ceaselessly against the hated *Kittim* the pagan Roman occupiers. They were devoted and ardent patriots who combined a devotion to the Torah with an intense love of their country and were ready to fight and die for both.[33] In fact, despite what is written in New Testament sources or implied by Church teaching, Judaism at that time embraced at least twenty-four parties and sects that were not regarded as heretical, but as integral parts of mainstream Judaism.[34] Furthermore, a devout Jew could sit at the feet of a teacher in any one or several of these groups at various times, in pursuit of spiritual knowledge and righteousness.

In addition to these important groups who made up the varied tapestry of religious belief in biblical Israel during the final century of the Second Temple period, there was a distinctive trend of charismatic Judaism that had Galilean roots;[35] there were also the various heirs of the mystical tradition of Egypt. One such sect, the Holy of Holies, became the focus for visionaries who imagined ascending directly to God's heavenly palace and approaching his celestial throne and there were many devout initiates preparing for this mystical ascent by special disciplines.[36] One form of mystical speculation mentioned in the Talmud, focused on the *maaseh bereshith* (the work of Creation) described in the first chapter of Genesis. Another focused on the *maaseh merkabah*, (the divine chariot) in the account of Ezekiel's vision. In that era, these mystical doctrines were carefully guarded and it was forbidden to expound them except to a few chosen disciples in the traditional manner of Egyptian initiation.

There was also the Ascents tradition in the Kabbala: ascent through the various degrees of enlightenment or gnosis – Ascents to the Higher Heavens – which is another variation of the Merkabah tradition, better known as *Hekaloth* mysticism.[37] The Kabbala itself, or the tradition that was received from Aaron, was the principal and most respected Jewish mystical tradition that was transmitted orally. One of its central tenets is the idea of the Zaddik or the Righteous One.[38] An obvious echo of the 'Righteous Man' described by Ezekiel that I cited earlier.[39]

Judaism was then, as now, a religion of studious piety where every possible interpretation of the Law was argued over, examined in detail and weighed carefully in application to everyday situations in life. This culture of analysis and debate gave rise to the age-old aphorism: 'Where you find two Jews, you will find three arguments.' In the theocratic state of Judea, the Torah was not just the Law of God, but also the law of the land and it was therefore impossible to make a religious statement without it also being a political one. This made it difficult, if not impossible, for the Romans to impose any political constraints upon the people of Israel without them being perceived as infringing upon the Jewish religion. With over twenty-four sects, each proposing different interpretations of basic law in a country occupied by the Imperial forces of pagan Rome, the potential for disaster was enormous.

With Herod's death, the kingdom was divided between his sons whose reigns were interspersed with periods of direct rule by corrupt Roman procurators. In that era nationalistic and religious fervour surfaced repeatedly in extremely violent confrontations. In the Talmudic accounts of this period, the first major rebellion was called Varus' War. To suppress this particularly violent rebellion, Varus dispatched his legions into the field, burnt Emmaus and Sephoris and enslaved the survivors of those cities.[40] Then, with ruthless Roman efficiency, he invoked the standard punishment for sedition by ruthlessly crucifying over 2,000 Jews.[41]

This rebellion, and its aftermath, was merely the first in a series of violent episodes signalling Jewish discontent with the Romans. When the Herodian kings and their Roman masters steadily increased taxation, the potentially explosive mix of religious fervour and political agitation gathered momentum. This was the turbulent reality that formed the actual backdrop for the birth, life and ministry of Jesus, not the gentle, rural atmosphere of peace implied by the Gospel accounts.

Robert Eisenman, the Dead Sea Scrolls and biblical scholar and director of the Center for the Study of Judaeo-Christian Origins at California State University, suggests that the fabrication by the Gospel story of a peaceful country where the Galilean fishermen cast their nets, the New Testament passages that depict Roman officials and soldiers as 'near saints', and the detailed descriptions of the vindictiveness of the Jewish mob, all have to be understood in the light of the fact that these accounts were written after the fall of Jerusalem and in total subservience to the brutal reality of Roman power.[42] Indeed, the Jewish historian Josephus, who worked under direct Roman patronage, stated that every historical account of that period suffers from two major defects: 'Flattery of the Romans and vilification of the Jews, adulation and abuse being substituted for real historical record.'[43] To complicate matters further, the Gospels were written a considerable time after the destruction of Jerusalem by the Romans in 70 CE. By then, Christian doctrine and mythology were already highly developed and, as a result, the 'Divine Saviour' of the Gospel stories has to be carefully distinguished from the very different Jesus of history.[44]

The Roman census that was cited as the cause of Mary and Joseph's journey from Nazareth to Bethlehem supposedly took place during the rule of Quirinius, the Roman Governor of Syria. This creates something of a problem for, according to the Roman records and the histories of Josephus, Quirinius began his rule over Syria in the year 6 CE, some ten years after the death of King Herod. Yet the Gospel stories tell us that Herod still ruled Judea. Indeed, when we consult the records of Herod's reign we find that no Roman census took place. Furthermore, Nazareth was supposedly in Galilee, an independent kingdom that at that time did not come under Roman rule at all.[45] The concept of a 'Virgin Birth' is another indicator that the Gospels owe far more to imaginative fantasy than to fact.

The earliest Christian documentation that we have, the Epistles of St Paul, were written within fifteen years of the crucifixion, yet they make no mention of the 'Virgin Birth' at all. Nor did such an idea occur to the writer of the Gospel of St Mark some twenty years later. No Jewish scripture, tradition or legend spoke of the coming Messiah being born of a virgin, but there were many such precedents in the pagan worlds of Greece and Rome.

As Jesus became increasingly popular as the God of a largely Gentile congregation, he, like other gods, had to conform to popular belief for his religion to be acceptable. Thus, the Gospels, which were written in just that era, took as their models earlier legends of virgins associated with pagan gods. The divine Jupiter had impregnated Danae and begat the god Perseus. The worship of Isis and the Horus child, another instance of virgin birth, was widespread throughout the eastern Mediterranean.[46] In the Greek myths, the virgin Persephone gives birth to Dionysus in a cave.[47] The Persian god Mithras, whose cult was extremely popular in the Roman Empire at the time of Jesus, was also supposedly conceived by a god and born in a cave. To add insult to injury, his official birthday of 25th December was hijacked by the new Christian religion to celebrate the alleged birthday of Jesus.

A similar situation exists in respect of the Gospel story of the visit of the Magi, the 'Three Wise Men', for that legend, according to the Dead Sea Scrolls scholar and historian of early Christianity Dr Hugh Schonfield, was of considerable antiquity long before the birth of Jesus. Indeed Schonfield claims that it had been used earlier in the same century, not in reference to the birth of Jesus but to the birth of his cousin, John the Baptist.[48] There is another strange coincidence to be found in accounts of the birth of John the Baptist for, according to the Mandean texts, Zechariah, John's father, is warned by an angel that Herod plans to kill the child and as a result sent the mother and child into the wilderness for safety.[49]

John the Baptist and Jesus

When we come to John the Baptist and his relationship with Jesus, modern historians using ancient documents are far more capable of filling in the gaps in the narrative than the authors of the Gospels. The devout Roman Catholic historian Paul Johnson claims that the example of the Essenes led to the creation of a number of Baptist movements in the Jordan valley, to the extent that the whole area between the Lake of Genasseret and the Dead Sea was alive with holy eccentrics, most imbued with Essene teaching. He is convinced that John was an Essene whose mission was the creation of an 'elite within an elite' within Israel[50] so that Israel as a whole nation could be purified and become a 'light unto the Gentiles'. John's position was thus firmly set well within the prophetic and mystical tradition of Judaism, indeed, some of his own disciples believed that he was the prophet Elijah come again.[51]

Another internationally renowned biblical scholar, John Dominic Crossan, after studying the relevant texts within the works of Josephus claims that John's baptism was not a ritual act that removed sin, but was a physical and external cleansing, symbolising that spiritual and internal purification had already taken place among his followers.[52] Historian Joan Taylor expanded upon this when she wrote:

> 'People placed themselves in the position of disciples of John
> [the Baptist] in order to learn how to be purified effectively
> both inwardly and outwardly. Once they felt fairly confident of
> their righteousness, by John's definition, then they came for
> immersion . . . Not all the people became his disciples. Once
> people were immersed, however, they would already have

accepted John's teaching and therefore become his disciples before this.'[53]

Yet, Holy Mother the Church has always denied any teaching role to John the Baptist in his relationship with Jesus. In contradiction to this, modern scholarship supports the 'heretical' view that Jesus was the Baptist's pupil. Which leads inevitably to the conclusion that the teachings of Jesus, far from being original, were part of a living spiritual corpus handed down from master to pupil in the initiatory tradition of old.

No wonder the Church has always denied any form of 'teacher and pupil' relationship between John and Jesus as this would pose huge problems for the hierarchy, for the Church would be seen to have been a trifle 'economical with the truth' in their accounts of these two inspired figures. It would appear that Jesus, far from being God and therefore perfect, must have been both human and a sinner who had already been restored to righteousness in order to qualify for baptism – a difficult concept for the Christian clergy to swallow. Thus Jesus, a devout Jew, was so committed to 'doing Torah' that he became a pupil of John the Baptist and needed ritual purification from sin before being baptised. From this, it is impossible to conceive that he *himself* ever thought he was divine. For him, as for all Jews in every age, that would have been the ultimate blasphemy.

The author A N Wilson reached a similar conclusion: that Jesus was a Galilean *hasid*, or holy man, a healer in the prophetic tradition, leading Wilson to the conclusion that: 'I had to admit that I found it impossible to believe that a first-century Galilean holy man had at any time of his life believed himself to be the Second Person of the Trinity. It was such an inherently improbable thing for a monotheistic Jew to believe.'[54]

The Synoptic Gospels of Matthew, Mark and Luke are, according to the modern scholarly view, founded to a considerable extent on an earlier lost common source that is known as Q. There is a startling consensus among scholars in respect of Q's content and style that has resulted in the virtual recreation of the document. Burton L Mack, Professor of New Testament Studies at the Claremont School of Theology in California writes:

'The remarkable thing is that the authors of Q did not think about Jesus as the Messiah or the Christ, nor did they understand his teachings to be an indictment of Judaism. They certainly did not regard his crucifixion as a divinely inspired, or saving event. Nor did they believe that he had been raised from the dead to rule over the world. They thought of him as a Jewish prophet whose teaching made it possible to live an attainable and righteous life in very troubled times. As a result they neither gathered to worship in his name, honoured him as a god – which to them, as devout Jews would have been the ultimate blasphemy – nor celebrated his memory through hymns, prayers or rituals.'[55]

Close and unbiased study of the Judaism of the Second Temple era soon reveals the a priori improbability of the doctrine of the deity of Jesus. He was born, raised and taught as a Jew; his followers were also ultra-strict Jews. The doctrine human 'divinity' is diametrically opposed to the Jewish concept of God and any Jew following the Torah who presented himself in such a manner would be stoned to death for blasphemy. Therefore, the obvious inference must be that the deification of Jesus was an intrusion from Gentile, heretical or external sources and was not fundamental to the integrity of Jesus' message. Proof of this can be found in the fact that Jesus' deification was staunchly resisted by the original apostles and those Jews who believed that he was the Messiah. This confirms that the whole idea was alien in origin and that Jesus himself could not have entertained it.[56] In stark contrast to accepted Jewish practice, however, the deification of humans was common among the heathens of Greece and Rome.

The Teachings of Jesus?

The Gospels and the Acts of the Apostles, with one or two exceptions, reveal far more about the theology of the authors than they do about the teachings of Jesus. However, the exceptions are fascinating, especially when they directly contradict Church teaching. The writer and historian of religion, ex-nun Karen Armstrong, comments on one passage in the Acts saying that, 'Certainly Jesus' disciples did not think that they had founded a new religion: they continued to live as fully observant Jews and went every day in a body to worship at the Temple.'[57] Indeed, Aristides, one of the earliest apologists for Christianity, wrote that the manner of worship of the first Jerusalem 'Christians' was fundamentally more mono-theistic than even that of the Jews. The teachings of Jesus were plainly not believed by his disciples and apostles to be either the foundation of a new religion or an indictment of Judaism, in fact the sole difference between them and their mainstream Jewish neighbours of any of the twenty-four sects of Judaism, was a fanatical adherence to Jesus' interpre-tation of the Law, underpinned by their belief that he was the Messiah.

Furthermore, the title 'Jesus of Nazareth' is a deliberate and calculated misnomer, for Nazareth did not exist at that time. His true title was Jesus the Nazorean, indicating his membership of a sect that was an offshoot of the Essenes. The initiatory and distinctly Gnostic nature of Jesus' teaching is made clear by a passage from the 'Gospel of Thomas' discovered among the Nag-Hamadi Scrolls in Egypt in 1945. In it he says clearly and unambiguously: 'He who will drink from my mouth will become like me. I myself shall become he, and things that are hidden will be revealed to him.'[58] Jesus as the teacher of righteousness initiated the elite among his Nazorean followers by a form of baptism, similar to that used by his teacher John the Baptist; proof of this was discovered by Professor Morton Smith in fragments of the 'Secret Gospel of Mark', which he found in the library of the monastery of Mar Saba in Israel.[59] According to Morton Smith, this Gospel was probably the one originally known as the 'Gospel of the Hebrews'.

We can only safely accept the reported sayings of Jesus in the New Testament Gospels when they can be authenticated by apocryphal works, or can be validated by the material covering the beliefs of Jesus' brother and successor James the Just. Others are more plausible when they are uncontaminated by pro-Roman bias or are consistent with mainstream Jewish belief.

When Jesus is quoted as saying, 'Go not into the way of the Gentiles and into any city of the Samaritans enter ye not: but go rather to the lost sheep of Israel',[60] this is entirely in line with Essene belief and may be taken as an authentic reflection of what he actually said. In contrast, the other saying attributed to him, 'Go ye therefore and make disciples of all nations, baptising them in the name of the Father and of the Son and of the Holy Spirit',[61] must be rejected as a complete fabrication as it is contrary to the Essene tradition in its instruction to preach to the Gentiles. Furthermore the use of the term, 'in the name of the Father and of the Son and of the Holy Spirit' only came into use when Christian theology was established many years later – it would be considered blasphemous by any Jew. The Jews only recognised one God, the Lord God of Israel.

A particularly crucial period to study is the one that commences with Jesus' entry into Jerusalem and ends with his crucifixion less than a week later. The deliberate staging of his triumphal entry into the City of David in the week before Passover[62] gave clear warning to the Romans that trouble was brewing, especially as one Gospel records that he was hailed with the words 'Blessed is the King of Israel'[63] a term that to the Romans was as an open call to rebellion. This would have been a painful reminder of a similar event that took place two centuries earlier, when the triumphant Simon Maccabeus entered Jerusalem to shouts of popular acclaim and was greeted 'with praise and palm branches' before purifying the Temple.[64] This clear note of warning to the Romans was thus amplified a thousandfold when Jesus upset the tables of the moneychangers in the Temple.[65] All this just before Passover when the city was bursting at the seams with Sadducees, Pharisees, Zealots, Hassidim and an assorted bunch of angry, apocalyptic fundamentalists, deeply imbued with nationalistic and religious fervour. The Holy City at Passover was clearly a religious and political powder keg and, to the Romans, Jesus' entry must have looked just like a burning fuse.

Pontius Pilate

The Roman Procurator was hardly the ideal candidate to deal with this potentially explosive situation. It is a matter of record that Pontius Pilate had a well-earned reputation for corruption, violence, robberies, and executions without the formality of a trial.[66] He had weakened the Sanhedrin by depriving them of their jurisdiction in religious matters and had saddled them with the responsibility of arresting anyone suspected of plotting against Rome before handing over the suspect to the Romans for judgement. The temple guards, acting under the instructions of the Sanhedrin, arrested Jesus and handed him over to Pilate.[67]

There was no night-time Sanhedrin trial of Jesus for blasphemy, that would have been illegal at that time; there was no appearance before Herod as recorded in the Gospels and, more importantly for history, there was no prevarication by Pilate over the fate of this Jewish trouble-maker. Why should he concern himself with the life of one man when his predecessor had crucified 2,000 Jews for sedition? The inescapable fact is that Jesus was indeed crucified by the Romans on a charge of sedition. He was certainly not tried by the Jews for blasphemy, as his teaching was completely in line with Judaic tradition – the Roman's standard punishment for sedition, rebellion and mutiny was crucifixion while the Jewish penalty for blasphemy as laid down in the scriptures, was death by stoning. He was tried and executed by Pontius Pilate[68] to nip an insurrection in the bud.

The True Successor to Jesus

When it comes to the truth about who was to succeed Jesus as leader of the disciples after the master's death, clues can be can be found in the New Testament, but the proof is located in the works of some of the early fathers of the Church and in a passage in one of the Apocryphal Gospels. Suppressed by the Church, the 'Gospel of Thomas' went missing for over 1,500 years until a copy was discovered among the Nag-Hamadi Scrolls in 1945. In it we find the following words:

'The disciples said to Jesus:
We know that you will depart from us.
Who is to be our leader?
Jesus said to them:
Wherever you are, you are to go to
James the righteous,
For whose sake heaven and earth came into being.'[69]

The phrase, 'for whose sake heaven and earth came into being' is a deliberate replication of the traditional Kabbalistic description of Noah of whom it was written: 'The Righteous One is the Foundation of the World'. A further reference to Jesus' appointment of James as his successor occurs in the *Pseudo-Clementine Recognitions*,[70] and according to Epiphanius, yet another father of the early Church and a historian of note, James was described as, 'the first to whom the Lord entrusted his Throne upon Earth'.[71] St Clement of Alexandria (c. 150–c. 215 CE) speaks of the election of James by the Apostles and not of an appointment by Jesus. Therefore it is established beyond all doubt that it was James and not Peter who was the true successor of Jesus. Even the New Testament acknowledges this, albeit subtly, when it delineates James as 'the first bishop of Jerusalem'.[72] The American biblical scholar Robert Eisenman takes this to its logical conclusion when he states that:

> '...James was the true heir and successor of his more famous
> brother Jesus and the leader at that time of whatever the
> movement was we now call "Christianity", not the more
> Hellenized character we know through his Greek cognomen
> Peter, the 'Rock' of, in any event, the Roman Church.'[73]

The falsehood inherent in the deliberate creation of the Petrine foundation myth forced the Church to marginalise the role of James the brother of Jesus whom they called James 'the Less'. Furthermore, despite the Church dogma that claims that Mary remained 'ever Virgin' and had no further children even the Gospels disclose that Jesus had brothers including James, Joses, Simon and Judas Thomas as well as several unnamed sisters.[74] This uncomfortable fact tends to explain Jesus' choice of one of his brothers to succeed him, for who would know his teaching best and be trustworthy enough to transmit it unaltered? His own brother would be the natural choice and James had a well-earned reputation for righteousness.

Another important cause for an embarrassment among Christian theologians began in the second century when, in its divinely guided wisdom, the Church decided that Mary the mother of Jesus was a virgin; that Jesus was her only child and that he was celibate. The fact that Jesus had several brothers and sisters was not the only awkward problem Church theology had to overcome; there was another – Jesus' allegedly celibate status. Jewish custom demanded that all men, especially rabbis, had to produce a family. The few exceptions to this are clearly recorded, one being James the brother of Jesus, who was described by the early Church fathers as a Nazorite who was 'dedicated to Holiness from his mother's womb'[75] and, as such, would undoubtedly have been celibate. The Dominican theologian and Dead Sea Scrolls scholar, Father Jerome Murphy-O'Connor, Professor of New Testament theology at the Ecole Biblique in Jerusalem stated in a BBC radio broadcast, that: 'St Paul was certainly married . . . Marriage is not a matter of choice for Jews, that's why you have so few in the early centuries who weren't married and that's why . . . Paul . . . must have been married because this was **a social obligation whose social fulfilment was obvious.**' [My emphasis][76]

The same reasoning used by Fr Murphy-O'Connor in respect of Paul must also have logically applied to Jesus. Furthermore, as a rabbi Jesus was subject to the 613 strictures of the Law and was bound to marry. More importantly, as heir to the Davidic throne it was strictly incumbent upon him to produce an heir.

The Marriage of Jesus

There is no mention in the New Testament that Jesus was unmarried and, if that were the case, it would have provoked considerable comment at the time. Indeed, some indications and traces of Jesus' marital status as well as clues to the identity of his wife can be found in the Gospels. A N Wilson, suggests that: 'The story of the wedding feast at Cana contains a hazy memory of Jesus' own wedding.'[77] And the Muslim scholar, Professor Fida Hassnain says of the same event:

> 'The question arises who is the guest and who is the bride? I would suggest Mary is the host for she orders the procuring of the wine for the guests, which Jesus deals with. One wonders whether it is *his* own marriage with Mary Magdalene, and whether the whole episode has been kept under camouflage ... I believe that Mary Magdalene behaved as the chief consort of Jesus, and he also took her as his spouse.'[78]

In the Gospel of John it is written that:

> 'And the third day there was a marriage in Cana of Galilee; and the mother of Jesus was there: and both Jesus was called, and his disciples, to the marriage. And when they wanted wine, the mother of Jesus sayeth unto him, they have no wine, Jesus sayeth unto her, Woman, what have I to do with thee? Mine hour is not yet come. His mother sayeth unto the servants, whatsoever he sayeth unto you, do it.'[79]

The story continues with the 'miracle' of changing water into wine and Jesus ordering servants to distribute it. Yet Jewish custom of that time would only permit the bridegroom or the groom's mother to give orders to servants at a wedding feast[80] – thus this was indeed Jesus' own wedding. Later we read of events that, read in any full knowledge of Jewish customs of that time, reveal the real nature of the relationship between Jesus the Nazorean and Mary Magdalene.

> 'Then Martha, as soon as she heard that Jesus was coming, went and met him: but Mary sat still in the house ... And when she had so said, she went her way, and called her sister secretly, saying, the Master is come and calleth for thee. As soon as she heard that, she arose quickly, and came unto him.'[81]

The Mary is Mary of Bethany, better known as Mary Magdalene, who is playing the role of a dutiful wife. In addition, the only woman permitted by Jewish custom and tradition to sit at a man's feet and in the Gospel of Luke we read: 'And she had a sister called Mary, which also sat at Jesus' feet and heard his word.' [82]

American Roman Catholic theologian Margaret Starbird was so angry at the 'heresy' of Jesus' marriage described in *The Holy Blood and the Holy Grail,* that she spent several years in research to refute it. Her spiritual and intellectual integrity were such that the book she published, *The Woman with the Alabaster Jar,*[83] is a superbly written, detailed exposition of the conclusive evidence demonstrating that Jesus married Mary Magdalene and founded a dynasty. The alabaster jar contained expensive perfume that Mary poured on Jesus head:

> 'While Jesus was in Bethany in the home of a man known as Simon the Leper, a woman came to him with an alabaster jar of very expensive perfume, which she poured on his head as he was reclining at table.'[84]

As a result, Western art and Church iconography nearly always portray Mary Magdalene as the lady with the alabaster jar. According to Jewish custom, and to other Near-Eastern traditions from Sumer, Babylon and Canaan, the king's head had to be ritually anointed with oil, usually by the royal priestess or royal bride in her ancient role of goddess. The Greeks called this ritual *hieros gamos,* or the sacred marriage. This ritual union with the priestess was crucial if the king was to be recognised in his divinely blessed and royal status, as the true 'anointed one' or the 'messiah'.[85]

Thus there were two very different views of Jesus, his nature, teachings and final days as well as two completely contradictory accounts of his appointment of the leader who was to succeed him. As for his teaching being either new or unique, that too is highly unlikely as he was heir to an age-old tradition of initiatory mysticism transmitted to him by his teacher, John the Baptist. One that after his death was carried on by the 'disciple he loved', John the Divine. Even the so-called central tenet of Christianity, 'Love thy neighbour as thyself' was far from new, indeed it was almost as old as Judaism itself and was a direct quote from one of the oldest and most respected books in the Torah, namely the book of Leviticus.[86]

We need to accept the realities of these opposing viewpoints if we are ever going to understand the hidden meanings encoded within Church symbolism by those who held a distinctly different view of Jesus from that promulgated by the Church. Let us therefore examine how one view became dominant to the exclusion of the other and how Church symbolism developed in the first centuries of the Church's existence.

SECTION 3

Early Christianity and the Development of Christian Symbolism

The man who became known as the 'Father of Christianity' was not Jesus of Nazareth, but Saul of Tarsus, better known as St Paul. His theology and his widespread mission to spread the 'good news' became the foundation of a faith that eventually dominated Europe and later the Western world. This new 'Church' became the arbiters of morals, good taste, art and architecture and developed a complex and ordered system of symbolism to both transmit and reinforce its message. Christianity, in one form or another, became the single most powerful unifying force in the development of European culture and its architecture and symbolism became the focal points in emerging Western civilization after the fall of the Roman Empire.

CHAPTER 5

St Paul, the Early History of the Church And the Foundations of Christian Symbolism

T he strange and complex character who became known as 'the Father of Christianity', despite his claim never to have met Jesus in the flesh, was Saulus, or Saul of Tarsus, better known as St Paul. His epistles claim that he was a Roman citizen and a Pharisee who spent some considerable time vigorously persecuting the followers of Jesus in the years immediately after the crucifixion.[1] Yet, after his miraculous conversion on the road to Damascus, this zealous opponent of Jesus' followers did an apparent religious volte-face and changed his religion and his name. Following an unexplained period of three years in Arabia[2] he then joined James the Just and his followers in Jerusalem, apparently learning the 'true way' as taught by Jesus.[3] Following this period of initiation he commenced a series of prolonged evangelical journeys that took him to some of the most important cities of the eastern Mediterranean. Yet, despite his undoubted evangelical zeal, he became the subject of scathing criticism by James' and Jesus' disciples in Jerusalem.

New Testament accounts and other sources make it abundantly clear that there was a fundamental difference between 'the Way', as interpreted by James and the original disciples and the new version taught by Paul. The conflict is mentioned, in a distinctly 'sanitised' manner, in the account of the Council of Jerusalem in The Acts of the Apostles. This revised version of events claims that, after heated discussion, Paul's teaching was deemed to be acceptable.[4] However, in the light of the absolute dedication to the Torah that was characteristic of James and the disciples; their strict prohibition against mixing with Gentiles; and their rigid adherence to the dietary laws of Judaism, this is an absolutely incredible scenario.

Paul's Expulsion from 'The Way'

Paul mixed almost exclusively with Gentiles and, in his view, the Covenant and its laws no longer applied; circumcision was no longer necessary for converts; and he taught that faith, and faith alone, was all that was required. In his study of the Dead Sea Scrolls and early Christian documents, the biblical scholar Robert Eisenman found records that enabled him to reconstruct a far more accurate and likely rendition of these pivotal events.

The word treachery occurs in the texts, referring to the factional strife within the community.[5] The dispute obviously hinged on Paul's preaching to the Gentiles and his repeated denial of the validity of the Torah. This led to a dramatic confrontation between a man called 'the Liar', namely Paul, and 'the Teacher of Righteousness', who at that time was most probably James the Just. Essenes' commitment to ritual purity, doing Torah and refusing to eat food sacrificed to idols, was absolute, and the strictures against social contact with Gentiles were rigidly enforced. In the Qumran Community Rule we find the following unequivocal statement:

> 'Any man who enters the Council of Holiness walking in the
> Way of Perfection as commanded by God and, whether overtly
> or covertly, transgresses one word of the *Torah* of Moses on any
> point whatsoever ... shall be expelled from the Council of the

> Community and return no more. No Man of Holiness shall
> associate with him in monetary matters or in approach *on any*
> *matter whatsoever.*'[6]

This is precisely what happened to Paul and as a result, Barnabas, who had been his constant companion up to this time, deserted him. Paul himself tells us this in his Epistle to the Galatians[7] which also lists his total repudiation of the Law; his teaching that salvation is by faith alone; and his denial of the Torah, which he claimed was worthless.[8]

Any analysis of the differences that separated the teachings of Paul and those of James and the other disciples in Jerusalem, clearly demonstrates that Paul had not only committed blasphemy in respect of his controversial views on the Torah, but that it was he who was responsible for the 'deification' of Jesus. The original disciples of Jesus, members of his family and Jews in general would have been outraged at the mere idea that Jesus was divine. To orthodox Jews this idea was the ultimate sacrilege.

The Gospels do not record any claim by Jesus to divine status, he never even claims the title of 'Son of God', indeed 'Son of Man'[9] is the only title he uses himself. If one scours the New Testament in its entirety, the earliest reference we have to the claimed divinity of Jesus, in chronological terms of documentation, is that found in one of Paul's Epistles when he writes: '... while we wait for the blessed hope – the glorious appearing of our ... great God and Saviour, Jesus Christ.'[10]

It was Paul who taught the notion that contradicted all of Jewish tradition from the time of Abraham onwards, that at Golgotha Jesus had become some form of vicarious 'sacrificial lamb' and had 'died for us'.[11] This idea was not merely repulsive in Jewish eyes, it was in complete contradiction to the experience of the patriarch Abraham. Since the time of Abraham, no Jew could perform a human sacrifice or become one, and those that transgressed this teaching were castigated for it. The sacrifice of an innocent man for the guilt of others also went against the basic religious principle that the innocent should not suffer for the guilty, enunciated centuries earlier by the prophet Ezekiel.[12] Thus Paul repudiated the Law, condemned circumcision and circumcisers – i.e. all Jews – brought back the pagan concept of human sacrifice and then deified Jesus.

The reaction of the staunchly Jewish community that centred around James the brother of Jesus in Jerusalem was predictable. Even the devoutly Roman Catholic historian Paul Johnson admits that from this time the evangelical mission of St Paul steadily lost ground to missions mounted by evangelists carrying written accreditation from James the Just in Jerusalem. Paul was scathing about this practice of accreditation and wrote: 'Or do we need, like some people, letters of recommendation to you ...'[13] Johnson makes it quite clear that if it were not for the destruction of Jerusalem by the Romans, Paul's efforts might well have been forgotten altogether.[14] Few, if any, Jewish disciples had anything more to do with him and Paul wrote that his colleagues and companions after his expulsion were Judeo-Greeks such as Timothy, 'whose mother was a believing Jewess',[15] the same description he applied to another of his converts, the Herodian Princess Drusilla[16] who was also a Roman citizen.

Paul's letters express considerable resentment and bitterness about his treatment and display his pain and anger at the charge that he was a liar and not a true apostle: 'Am I not free? Am I not an apostle? Have I not seen Jesus our Lord? . . . Even though I may not be an apostle to others, surely I am to you!'[17] In a later letter he writes: '. . . and for this purpose I was appointed a herald and an apostle – I am telling the truth I am not lying . . .'[18]

One early father of the Church, Iraneus, Bishop of Lyon (c. 130–c. 200 CE), quotes one Ebionite document that describes Paul as 'an apostate of the Law'.[19] The Ebionites, or 'the Poor', was the name by which the original disciples of Jesus were known both during and after James' ministry. The Kerygmata Petrou, another Ebionite document of the early second century CE, describes Paul as, 'an apostate of the Law', the 'spouter of wickedness and lies' and 'the distorter of the true teachings of Jesus'. This document is derisive of Paul's alleged visions and of his conversion on the road to Damascus. It brutally describes these as, 'dreams and illusions inspired by devils'. Thus it can clearly be seen that the family and disciples of Jesus looked on Paul with complete contempt.

From Paul's own letters we can see that this attitude was mutual. He describes his position vis-à-vis the first 'Christian' community in Jerusalem, in the following terms:

> 'Therefore stand fast in the freedom with which Christ has made us free and do not [submit] again to the yoke of slavery … Everyone who accepts circumcision is obliged to do the whole Law. Whosoever is justified by the Law **are set aside from Christ**'.[20] [my emphasis]

The Pauline epistles were regarded by James as blasphemous and gratuitously insulting, denigrating as they do circumcision, circumcisers, and the Law. He was also derided for adopting a two-faced approach, or, to use Paul's own words, of being simultaneously a 'Law-Keeper to those who keep the Law' and a 'Law breaker to those' who did not.[21] It is not surprising, therefore, that this quarrel did not end with Paul's expulsion from the first Christian community in Jerusalem. Indeed it soon turned from bitter, verbal argument to an act of murderous violence.

The Assault on James and Paul's Arrest

Recorded in the *Pseudo-Clementine Recognitions* and in a lost work about James from which Epiphanius quotes several passages, the *Anabathmoi Jacobou – the Ascent of Jacob* is the almost incredible accusation that Paul assaulted James the brother of Jesus and tried to kill him. Paul threw James headlong down the steps of the Temple and broke his legs. The most scholarly and superbly researched study of this appalling event can be found in Robert Eisenman's master-work, *James the Brother of Jesus*.[22] After this, Paul was arrested.[23] The Acts of the Apostles claims that this was because he had inflamed the Jewish mob at the Temple by preaching the Gospel. The truth would appear to be that this was a protective arrest to save the Roman Citizen Paul from a mob that wished to kill him for his attempt on the life of James the Just, who was supremely popular with the people. When warned of another plot to kill him, the Roman arresting officer[24] took Paul to Caesarea under an escort of 200 soldiers, 70 cavalrymen and 200 spearmen.[25] This was a suspiciously large escort for a Jewish blasphemer whom the Romans would normally have left to the court of the Sanhedrin and the inevitable sentence of death by stoning.

No Christian scholars have ever questioned why such an expenditure of scarce military resources should be employed to protect Paul at a time of potential rebellion. Yet, the most probable answer can be found within the New Testament: Paul is not only a Roman citizen, but also a member of the Herodian ruling family and a long-term friend of Rome. These uncomfortable facts can be found in one of Paul's own letters where he wrote: 'Greet those who belong to the household of Aristobulus. Greet Herodian my relative.'[26]

Aristobulus was the son of Agrippa I's brother, Herod of Chalcis, whose son was known as 'Herodian' or 'the Littlest Herod'. These politically charged family links explain how Paul became a member of the temple guard authorised by the high priest to persecute the followers of Jesus. The nationalistic zealous members of the Jesus group were a prime target for the Sadducees of the Temple bent on suppressing rebellion against their Roman masters. A N Wilson claims that: 'It does not seem unreasonable to suppose that he was in the same position in the temple guard when Jesus was arrested.'[27]

The political 'clout' that flows naturally from royal connections also explains Paul's comfortable status during his two-year 'imprisonment' at Caesarea under the orders of the Roman governor Felix.[28] Also within The Acts of the Apostles, we discover that Felix was married to a Jewess called Drusilla, a daughter of Agrippa I and the sister of Agrippa II. After divorcing her first husband she married Felix[29] who was the brother of Nero's favourite freedman, Pallas. Josephus recounts that the first Antipater, father of Herod the Great, was awarded hereditary Roman citizenship for services to Caesar.[30] Therefore Paul and Drusilla, as Herodians related to King Agrippa II,[31] inherited a highly privileged position which they exploited to the full. The epistle to the Philippians, mentions one of Paul's converts, Epaphroditus, a senior advisor of the Roman Emperor Nero.[32] He stressed this important connection later in the same letter with: 'Greetings, especially those in Caesar's household.'[33] Paul or Saulus, as the Romans and Herodians knew him, had friends and relatives in very high places.

This explains how Paul, allegedly a humble tent-maker, managed to travel the world with comparative ease, had so many 'miraculous' escapes from prison and was so frequently welcomed as the guest of people of power and political influence. The community at Antioch, who, according to the biblical scholar Robert Eisenman, were the first group of believers to be called Christians, were mainly drawn from members of the Herodian family. These Herodian and pro-Roman links go some way to explain why Paul neutered Jesus' message so thoroughly. He stripped it of all Jewish and nationalistic intent and then diluted it further with a series of instructions to obey all lawful authorities. Paul, like Herod the Great, wore his Judaism very lightly. If that were not so, it is difficult to conceive how any Jew of a studious and devout Pharisaic background could preach the anti-Semitic and anti-Torah message he repeatedly stressed in his epistles.

Thus Paul's message of subservience to 'lawful' Roman authority and his preaching of a New Covenant that denied the Torah was the complete negation of the teaching of Jesus and his brother and successor James. James' almost fanatically Jewish stance had distinct and overt political dimensions. James' pro-Torah, nationalistic, anti-Herodian and anti-Roman policy inevitably resulted in a head-on collision with the authorities in Jerusalem – the Sadducee high priests – and their principal ally, Paul's influential relative King Agrippa II.

The Murder of James the Just

The inevitable collision occurred after King Agrippa appointed a new Sadducee high priest, Ananus, who convened a meeting of the Sanhedrin to try James for blasphemy. The *Mishna Sanhedrin* listed procedures for the execution of men deemed popular with the people and recommended that the priests gather around the condemned man to jostle him and cause him to fall from the temple wall. Then the victim was to be stoned and have his brains beaten out with clubs.[34] This is precisely what happened to James. The brother of Jesus was cast down from the temple wall, stoned and then given the *coup-de-grâce* with a fuller's club.

One early Church father, St Jerome (342–420 CE), who first translated the Bible into Latin wrote that: 'James was of such great Holiness and enjoyed so great a reputation among the people that the downfall of Jerusalem was believed to be on account of his death.'[35] Later in the third century both Origen the Theologian, and Eusebius, Bishop of Caesarea, claim to have seen a copy of Josephus, probably the Slavonic version, which states that the fall of Jerusalem was a consequence of the death of James, *not the death of Jesus*; a highly significant admission by two of the most influential early fathers of the Church.[36]

It was after this traumatic murder that the Ebionites and the other members of the ma'madot, led by James' 'cousin' Simeon, left Jerusalem and crossed the Jordan into Pella.[37] The descendants of the family of Jesus known as the *Desposyni*, retained the hereditary leadership of the Ebionites for the next 150 years.[38] In Jerusalem and Judea, opinion among the Jews was sharply divided: the Zealots actively fomented rebellion against Rome; the Sadducees, 'Hellenisers' and Herodians tried every means within their power to oppose any rising; while many others simply wanted to live and worship in peace. However, the murder of James proved to be the catalyst; with his death, the die was now cast and preparations for war soon came into the open.

Paul's Role in the Fall of Jerusalem?

Despite the fact that the Church has always insisted that Paul was martyred in Rome, being beheaded in or about the year 66 CE and citing 'oral tradition' as their source, one contemporary historian tells a very different story about Saul, the kinsman of Agrippa. Josephus writes that when the Jewish Zealot forces occupied Jerusalem in 66 CE:

> The men of power [the Sadducees], perceiving that the sedition
> was too hard for them to subdue . . . endeavoured to save
> themselves, and sent ambassadors, some to Florus [the Roman
> Procurator] . . . and others to Agrippa, among whom the most
> eminent was Saul, and Antipas, and Costobarus, who were of
> the king's kindred.'[39]

The messengers to Florus and Agrippa were to request prompt military action by the Romans to subdue the rebellion before it got out of hand; a motivation completely in accord with Paul's oft-expressed philosophy of 'obey lawful authorities'. When this attempt failed, the insurrection became unstoppable and when, in the early months of the insurrection, the Jews repeatedly defeated the Romans, Saul is mentioned by Josephus again, this time as a member of a deputation sent to the Emperor Nero at Corinth – then called Achia: 'Cestius sent Saul and his friends, at their own desire, to Achia, to Nero, to inform him of the great distress they were in . . .' [40]

Subsequent to this meeting Nero appointed Vespasian as commander of the legions in Palestine. After four years of prolonged and bitter fighting, Jerusalem was besieged and fell to the Romans amid unprecedented scenes of carnage. The city's surviving inhabitants were put to the sword, crucified or sold into slavery. The Holy City itself and the Temple were razed to the ground. At a stroke the Jewish people were deprived of the central shrine of their religion, the home of the Lord God of Israel, and the spiritual heart of their culture and traditions was destroyed. Everything had now irrevocably changed for the Jews, for the true followers of Jesus and for the entire world. Paul's followers now had the field to themselves and all who could testify to the true teachings of Jesus were either dead, on the run from the Romans, or scattered and in hiding.

The Early Church

It would be grossly inaccurate to speak of 'the early Church' in a manner that implied any degree of cohesion, organisation or shared beliefs until many decades after the fall of Jerusalem. The leaders of the original

Christian community, or Church, in Jerusalem, Peter and James, were both dead and Paul had simply vanished without trace and their joint legacy was a collection of disparate small congregations dotted throughout the Middle East founded by a wide variety of evangelists each of whom had preached their own highly individual version of the 'Good News'. The leadership vacuum left by the destruction of the 'Christian' community in Jerusalem was not filled for some time. The Christians at Antioch fell under the sway of a variety of Gnostics and it was not until some seventy or eighty years later that the congregation in Rome slowly began to gain precedence. Paul Johnson claims that: 'Christianity began in confusion, controversy and Schism and so it continued. A dominant orthodox church, with a recognisable ecclesiastical structure, emerged only very gradually... As with all such struggles, it was not particularly edifying.'[41]

The structure of the early Christian Church, when it did begin to take shape, displayed a high degree of earlier Essene teaching, tradition and practice.[42] The emergent Church used a handbook known as the *Didache*, or 'the teaching of the Lord' as its model and passages from it were frequently quoted in letters to newer Christian communities. The *Didache* and the *Community Rule* of the Essenes, found amongst the Dead Sea Scrolls, are startlingly similar. The first 'Christian Church' in Jerusalem, for example, was led by a triumvirate of elders, based on the Essene model. The three leaders were referred to as 'the Pillars', and are listed as James the brother of Jesus, the 'first Bishop of Jerusalem', Simon-Peter and John.[43] Thus the well-respected use of 'pillar' symbolism had evolved further from its Egyptian use as a sign of divinely inspired wisdom or gnosis, through its signification of the divine presence during the Exodus, to symbolise a pillar as a 'righteous' individual who has attained enlightenment.

However, there is little sign of enlightenment to be found in the bitter disputes and quarrels between the leaders and emergent theologians drawn from the many and varied strands of 'Christian' belief. It took over two centuries for order to begin to emerge from the chaos of those early years. These continual and venomous controversies simply reflected the complete instability of belief in the early centuries of the Church. Even with the later establishment of an accepted canon of New Testament writings, the controversies did not cease; but this did prove to be a turning point in Church history that favoured those who were trying to establish an institutional Church.

The newly approved Gospels were accorded the respect of a new 'Divine Law' that demanded universal acceptance and respect. The concept of Law implied authority, but whose authority? The Church's authority! Who wielded that authority? The men who led the Church, of course. The 'Pillars' of the first Christian community in Jerusalem had a degree of authority and charisma deriving directly from their association with Jesus. That was now invested in the bishops and deacons of the new Gentile Church. False pedigrees asserting apostolic descent were confected to validate the spurious authority of the new leaders, the most famous being the Petrine foundation myth that was used to buttress the claim of the Bishop of Rome to exert supremacy over the entire Christian community. A situation compounded by the fact that Rome was the capital of the entire empire.

After Constantine the Great became Emperor of Rome and made Christianity a *religio licta,* an approved religion, things began to move very much faster. The Council of Nicea in 325 CE was convened by Constantine to end all controversy over the nature of Jesus, buttress the power of the clergy and condemn heresy in all its forms. In reality it gave the Church a power base that it has continued to use, enlarge and exploit ever since. However as a means of ending disputes, it was a failure. After Nicea, as a result of the repression that was institutionalised at that Council, dissent went underground, doubtless encouraged by the example of Priscillian of Avila who was the first Christian to be burnt alive for heresy in 383 CE.[44]

For the first two centuries of Christianity, congregations met mainly in private houses belonging to one or another of their members. It was not until considerably later that the Church began to own property and it was not until after the Council of Nicea that Church Symbolism began to develop in any coherent manner. In the early years, however, there was a pressing need for some universally accepted means of recognition between members of far-flung congregations who travelled far from home for reasons of trade or as slaves being sold from one place to another. Perhaps the earliest such Christian sign of recognition was the *Chi Ro* monogram formed by superimposing X(chi) and P(rho) the first two letters of the Greek word Christos. The resultant six-armed figure greatly resembled the spokes of a wheel, which was sometimes enhanced as the number of spokes increased to eight with the addition of a horizontal bar representing the horizontal arm of the Cross (see figure 8). The initial letters of the Greek words alpha and omega were also used reflecting the passage describing Christ in The Revelation[45]; also the word *Icthus*, meaning 'fish'. This was taken from the Greek words *Iesous Christos Theou Huois Soter*, which translates as 'Jesus Christ, Son of God, Saviour'. Thus the fish itself was portrayed along with birds, animals whose symbolic significance was readily recognisable to the Christians, but completely obscure to the uninitiated.

As the Church grew in size and power, other representations of the dove, the phoenix, the peacock, the lamb, loaves of bread and the vine began to come into common Christian usage and laid the foundation for the birth of formal Christian symbolism and art.[46]

Figure 8

CHAPTER 6

The Consolidation of Christian Europe and the Foundations of Church Symbolism

Heresy remained an ever-present problem for the growing Church. A problem that was largely solved by St Augustine of Hippo when he defined heresy as *the distortion of a revealed truth by a believer or an unbeliever*. The pivotal term, *a revealed truth*, was itself defined by the Church hierarchy as: *what the Church itself had declared to be revealed truth*. This useful, if somewhat circular and self-serving definition, was then used by Church leaders to establish a total monopoly on all access to the sacred.[1] The Church's very need to survive caused it to refute anything it viewed as heretical with increasing venom and also led to the rise of dogmatic statements of belief that papered over areas of dispute with dictatorial rigidity. The growing and ever more powerful Roman Church brooked no rivals, either within Christianity or in the pagan world, and campaigned vigorously and effectively for the closure of temples and centres of worship of rival faiths and then hijacked these well-established sacred sites for its own use. Thus the great Greek mystery temples of classical antiquity were abolished and their oracles silenced for all time.[2]

With the decline of the Roman Empire, the Church became the principal lawmaker for the newly converted peoples of Europe and their customary laws were given written form by the clergy who were the scribes, codifiers and final arbiters against whose decisions there was no appeal. Thus being the self-appointed and sole literate guardians of history, the priests wrote down the oral legends and myths of the various tribes, omitting all that was offensive to Christian teaching, retaining this, adding that, subtly changing people's ancient histories and creating the mould for a new, essentially Christian, culture.

In this pervasive way the Church was not only able to distort the histories of entire peoples, but also devalue any pagan rivals in the religious field.[3] This all-embracing process was strengthened by the incorporation of pagan festivals into the emerging Christian calendar: Easter took over from the festival of Astarte – the Phoenician goddess of love and fertility, the feast of St John the Baptist replaced the much older pagan celebrations of the summer equinox; and the celebration of the winter equinox was amalgamated with the birthday of Mithras on 25th December to become the feast of Christmas.

Much of Mithras' own mythology was incorporated into the Christian story, for legend recalls that at his birth shepherds adored him, and that after performing a variety of good deeds for his followers, he too celebrated a last supper with them before ascending to heaven. Mithras, in the form of *Sol Invictus* – the god worshipped by Constantine the Great – was supposed to return to Earth at the end of time and judge the human race.[4] A chain of events that seems a trifle bizarre for any Christian who believes that Christianity is either unique or very different from its predecessors.

The Church Tightens its Grip

It was not only the doors that gave access to the ancient spiritual and cultural heritage of its congregations that were closed by the Church. In its march towards total control, power and authority it feared any access to the realms of either sacred or secular knowledge that it did not itself monopolise. Education was restricted to the clergy to the extent that the first Holy Roman Emperor, Charlemagne (c. 742–814 CE), could barely write his name. By restricting access to books, education and understanding, the Church revealed its real objective - absolute power and control over kings, emperors and princes; over territories, peoples and individuals; over everyone in this world and their entrance to the next.

However in seeking to monopolise all access to the sacred and claiming sole rights over all spiritual knowledge and revelation, the self-appointed guardians of Divinely Revealed Truth had initiated a course of action that was to be paid for in blood over the ensuing centuries of repression and persecution that culminated in the Inquisition. The Church was corrupt and its influence on intellectual life stultifying. Yet, in the field of architecture and art, it was the true saviour of European culture.

The Development of Christian Symbolism

In the Dark Ages the literacy of the clergy led to the development of some of the most beautiful symbols of early Christianity. The pictures of the evangelists, which were the only illustrations in early manuscripts, became by the tenth century an assertion not only of faith but also of the almost divine accomplishment of learning.[5] While historians generally consider the tenth century almost as dark and barbaric as the seventh, the art of both centuries is astonishing. Princely patrons such as Lothar and King Charles the Bald of France, commissioned large quantities of manuscripts encased within jewelled book-covers, as well as superbly crafted reliquaries as gifts to other rulers or influential bishops.[6] In these beautiful religious artefacts, an appetite for 'gold and wrought gem-work' was no longer perceived solely as a symbol of a warrior's courage but was now used to celebrate the glory of God. By the tenth century Christian art had largely adopted many of the characteristics it was to retain throughout the Middle Ages.[7]

Before we study the individual examples of the many symbols of Christian faith, we need to gain an understanding of the context in which they must be read, understood and experienced. In the early years of the second millennium, Christian symbolism became an important unifying force, tying together many artistic, mythical and legendary traditions of the conquered people's pagan past, which were woven together by the common thread of Christian belief.[8] Thus many Christian symbols tend to share common ground with symbolic meanings in pagan religions.[9]

Representations of the Crucifixion, the redemptive act at the very heart of Christian faith, were rarely used in the early years when Church symbolism was developing, indeed, in early Christian art it is hardly ever used. The reason for this was pragmatic not theological, for the early Church needed converts, and it was believed that depictions of the Crucifixion would not encourage them to come forward. Thus early Christian art was far more concerned with the miracles of Christ, his healings and other inspiring aspects of faith such as the Ascension and the Resurrection.[10]

However, as time progressed, various forms of equal-armed crosses came into use, and again it should be noted that the use of the cross as a spiritual symbol considerably pre-dates Christianity. Two of the earliest forms are the *swastika* from India and the *ankh*, or ansa, mentioned earlier, from ancient Egypt. The swastika symbolised sacred fire and fruit-fulness and was attributed to Maia who was a goddess of fertility. The ankh was a hieroglyphic sign for life, or the living. Thus both of these cross-shaped symbols from different cultures were life affirming.[11] When the long-stemmed cross did creep into use, it often carried pagan symbolism with it, for example, it sometimes symbolised the Cosmic Tree, *the axis mundi* which was given a biblical or Christian gloss by being described as representing the Fall or the Tree of Knowledge of Good and Evil now transformed into the Tree of Eternal Life, uniting the two Adams.[12]

The Church's habit of using ancient religious sites of sacred significance followed Roman Imperial usage for the Romans almost invariably took over existing sacred sites and built temples on them and, as often as not, merely Latinised the name of the original deity and continued worship as before. Therefore, on approaching any village of real antiquity, the first building that comes into view is generally the church which usually stands upon raised ground because ancient churches, and their later replacements, were often built on a raised site with some pagan religious significance.[13]

Perhaps the best known example of this is Chartres Cathedral which, as we shall see later, was built on a mound sacred to the ancient Druids. Another pagan habit adopted by the Church was that of facing eastwards for worship. This is where the sun rises and is another example of a practice that pre-dates Christianity by many centuries. The Church insisted on the continuation of this practice and made it mandatory citing the Bible as justification, for example, 'the glory of the Lord was coming from the east'.[14]

Biblical Inspiration

The basis for the foundation of Christian symbolism was the Bible, the scriptural source of Christian belief, so it was inevitable that relevant stories from within its pages came to be presented in visual form. Narrative cycles from the Holy Scriptures became the principal subjects of Christian art in the West. Thus visual representations of the mysteries of the Creation, the Incarnation and the Resurrection became the central core around which all other symbolism revolved.

To accommodate and regulate this in a standardised manner that was in accord with Church teaching, predicated an evolving iconographical system that was developed by the clergy who then commissioned its creation in stone, glass or paint. In Christian art, right up to the Renaissance, it is not unusual to find two or more related episodes from a biblical narrative, that are described as a 'type' and it's 'anti-type'.[15] Each type, or precursor has its corresponding image or anti-type; the type depicts an idea, an individual or event from the Old Testament that prefigures or acts as a prophecy of its anti-type, the corresponding idea, person or event described in the New Testament.[16] For example, the story of Jonah and the Whale is held to prefigure the Death and Resurrection

of Christ as recounted in the Gospels: 'For as Jonah was three days and
three nights in the belly of the whale, so will be the Son of man three days
and three nights in the heart of the earth.'[17]

Several types occur in the biblical accounts of the Exodus: the
Passover Lamb prefigures the Paschal Lamb; the forty years in the
wilderness of the people of Israel equates to the forty days spent by Jesus
in the wilderness; manna, the food from heaven, is matched by its anti-
type, Christ the living bread; the story of Moses and the brazen serpent
predicts the Crucifixion and the Redemption; Moses striking water from
the rock is linked to the concept of Christ, the living water.[18] The classic
linkage between the beginning of the history of the people of Israel and
the fulfilment made by Christ can be seen in the type where Isaac is
carrying the wood on which Abraham intended to offer him in sacrifice
and the New Testament anti-type of Jesus carrying the Cross on the road
to Calvary.

Symbolism demonstrating the difference between the 'old' and the
'new' covenants are shown in a variety of ways; for example by the duality
of darkness and light; the flesh and the spirit; and, ultimately, by death
and life itself.[19] As well as events portrayed in the Bible, passages from
apocryphal works such as *The Book of James* were also used along with
subjects from non-biblical sources such as the Bestiaries.[20] Another
relative gold mine for the artist could be found in the lives, real or
imagined, of the multitude of saints into whose ranks many local gods of
the pagan era had been absorbed. Primacy among these, in each church
or cathedral, would be given to the patron saint of the district or of the
building.

New Testament Symbolism

The birth, life and ministry of Christ and, of course, the redemptive act of
the Crucifixion became the most important themes within Christian
symbolism. Not only was Jesus represented by the familiar images of the
bearded and compassionate figure so well known to all of the Christian
faith, he was also represented symbolically by a variety of other images

that were associated with him both in Holy Scripture and Church teaching and tradition. These include: the sun, the star, the branch, the fountain, the vine, the pelican, the snake, the fish in the form of *icthus*, and the Lamb of God.[21] Over the west front of many cathedrals we find carvings of Jesus enthroned in Majesty; Jesus Crucified and other references such as the Lamb of God, surrounded by people intimately connected with Jesus, such as the Virgin and Child.[22] It is common to find carvings of the Last Judgement with the saintly en route to heaven and the sinners on their way to hell, portrayed in great detail and usually placed for dramatic effect immediately underneath the carvings of Jesus himself in the central tympanum of the main entrances to many cathedrals.

Carvings of the four Evangelists are identified by specific symbols said to derive from a vision experienced by Ezekiel that in its turn harks back to ancient Babylonian symbolism: those of St Matthew by a man or an angel; those of St Mark by a lion which is often winged; St Luke by a bull, again sometimes winged; and St John by an eagle. All four symbols are often found grouped together, either at the four points of a cross, or in series on a panel. They can also be found next to figures representing each of the Evangelists to identify which is which.[23]

St John the Baptist is usually portrayed as a tall, bearded, emaciated figure clothed in animal skins held together with a belt and holding a tall, long-stemmed cross or a representation of the Lamb of God (see plate 1). He can also be symbolised by a head on a dish, or a figure with reeds at his feet or by an axe at the root of a tree.[24] The symbolism of the axe for John the Baptist, derives from his words recorded in the Gospel of St Luke: 'Every tree that does not bear good fruit will be cut down.'[25] That of the reeds arises from the words of Jesus used in the same Gospel: 'What did you go to the desert to see? A reed swayed by the wind? No. A prophet? Yes.'[26]

The figure of St Peter is also bearded, as are most of the disciples and Apostles, and he can be identified by the keys, usually two in number, that he carries in his hands. Like most martyrs he is sometimes depicted carrying the instrument of his martyrdom, in his case a cross carried upside down. St Paul, like the Evangelists, is depicted as having a pointed beard and a receding hairline, usually carrying a book and the sword which, according to Church tradition, was the instrument of his martyrdom.[27] Mary Magdalene is portrayed as a young woman with long hair wearing a red dress and carrying a pot or alabaster jar of ointment (see plate 28).[28] A figure carrying a scroll or book not only signifies one of the Evangelists, but can also indicate a Doctor of the Church, the founder of a religious Order or any learned and holy person.

The important dogma of the Holy Trinity is represented by an equilateral triangle which is one of the oldest Christian symbols, the equality of the sides and the angles express the equality of the three persons of the Trinity: Father, Son and Holy Ghost. Two interwoven triangles forming a six-pointed star are also commonly found and are used to express a reference to the Creation – for, in Christian theology, a six-pointed star is an ancient symbol of creation and the two interlacing triangles represent the eternal nature of the Trinity that was present at the Creation.[29] The six-pointed star also represents the Seal of Solomon, a hieroglyph for Wisdom (see figure 9). It is also known as the Star of David indicating descent from the Royal House of Israel. Other symbols that represent the Holy Trinity are three-petalled flowers such as the fleur-de-lys, the clover and the shamrock.[30]

Figure 9

Those who codified Christian symbols borrowed heavily from the world around them and made many analogies between nature and Christian doctrine. Thus the low-growing violet was transformed into a symbol of humility.

The circle, considered by the ancient Greeks to be the perfect shape, as a perfectly balanced figure that was seemingly eternal without either a beginning or an end, was, as a result, used as a symbol of the Divine, or of eternity. Other symbolic representations of God the Father include, the *Manus Dei*, or the Hand of God; the all-seeing eye, using the Egyptian symbol of the Eye of Horus, expressing God's omnipotence and all-seeing nature; a cloud or an aureole standing alone.[31]

One was used to express the unity of God.

Two was used to symbolise the two-fold, human and the divine, natures of Jesus and was also used to represent both the Old and the New Testaments.

Three was extensively used as a symbol of the Trinity.

Four for the Four Evangelists and a square or a cube symbolised the earth.

Five symbolised the wounds of Jesus.[32]

Seven is a powerful mystical number that appears repeatedly throughout the Bible, usually associated with perfection. It is the magical number of all known spiritual paths.[33] Theologians stress the importance of the seven virtues and the seven deadly sins. Sevenfoldedness is the most important key to unravelling the Revelation of St John. Within that mysterious work there are the seven stars; the seven golden candlesticks; the seven messages; the seven angels of the seven churches; the seven seals; the seven trumpet blasts and the seven vials of wrath. It was also a number of supreme importance to the religions and initiatory systems of all the civilizations that preceded the time of Jesus, whether their origins were Mesopotamian, Egyptian, Greek, Celtic or Roman.

'The number seven symbolises the movement of life in space and time. The seven days of the week, the seven colours of the spectrum, and the seven notes of the scale remind us that birth and death bear witness to eternal life in an eternal becoming.'[34]

Eight, or the octagon, symbolises Jesus, unifying God and Earth. An octagon is perceived as being halfway between the circle, representing God and the square signifying the earth.

Nine is the number of the angels, for there are nine choirs of them.

Ten is the number of the Commandments.

Twelve refers to the twelve disciples, the twelve tribes of Israel[35]
and, in architectural terms, the twelve doors to a cathedral
symbolise the twelve gates to the Holy City.[36]

All the carvings that can still be seen in the churches and cathedrals of
northern Europe were originally brightly coloured, and in the vast
majority of churches in Italy and Spain, they still are. While the brown
cloak in which Christ is usually clothed and the traditional blue and
white garb of the Blessed Virgin Mary are common, no absolute binding
convention was developed in respect of symbolic colours, but some of
the more common usages are listed below. When it comes to the
symbolism of Church ritual, however, a strict symbolic use of colour was
established.

Ritual throughout the traditional church year is strictly colour-coded
and the colour of the fabric used on the altar and for the vestments of the
priest changes according to the liturgical season. The standard colours
are green, purple, white and red.

Green represents new life and in liturgical practice is used
whenever the other colours are not appropriate.

Purple symbolises repentance and is mandatory during Advent
and Lent.

White, the colour of purity, is the liturgical colour of Christmas
and Easter,

Red, the colour of fire, symbolises the season of Pentecost when
the tongues of fire descended upon the disciples.[37]

Black is the liturgical colour of mourning and in symbolic terms
when black and white are used together, this represents purity
as, for example, in the *Beauseant*, the battle flag of the Knights
Templar and on the habits of Dominican friars.

Blue, as I have mentioned, is traditionally associated with the
Virgin Mary, and also sometimes with Jesus for blue, as the
colour of the sky, is used to symbolise heavenly love.

Brown, which was often used as the colour of Jesus' robes, was imitated in the simple dress of the Franciscans, a replication of poor peasant dress that came to represent renunciation of the world.

Gold, held to be the colour of light carries the same symbolic meaning as white.

Green became the colour of life in its triumph over death, just as spring overcomes winter.

Grey, the colour of ashes, symbolised the death of the body, and the qualities of both repentance and humility. In some representations of the last judgement Jesus is garbed in grey.

Purple, the liturgical colour of penance, was also the colour of imperial power hence God the Father is sometimes shown in a purple mantle.

Red is not only the liturgical colour of Pentecost; it is also the colour of the passions, either good or bad, although it is most often used for love. Mary Magdalene is also often shown in red to show her love and Jesus is often depicted wearing a red cloak. Being the colour of blood, red is sometimes used for the clothing of martyrs.

The Bible contains several references to white being the colour of purity and innocence. It is also held to symbolise spiritual transcendence; thus in depictions of the Transfiguration, Jesus is shown in robes of dazzling whiteness and the risen Christ may be portrayed in white. The colour yellow is sometimes used as a variant of white or gold to represent light and is often used for halos in stained glass. It can also be used to indicate treachery and deceit and Judas Iscariot is sometimes shown wearing yellow.[38]

These broad outlines of the general principles of Church symbolism in western Europe are simply an introduction to a vast and complex subject. Let us now proceed to a more detailed examination of specific examples to illustrate the points already covered that can be found in that period of superlative creativity that gave us the glories of Gothic architecture.

CHAPTER 7

The Glory of the Gothic

T he dedicated monks, masons and architects who created the Romanesque style of church building in about 1000 CE had been forced to come to terms with decades, if not centuries, of terror caused by war, migrations and the Viking incursions of the Dark Ages, which only added to the confusion arising from the imposition of Christianity on pagan Europe. The models they drew upon were those of Roman and classical eras admixed with those from early Christianity in both Europe and Byzantium. This resulted in a series of massive stone churches which the poetic English historian William Anderson described as 'castles of the spirit, as opposed to stone castles of the new feudal overlords'.[1] Cultural historian Kenneth Clark described the artistic creativity of the Dark Ages and the Romanesque era, in the following terms: 'It is arguable, that western civilization was saved by its craftsmen.'[2]

Indeed, the massive achievements of the men who created Romanesque art and architecture is nothing short of heroic. They had to devise or rediscover a whole raft of techniques in building and sculpture that had been lost since the great days of classical Greece and Rome. The range of possibilities inherent in the architectural and sculptural styles they developed, however, proved far too limited for the explosive eruption of new thinking, feeling and perception that arose, as if by magic, in the twelfth century. An era in which theology made rapid developments and brought a new and definitive emphasis on the salvation of the individual soul; it was the time of the birth of scholastic philosophy and, above all, for the ordinary people it was the age of the rediscovery of the principle of the Eternal Feminine that manifested itself in

Mariolatry and the lyrics of the troubadors.[3] A form of veneration that carried with it strong echoes of the worship of the Earth Mother in the Neolithic era and the veneration of the goddesses of pagan times.

The sudden rise of Gothic architecture signalled not merely a significant advance in form and beauty, but also inherent within its art an explosion of creativity, doctrinal change and hope. All given lasting form in those outstanding 'prayers in stone', the Gothic cathedrals of northern Europe that still intrigue and entrance us today. The nineteenth-century architectural genius who restored so many of our ancient buildings, Viollet Le Duc wrote of this era: 'The medieval artists have made the Christian Temple, as it were, a new creation, in which, as in an epic poem of mortar and stone, they have incorporated every creature of the visible and the invisible world.'[4]

All this was clearly expressed in the new style of architecture that was enriched by a devout idealism, in a manner that has never yet been surpassed. These new Gothic 'Temples' were created as earthly representations of the 'heavenly Jerusalem' described in the Revelation of St John. Each cathedral, like the heavenly city, had its four walls, each with three gates, to allow all to enter in the name of the Blessed Trinity; one set of three gates set in each of four walls, twelve in all symbolising the twelve precious stones, the twelve Apostles on whom the very Church itself was built.[5] The central space of each church or cathedral was flanked with columns, reminiscent of the sacred groves in which our pagan ancestors worshipped.[6] The entrances, porches and doorways were superbly decorated with carvings symbolic of the major precepts of Christian faith. Wall paintings, stained-glass windows and sculptures pointed the way directly to the righteous, religious and holy way of life and, thereby, to the redemption of the individual's soul.

The craftsmen who devised this evocative symbolism knew that it reflected the universal nature of Christianity. The artistic wealth they created operates on every level and so Christian symbolism has come to mean many different things to individual people, yet each symbol is there to redirect one's faith when it falters. The symbols are unobtrusive, yet evocative. They act subtly and subconsciously in such a manner that the faithful require no explanation of them and yet all continue to work invisibly and of their own accord in a realm far beyond the conscious mind of man.[7] Medieval churchmen understood only too well that images are truly eloquent teachers. Indeed, St Thomas Aquinas, that great theologian stated simply that: 'Man cannot understand without images.'

The First Gothic Church

Abbot Suger, who gave us the first Gothic building in Europe at St Denys in Paris, was both direct and explicit about his intentions:

> 'Bright is the noble work; being nobly bright the work should brighten the minds, so that they might travel, through the true lights, to the True Light where Christ is the true door.
> **The dull mind rises to truth through that which is material**
> and in seeing this light, is resurrected from its former submersion.'[8] [My emphasis]

Abbot Suger and the architects and craftmasons who created the Gothic style were men of exceptional boldness and originality who achieved something truly extraordinary in addition to the lasting architectural heritage they left us. They created what became an international organisation that over the succeeding 400 years, from about 1140 to 1540, trained successive generations of artists of pure genius; men who maintained the superbly high standards of their art in a manner which allowed it to continue to evolve in a manner that could adequately reflect the fashions and requirements of the changing times. For over four centuries they remained the supreme masters of applied science and technology. Because of their range of skills and insight, they became known to succeeding generations as the Gothic Masters.[9]

The Medieval Craftmasons

Initiatory Orders were, of course, nothing new for they had always existed among the craftsmen who built the churches, cathedrals and castles of

Figure 10

Europe. All observed traditions of chivalry and morality within their craft. They were united by humility towards the work upon which they were engaged and they were men who knew how to use a pair of compasses.[10] Raoul Vergez, a companion-carpenter of the Duties who rebuilt most of the church spires in Brittany and Normandy after the Second World War,[11] claimed that they all shared the same bread, one of the hallmarks of a true fraternity. Those who know how to use a pair of compasses are men who have been initiated into the secret knowledge of 'sacred geometry'. These qualifications admitted them to the status of 'mason'. The allegedly 'divine' origins of their skills is commemorated by the English author Ian Dunlop who wrote that: 'It is not uncommon in medieval illumination to find God the Father represented as the "*elegans architectus*" holding a large pair of compasses' (see figure 10).[12]

The initiated masons qualified by passing through three ascending degrees: apprentice, companion and master mason. Apprentices learnt their trade moving from site to site in what was described as a *Tour de France*, receiving instruction from skilled and initiated men known as *companions*. When they had attained the required levels of skill, their masters initiated them in secret conclaves known as *cayennes*. The Children of Solomon were the Masonic brotherhood who built the great Gothic cathedrals of France. Named after King Solomon, the legendary constructor of the first Temple in Jerusalem, they were taught the principles of sacred geometry by Cistercian monks.

There was a mysterious and, as yet, indefinable relationship between the Children of Solomon and the controversial Order of the Templars. It is difficult to discern whether the craftsmen were a part of the knightly Order, affiliated to it, or simply employed by the Knights of the Temple. What is indisputable is that the Templars, acting on instructions from Bernard of Clairvaux, gave a rule to the Children of Solomon in March 1145, prefaced by the words:

> 'We the Knights of Christ and of the Temple follow the destiny that prepares us to die for Christ. We have the wish to give this rule of living, of work and of honour to the constructors of churches so that Christianity can spread throughout the earth not so that our name should be remembered, Oh Lord, but that Your Name should live.'[13]

Indeed, the Children of Solomon did have some form of intimate connection with the knightly Order, for they received considerable privileges from both the Church and the State that included freedom from taxation and immunity from prosecution by the constructors of other buildings. It is also interesting to record that, at or about the time the knightly Order was suppressed, the Children of Solomon alone among the Masonic Orders forfeited all their privileges.

Gothic Symbolism

Fred Gettings, the English architectural historian, records that the Order of the Knights Templar was closely involved in that highly creative era of cathedral construction known as the Rise of the Gothic. 'The Knights Templar who were founded ostensibly to protect the pilgrimage routes to the Holy Land, were almost openly involved in financing and lending moral support to the building of Cathedrals throughout Europe.'[14]

While the Templar Order played a significant part in financing the construction of many of the Gothic cathedrals in France, their influence on esoteric symbolism will be dealt with in some detail in later chapters. What is important to note now is that their financing of cathedral construction and the role played by their protégés – the order of craftmasons known as the Children of Solomon – helped to create many of the Gothic masterpieces that carry some of the most beautiful and inspiring Christian symbolism in Europe.

According to Christian teaching, mankind is a strange mixture of saints and sinners and the repentant sinner can only be saved from eternal hellfire and damnation by the redemptive sacrifice of Jesus on the Cross at Golgotha. The Church, both as a body and in the form of churches and cathedrals, is a perpetual avowal of that belief. Perhaps nowhere is that more evident than in the cathedral of Notre Dame de Paris. Every carving on this ornate masterpiece is a celebration of the redemptive nature of the mission of Jesus and the deep Old Testament roots of both his spiritual and ancestral heritage. The huge triple doorway so familiar to tourists and pilgrims alike, appears to dominate the entire west front of this vast cathedral, although, in fact, it only takes up less than ten per cent of its surface area.[15] Stretching right across the entire width of all three portals and surmounting them all is a line of twenty-eight statues. These are relatively modern replacements for those destroyed during the French Revolution. They were destroyed as, being crowned, they were perceived to be Kings of France, in fact they represented the ancestors of Jesus as listed in the Gospel according to St Matthew and ranged from Jesse, the father of King David, to Joseph the father of Jesus.[16]

By some miracle their heads survived the destruction, were preserved and can now be seen in the Musée Cluny. In this museum off the

Boulevard St Michel, other carvings from the cathedral can be found along with large portions of the Pillar of the Nautes discovered during excavations under the cathedral choir conducted in 1710. The Pillar demonstrates that the Romans had taken over a Celtic place of worship on the site and erected a temple there dedicated to both of the gods Jupiter and Mars.[70] Later Christians erected their first church on the same site dedicated to St Etienne in the late fifth or early sixth century.[18] Near the north wall of the Cathedral of Orleans lie the ruins of another Roman temple showing clearly that this hijacking of ancient sacred sites by both the Romans and the later Christians was a matter of continuing and deliberate policy.

Notre Dame de Paris

The arch of the main central portal of the Cathedral of Notre Dame de Paris is composed of six superbly carved ribs decorated with patriarchs, prophets and kings from the Old Testament and, on the inner ribs, a plethora of saints from the Christian era. This merely provides a stunning backdrop to the central theme of the redemptive nature of Jesus' sacrifice. Enthroned in glory, Jesus is depicted barefoot with his feet resting on a carving of the New Jerusalem (See plate 2). His pierced hands are uplifted in an all-embracing and welcoming blessing. The divinity of Jesus is indicated in the traditional manner by a halo containing a cross. On his right stands an angel carrying the nails that pierced his hands and the spear that pierced his side. On his left is another angel bearing the sacrificial Cross on which he died. To the right the angel carrying the nails and spear is flanked by Mary the Mother of God, and that on the left is accompanied by St John the Divine, the disciple whom Jesus loved.

Two important panels beneath the figure of Jesus display the central message of redemption and the wages of sin. On the lower panel the dead, including various prophets of the Old Testament and figures from the Christian era, are shown awakening from their slumber as angels on either side blow the Last Trump. Above them, in a separate panel, is what they are awakening to – what in Christian doctrine awaits us all – the Last

Judgement. The Archangel Michael takes centre stage holding a pair of balances to weigh the soul of every person, judging them according to the love that they have shown while on Earth. Demons can be seen pulling downwards on the scales, in a last desperate effort to affect the outcome. To the angel's right stand those people who have already been judged as righteous, in attitudes of prayerful contemplation with their eyes focused lovingly on Jesus enthroned above them. To the left, escorted by grinning demons of fearsome aspect, the damned are chained together and bound for hell.

Separating the two doors of the central portal is a larger-than-life-size figure of Jesus, his right hand raised in blessing, his left carrying a book, the sacred scriptures of the New Covenant – the Gospels. Under his feet the serpent of evil and a lion are trampled into the dust. The entire central double-doorway is flanked by carvings of the twelve Apostles, six on either side. Peter holds the Keys of the Kingdom, the four Evangelists carry copies of the Gospel and, where appropriate, certain of them carry the instruments of their martyrdom. On either side of the central door are carvings of the seven virtues and the seven vices, as well as others showing Old Testament scenes, including one of Job reflecting on his misfortunes and accepting them as 'the will of God'.

To the right of the main portal is that of St Anne, the mother of the Virgin Mary. The central feature of the main tympanum above it is the Madonna and Child (see plate 3). Mary is enthroned in glory, crowned as the Queen of Heaven. Jesus is seated on her lap with his right hand raised in blessing. The Madonna is flanked by angels on both sides, the one on her right is accompanied by the figure of a bishop, commonly believed to be Maurice de Sully who instigated construction of the cathedral. To her left, the angel is accompanied by a king, who supposedly represents King Louis VII. Between the two doors is the serene figure of St Marcel, one of the popular patron saints of the city at the time of the cathedral's construction. St Marcel is carrying a bishop's crook which is inserted into the mouth of a dragon under his feet, symbolising the triumph of good over evil or, at another level, the mastery of Sacred Gnosis.

The third portal is also dedicated to the Holy Virgin, but in this superbly carved doorway, it is her death and glorification that is being celebrated. The highest carving in the tympanum shows Mary being crowned by an angel as the Queen of Heaven, enthroned in glory in an attitude of prayerful obeisance to her son Jesus, whose right hand is raised, blessing his mother. Beneath this panel is another where Mary is depicted in death, being laid to rest surrounded by disciples. The link to the Old Testament is made explicit by the fact that the body of Mary resting on her bier which, in its turn, is supported by a carving of the Ark of the Covenant. Thus Mary is the bridge between the Old Covenant and the New in the person of her Divine Son.

Beneath the main tympanum is a larger-than-life-size statue of the Madonna and Child separating the two doors. Mary is shown standing on a detailed carving of 'The Fall'. Adam and Eve are carved, complete with fig leaves of course, clasping their hands around the Tree of Knowledge and clutching an apple, the forbidden fruit, encouraged by a serpent entwined around the tree. The serpent has a human torso, which is clearly that of a naked woman, a graphic representation of the Church's ambivalent bias against both the generative act and the female sex (see plate 4).

One early father of the Church, St Augustine of Hippo, had confected the dogma of Original Sin whereby, he claimed all men were doomed to eternal damnation by the sexual act that conceived them, unless, of course, they sought the solace and redemption that only the Church itself could bestow for 'outside the Church there was no salvation'. So, in the view of this loving theologian, a man could live a saintly life, but, as a direct consequence of Original Sin, he was damned unless he sought the solace of the Church. Augustine's anti-feminine bias was made clear when he described all women as 'Vessels of Excrement', yet oddly he did not clarify this statement to exclude the Holy Virgin. His teaching formalised the Church's strange attitude towards God's gift of sex, an uncomfortable ambivalence that still distorts the lives of millions of believers today.

St Marcel is not the only saint of local importance depicted on the west front of Notre Dame de Paris. A detailed carving of St Denys, the legendary 'first bishop' of Paris is shown flanked by angels. The saintly bishop carries his head in his hands, complete with bishop's mitre. This carving can be found in the row of figures to the left of the three portals. St Denys was martyred at Montmartre by being beheaded and, according to a well-respected legend, he then picked up his head and marched down the hill, thereby setting a precedent that other French martyrs followed with gusto.

The bases of all three portals are decorated with carvings showing the signs of the zodiac. The Church's antipathy to the arcane art of astrology came much later for, bizarre though it might seem, Divinely Revealed Truth is a constantly evolving process that only later declared that astrology was anathema. Beneath each sign of the zodiac are small circular insets containing carvings of peasants and others at work in seasonal activities consistent with the time of years depicted by the sign of the zodiac above them (see plate 5). Similar carvings are replicated in greater detail on the west front of the Cathedral of Amiens.

Amiens Cathedral

The Cathedral of Amiens is the largest cathedral in France with a vault that soars heavenwards for 140 feet (42.5 metres). It is without doubt the most sublime example of Gothic architecture in Europe, *l'eglise ogivale par excellence*. A slightly later development of the Gothic style known as *Rayonnante*, the quality of light within its walls comes as a delightful surprise after the comparative darkness within Notre Dame de Paris for example. The feeling of space and of the light that floods the interior is heightened by the simple, severe lines of the pillars surmounted by Gothic arches and the glorious ribbed vaulting that seem to replicate Almighty God himself supporting the vaults with his fingers. The tympanum over the central door in the west front replicates the fundamental Christian themes celebrated at Paris, with only minor differences of design. Christ is again seated in glory displaying the wounds of the crucifixion, only in this instance his close companions are Mary on his right and St John the Divine on his left, Mary being flanked by an angel carrying the Cross of Redemption and St John by an angel carrying the nails and spear. Immediately beneath their feet are the saved and the damned; the righteous, fully clothed and serene of countenance en route to heaven and the damned, naked and troubled, being led into hell. Beneath them is the archangel Michael weighing the souls of the dead for judgement, surrounded by those awakening from sleep as the Last Trump sounds. (see plate 6)

The main doors are separated by a large statue of Jesus in the act of blessing carrying the Gospels in his hand. This statue, known as *Le Beau Dieu D'Amiens* (see plate 7), is flanked by two banks of prophets from the Old Testament on either side of the doors, thus stressing Christ's validity in both prophetic terms and spiritual ancestry indicating that the veil of the Old Testament is drawn aside by Jesus to reveal a New Covenant between man and God. This New Covenant is celebrated by carvings of the twelve Apostles reinforcing the continuity of the Christian message of hope and redemption.

These glorious examples of medieval sculptural art can be found replicated in one form or another on all the great cathedrals of Europe, the parish churches and the small chapels. Only Britain is almost bereft of them, thanks to the iconoclastic puritans of Cromwell's army whose wholesale vandalism in the name of God destroyed some of the finest artwork in England's heritage.

But what of those who had a different perspective on the life and work of Jesus? They too have left their mark on certain of the great churches and cathedrals in Europe. Their message was kept alive and encoded secretly, yet in plain sight; secretly for fear of persecution and unseen by all save the initiates who, following the hidden streams of spirituality that had irrigated the barren wastelands of the Dark Ages, were now, with the flowering of the Gothic age, tentatively seeking to come into the open.

SECTION 4

The Hidden Streams Come to the Surface

The hidden streams of spirituality, guided by the descendants of the ma'madot, the hereditary families of the high priesthood of Jerusalem, had kept alternative views of Jesus and his teaching alive for over one thousand years, albeit in conditions of the utmost secrecy. These priestly families, who became known amongst themselves as 'Rex Deus' had defied the repressive Church hierarchy and passed down their secret teachings in a manner that was tried and tested: fathers taught sons and daughters as the initiates of ancient Egypt had taught their novices. Within the Rex Deus group of families there was another even more select group, the *Desposyni* or the descendants of the Master.

The collective intent of all the Rex Deus families was to preserve the true teachings of Jesus until such time as they could be spread beyond the families to carefully selected disciples, secretly and without fear of persecution. In the meantime, they took no part in doctrinal disputes and outwardly practised the prevailing religion of the time while secretly passing down the generations within the families, the true nature of the initiatory teaching of Jesus the Nazarene as he received it from John the Baptist and transmitted it, in his turn, to John the Divine. Thus vital spiritual truths continued to be transmitted from master to pupil and flourished secretly under the seemingly obedient mask of outward

Christian conformity. These beliefs began to take tangible, physical shape in the late twelfth century in both formal symbolism and in architecture

The foundation of the Knights Templar, the actions of Bernard of Clairvaux and the creative explosion that accompanied the building of the early Gothic cathedrals, were all signs that the hidden families of Rex Deus were slowly and cautiously beginning to use the tolerance of the times to pass on their message to a wider public. They encoded their heretical message within mainstream Church iconography, in allegory and fable and in the new Gothic form of architecture itself.

CHAPTER 8

Sacred Geometry and 'La Langue Verte'

T he symbolic image of God the Divine Geometer or Divine Architect who, compasses in hand, created the universe, was probably inspired by the scriptural verse: 'Thou hast arranged all this by measure, number and weight.'[1] This geometric symbolism of his image was extended by the biblical passages describing the form and precise dimensions of certain structures: Noah's Ark, the Ark of the Covenant, the Tabernacle, the Temple of Solomon and the Heavenly City of the New Jerusalem. The dimensions of the Temple of Solomon held a particular fascination for the Craftmasons.[2] Furthermore, the Divine Geometer or, as the Craftmasons called him, the Great Architect of the Universe, compasses in hand, divided the light from the darkness, and heaven and earth from the waters. It was believed that Pythagorean geometry in which 'all things are known to have number', was the perfect vehicle of expression of the inherent harmony that is to be found within nature and the universe.[3] For as John James the architectural historian has written: 'Creative work without some sense of unity throughout it is not art, which is why even under medieval contracting conditions the masters developed a technique to ensure some sort of unity.'[4]

So the artistic and architectural representation of the sacred developed into a form of science governed by fixed and secret laws that could not be transgressed at the whim of any individual. This principle was encapsulated in an aphorism of great importance to the medieval Craftmasons

– 'Ars nihilni scienta est' – art is nothing without knowledge. The great Gothic cathedrals of the medieval era were not built just to be seen from the perspective of man, but the viewpoint of Almighty God himself. Other considerations were completely irrelevant to those people, Craftmasons and clergy alike believed that they were building an earthly representation of paradise. God's purpose given architectural form. Only through the discipline of sacred geometry could that be achieved. In architecture there was not one decision that was not made through geometry.[5]

Sacred Geometry

The new science of scared geometry rested firmly on a reasoned belief in the virtue of numbers and the Craftmasons of the medieval era 'knew' that numbers were endowed with an occult power. St Augustine of Hippo believed that numbers were the thoughts of God and said: 'The divine wisdom is presented in the numbers impressed on all things.' An idea developed by Émile Mâle when he wrote that: 'The construction of the physical and moral world alike is based upon eternal numbers.'[6] The significance of numbers in expressing the divine order of things was not restricted to the architects of Classical Greece or to the medieval students of sacred geometry. It was known and respected by the followers of the tradition of the Kabbala, the supreme vehicle of transmission of the inner and mystical aspects of Judaism.[7] Thus, paradoxically, cathedrals built to celebrate the 'heresy' first propounded by St Paul, harked back in their construction to an ancient Judaic tradition that was far closer in fact to the true teachings of Jesus. So, discovery of the geometric laws of the universe mingled with ancient Jewish mystical tradition to produce the Gothic architecture of the great Christian churches and cathedrals of western Europe.

Therefore symbolism is not simply restricted to sculpture, paintings and stained glass, it includes the architecture as well. The symbolic imagery of the paintings and sculptures of the medieval cathedrals often may appear to be a two- or three-dimensional form of 'teaching board' for the instruction of the illiterate, but for the Craftmasons who built them, the real mysteries were expressed in the architecture; beneath the decorative and inspirational sculptures there vibrates a deeper resonance within the very building itself.[8] Indeed the patterns inherent within sacred geometry were, to the master masons who used it, tangible signs that they had tapped into a higher level of consciousness that would guarantee the building's stability. The use of appropriate patterns symbolised a pact with the Divine Architect in which he pledged that he would maintain the building in its allotted place.

Two modern architectural scholars John James[9] (see figute 11) and George Lesser[10] (see figure 12) applied different sets of geometrical patterns to the ground plan of Chartres Cathedral and another very different variation was devised by the French mystical writer, Louis Charpentier.[11] (See figure 13) While each of these geometrical patterns contain considerable differences from one another, they all have as points of focus, the centre of the Labyrinth in the nave, the central point of the transepts (now the site of an altar) and the high altar in the choir. Each, different from the others though it may be, is equally valid and none of them are mutually exclusive. As Colin Ward explained, the master masons of the medieval era:

' …gloried in multiplicity as part of the divine order and hence we should not be surprised when we find more than one geometric system inhabiting the one place, each flowing over the other, while being locked together at a few essential points like the Labyrinth and the altar, which thereby express the most sacred and meaningful locations in the building.'[12]

It is no wonder, therefore, that the study of sacred geometry is one that has occupied many gifted and skilled architects for a lifetime. The problems of analysis are extremely complex and far beyond the scope of a work such as this. Furthermore, despite the many assertions that sacred geometry was the sole preserve of the hidden streams of spirituality, this is simply not so. Sacred geometry is not only the preserve of both

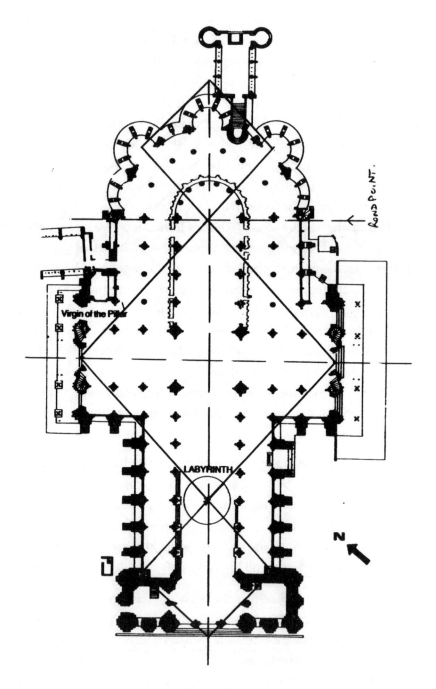

Figure 11

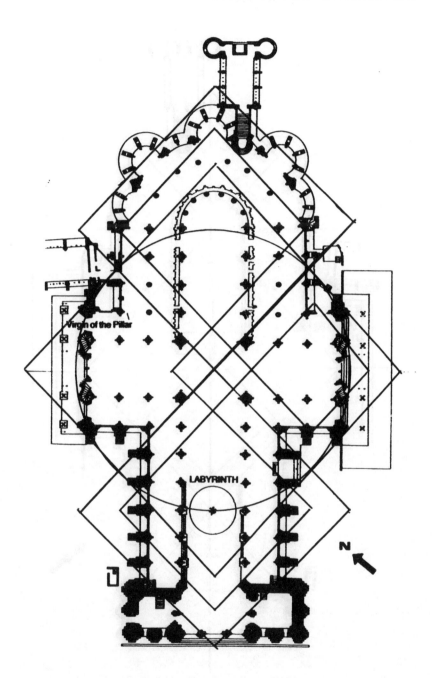

Figure 12

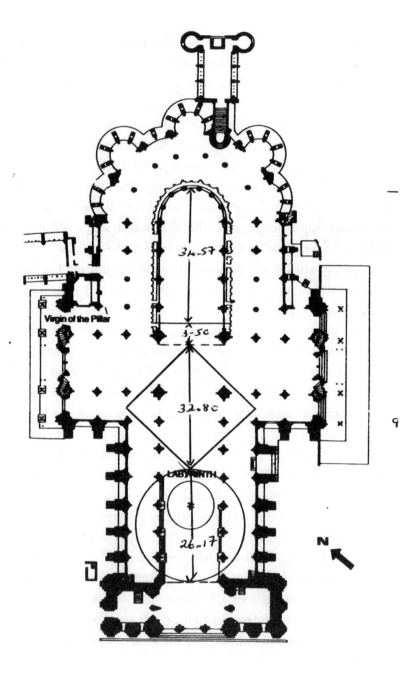

Figure 13

mainstream Christianity and the hidden streams, it transcends all religious boundaries and is detectable in the sacred buildings of all creeds and cultures, as the work of that gifted architectural scholar Keith Critchlow amply demonstrates.

On occasion certain geometrical features do have occult significance and examples of them will be dealt with in due course. In the mainstream of sacred geometry, however, irrespective of the unit of measurement being used, the systems of proportion being used were the *ad quadratum* designs based upon the square, symbolising the earth and the *ad triangulum* shapes derived from the equilateral triangle which, as I have explained earlier, is symbolic of the Holy Trinity.

The effects of the sacred geometry of the Gothic era can hardly be exaggerated. That poetic architectural historian William Anderson wrote that a Gothic building 'creates a new state in us, the state of intensified aesthetic delight which is like singing in the mind'.[13] A result that, in special sites such as Chartres for example, aided by artificially enhanced telluric forces and the energy of certain qualities of light filtering through the stained glass, become truly transformative, inducing a higher state of consciousness, a tangible initiatory state. Thus the use of sacred geometry could be sacramental, sometimes initiatory, and always symbolic of the Divine. Indeed the rule of the Craftmasons who built the Gothic cathedrals states clearly that they used their craft: 'not so that our name should be remembered, Oh Lord, but that Your Name should live.'[14]

This divinely inspired art form included many skills such as engineering, building and design. The knowledge base of these, according to the traditions of the Craftmasons, had been handed down from master to novice in an unbroken chain of transmission from the earliest times until the fall of Jerusalem in 70 CE. This same unbroken chain of teaching had preserved, enhanced and passed on the secret knowledge required for the construction of sacred buildings by the ancient Egyptians and biblical Israelites.[15]

After the fall of Jerusalem, the knowledge of sacred geometry was apparently lost until crusading knights of the newly formed Templar

Order returned from the Holy Land in 1128. Inevitably, certain questions arise from the strange juxtaposition of the Templars' return from Jerusalem and the sudden explosion of building in the Gothic style that followed, namely: Did the Templars find the keys to this new form of building in the course of their excavations under the Temple Mount? Or were there other influences originating in Jerusalem that can clarify the origins of this new form of architecture?

The Rise of the Gothic

In earlier works I suggested one possible source, namely documentation they may have discovered under the Temple Mount, but I proposed this idea in the absence of evidence of any viable alternative and have always had some reservations about it.

Two learned historians of note – the gifted Englishman, William Anderson, and the French scholar, Jean Boney – both claim that the Gothic arch was introduced from Islamic culture.[16] My good friend and colleague, Gordon Strachan, has now elaborated this idea in highly credible detail. I first met Gordon at a seminar in Edinburgh organised by Keith Critchlow. Gordon's suggested origin for the Gothic arch is not only completely credible but also has the merit of simplicity. Furthermore, it is wholly consistent with what we know of cultural inter-change at the time of the First Crusade and thereafter.

Gordon is convinced that the origin of the pointed arch that is the foundation of the Gothic style of building lies outside Europe. Like William Anderson and Jean Boney, he agrees that its origin is Islamic, but he goes further and claims that it came from the Holy Land. Gordon wrote that the Gothic arch resulted from, 'a unique blending of indigenous building skills with the architectural genius of Islam'.[17]

It is demonstrably true that the Templars, during their first period of nine-years residence in Jerusalem, met many members of the Sufi Orders who were undergoing a revival in their fortunes at that time.[18] The Sufis were the main mystical order of Islam who were devout believers in a mystical form of inter-faith pluralism epitomised by the words of

Jalaluddin Rumi: 'The religion of love is apart from all religions. The lovers of God have no religion but God alone.' A fruit of a similar initiatory pathway to that followed by the Templars and the Rex Deus families back in Europe. It was as a result of their contact with the Sufis that, Strachan claims, the Templars learnt the geometric method used to design the Islamic *mukhammas* or pointed arch. They put this to the test in Jerusalem building a three-bayed doorway with pointed arches on the Temple Mount that can still be seen today.[19]

Thus knowledge of sacred geometry gained an immense boost from contact between the initiatory Orders of both faiths, the Templars and the Sufis, and the end result was the development of the pointed arch into a totally new style of sacred building. Thus the result of inter-faith co-operation can still be seen and appreciated in the flowering of artistic and religious expression of the medieval Gothic cathedrals. Two well-known mystical writers of the twentieth century noted the importance of Templar influence on these buildings in the last century. First, the twentieth-century mystical writer Ouspensky speaks of the link between the new sacred architecture and the hidden streams of spirituality:

> 'The building of cathedrals was part of a colossal and cleverly devised plan which permitted the existence of entirely free philosophical and psychological schools in the rude, absurd, cruel, superstitious, bigoted and scholastic Middle Ages. These schools have left us an immense heritage, almost all of which we have already wasted without understanding its meaning and value.'[20]

The renowned twentieth-century French initiate, Fulcanelli remarked that a church or cathedral was not merely a place of worship, or a sanctuary for the sick and deprived, but also a place of commercial activity, public theatre and secular beliefs.

> 'The Gothic cathedral, that sanctuary of the Tradition, Science and Art, should not be regarded as a work dedicated solely to the glory of Christianity, but rather as a vast concretion of

ideas, of tendencies, of popular beliefs; a perfect whole to which we can refer without fear, whenever we would penetrate the religious, secular, philosophic or social thoughts of our ancestors.'[21]

He too made the link between the heretical streams of spirituality when he described Gothic cathedrals as a form of philosophical 'stock exchange' where lingering pockets of arcana and heresy were flouted under the noses of an unsuspecting clergy.[22]

Esoteric Symbolism and *La Langue Verte*

Fulcanelli, and his biographer Kenneth Rayner Johnson, both state categorically that Gothic architecture, which was the fruit of the Templar's knowledge of sacred geometry, was not only a superb example of architectural beauty but also a three-dimensional code that carried its hidden message in an architectural form of *la langue verte*, the green language, or the language of initiation. Some years earlier, towards the end of the nineteenth century J F Colfs had written that: 'The language of stones spoken by this new art, [Gothic architecture] is at the same time clear and sublime, speaking alike to the humblest and to the most cultured heart.'[23]

La langue verte arose from the demands incumbent upon all initiates and heretics to disguise the details of their conversations from casual eavesdroppers such as the clergy. Heretics had to learn to talk using a verbal code, so that they could communicate freely without putting their lives or their freedom in jeopardy. Over the centuries this useful barrier against persecution became not only the language of heretical initiates but also of all the poor and oppressed who needed to keep their conversations secret from their lords and masters. *La langue verte* was thus the medieval ancestor of cockney rhyming slang and the mid-twentieth-century development of 'hip-talk' or 'rap' in the American inner-city ghettos.[24]

A similar form of camouflage was developed to communicate heretical ideas under the guise of normal Christian symbolism where very different interpretations would apply provided certain visual clues could be discerned by observant and aware initiates. If there were no clues, then the standard church interpretation applied; if the clues were present, then an esoteric, or hidden meaning would be more relevant.

Knowledge, as information, can be acquired through many forms of learning. In the case of esoteric symbolism, however, a very different kind is involved – one that is frequently referred to as 'real' knowledge. Knowledge that cannot be acquired from a book, but that can be brought out by a teacher or stimulated by a symbol for it is the sacred knowledge, or Gnosis, that already exists within each person on a very subtle, unconscious level. This innate knowledge is sometimes called our intuitive or sixth sense, and provides us with a perception of the truth that appears to come from inside man himself.[25] This way of knowing transcends all outward religious forms, for one of the Hadiths of the Prophet states: 'He who knows himself, knows his Lord.'

In the traditions of the hidden streams, a similar expression incorporating several hermetical ideas can be found in one of the Gnostic Gospels: 'When you make the two One, and you make the outer even as the inner, and the above even as the below ... then shall you enter the Kingdom.'[26] The Hermetic ideas, supposedly Greek in origin, owe their true foundations to ancient Egypt, hence the 'as above so below' reference in the passage from the Gospel of Thomas. For all initiatory ideas within biblical Judaism have their real origins in Egyptian initiatory mysticism. Sacred geometry, therefore, encompasses both mainstream Christian symbolism and aspects of the hidden stream of initiatory revelation as taught by Jesus the Nazorean. However there was one widespread form of symbolism that was used in the early years of Gothic building that seems to defy any rational explanation, and that is alchemical symbolism.

Alchemical Symbolism

On the magnificent west front of the Cathedral of Notre Dame de Paris, a pier decorated with carvings representing the medieval sciences, including alchemy, divides the entrance bay. Alchemy, an allegorical representation of the hidden paths of initiation, is symbolised by a woman seated on a throne with her head touching the clouds. Her left hand holds the sceptre of royal power and her right supports two books – one open, the other closed. The open book represents the exoteric path, or mainstream Christian way, the closed one symbolises the esoteric pathway of illumination. Between her knees with the upper portion resting against her breast is a ladder with nine rungs, the *scala philosophorum*. (See figure 14.)[27] Nicolas Valois describes the symbolism in the following manner: 'Patience is the Philosopher's ladder, and humility is the door to their garden; for whosoever will persevere without pride and without envy, on him God will show mercy.'[28]

Fulcanelli described this statue in relationship to the cathedral as like the title page to a book; the cathedral being the book which he described as an occult Bible, but one wrought in stone, which carries within its

Figure 14

massive pages the hermetic secrets of *the Great Work*. Traditionally the alchemical process itself is divided into the 'lesser' and the 'greater' work. Each consists of three stages. According to the alchemical writer, Titus Burchkhart:

> 'The first three stages correspond to the "spiritualisation of the body", the last three to the "embodying of the spirit" or the "fixation of the volatile". Whereas the "lesser work" has as its goal the regaining of the original purity and receptivity of the soul, the goal of the "greater work" is the illumination of the soul by the revelation of the spirit within it.'[29]

Thus alchemy, far from being a search for the philosophers stone is a euphemism for the alchemical process of transmuting the 'base metal' of imperfect man to the 'gold' of spiritual perfection. An allegory for the hidden and heretical pathway of initiation.

For Fulcanelli, the Virgin Mary, to whom the cathedral is dedicated, is, when stripped of the ill-fitting theological clothes of dogma, nothing less than the Eternal Feminine; the personification of the principle of the Great Work itself.[30] Even Christian dogma in all its complexity sometimes gets close to the principle of eternal truth, such as when it describes the Virgin as a *vas spirituale* – the vase containing the spirit of all things. The French eighteenth-century scholar, Etteila wrote that: 'On a table breast high to the Magi were, on one side a book or a series of golden plates of the book of Toth, and on the other side a vase full of celestial liquid ... the secret, the eternal mystery was therefore in that vase.'[31]

Church teaching describes the Virgin as *the Seat of Wisdom*, thereby consciously or unconsciously, echoing the teachings of the hidden stream. The plethora of alchemical symbolism in the main portal of Notre Dame is a bizarre preparation for entering one of the main Christian cathedrals in France.

Another carving of considerable interest can be found in the north portal of the same cathedral. Carved on a cornice in the middle of the tympanum is a representation of a sarcophagus and on it are seven symbols representing in turn the seven planetary metals: the Sun represents gold; Mercury, quicksilver; Saturn, lead; Venus, copper; the Moon, silver; Jupiter, tin; and lastly, Mars represents iron. In describing this carving, Fulcanelli quotes the Master Jean d'Houry in words that we will find very pertinent when I describe the post-Templar pilgrimage of initiation: 'Look at the sky and the spheres of the planets, you will see that Saturn is the highest of them all, succeeded by Jupiter and then by Mars, the Sun, Venus, Mercury and finally the Moon.'[32]

Alchemical symbolism is not restricted to those carvings already mentioned, it can be found stretching right across the lower parts of the triple doorway of the west front of Notre Dame de Paris. And Paris is not alone, the quatrefoil carvings that decorate the west front of Amiens cathedral, like those of the zodiac and the work of the seasons already mentioned, replicate in superbly carved detail, those on the façade of Notre Dame de Paris. From this we can discern several facts: firstly, the hidden streams of spirituality had slowly started to come out into the open and give clear signposts to the 'true' path, the pathway to initiation. Secondly, Church doctrine is a constantly evolving body that, from time to time, will happily tolerate that which it later anathemises. And finally, in times of potential persecution, allegory was the safest way to pass on heretical messages to other initiates and eventually to the wider public.

CHAPTER 9

The Hidden Streams Within the Church

St Bernard of Clairvaux and the Knights Templar

I n the early years of the twelfth century a linked chain of events in the County of Champagne revealed that the Rex Deus families were making a bid to exert a profound influence on the Church whose dogma they detested. Firstly, certain bizarre decisions made by the family of an obscure nobleman, Bernard de Fontain, heralded a bid for power by the Rex Deus group that was unprecedented. Bernard's family were shocked when he first announced his intention to join the small and struggling monastic Cistercian Order. After their initial resistance, their attitude underwent a dramatic and complete volte-face, a total reversal for reasons that are far from clear. Not only did Bernard's family's opposition to his plans evaporate completely, stranger still, most of his male relatives and many of his friends chose to follow him into the Order and thirty-two of them became novices with him when he joined in 1112.[1]

Whatever the reason for this change of heart may have been, it must have been a very compelling one. This uncharacteristic outburst of religious fervour among Rex Deus members involved Bernard's elder brother, the heir to the family estates, his two younger brothers and his uncle, the Knight Gaudri of Touillon. The new recruits from the wider de Fontain family and close friends from Rex Deus more than doubled the size of the struggling Cistercian Order.[2] Stranger still, the vast majority of these new religious zealots owed feudal allegiance to one important nobleman, another scion of the Rex Deus group, Count Hughes I of Champagne.

The Counts of Champagne were not just among the leading members of Rex Deus, but were virtually independent princes who ruled lands larger than Wales to the east and south-east of Paris, owing nominal allegiance to the Kings of France, the Holy Roman Emperor and the Duke of Burgundy and were linked by blood and marriage to the Capetian Kings of France, the Norman and Plantagenet Kings of England and the St Clairs of Normandy and Roslin. Hugh of Champagne met in a secret conclave with other Rex Deus members from the families of de Joinville, Brienne, Chaumont and Anjou[3] before departing for the Holy Land from where he returned in 1108.

The Count was openly involved in Gnostic spirituality, for under his protection the respected Jewish scholar Solomon ben Isaac, better known as Raschi, founded an internationally renowned Kabbalistic school at the county seat of Troyes in 1070[4]. On his return from another visit to Palestine in 1115, Count Hugh made a substantial donation of land at Clairvaux to the new Cistercian Order enabling it to found a new Abbey and Bernard de Fontain was appointed its first prior[5] and was joined there by two brothers of a certain André de Montbard, who later became one of the founders of the Templar Order.

Bernard of Clairvaux

Bernard of Clairvaux, as he now became known, rose with astonishing speed to a position of incontestable leadership in the Church of his time, becoming personal adviser to one pope who had previously been his pupil and outside the church he exerted immense influence in purely secular affairs, advising kings, emperors and influential members of the nobility. His deep commitment to initiatory teaching was no secret and he preached over 120 sermons based on the Song of Songs by King Solomon.[6] He extended the influence of this teaching by giving spiritual guidance to the Children of Solomon.

Bernard rapidly became one of the most powerful men in Europe in the early twelfth century, and played a considerable, if somewhat mysterious, role in the second stage of the Rex Deus bid for power, the foundation of the Knights Templar.

Nine years after the foundation of the Templars he wrote a discourse on the Order, *In Praise of the New Knighthood*, which he addressed to Hughes de Payen one of the co-founders of the Order and its first Grand Master. In the last paragraph of this document we read: 'Hail, land of promise, which, formerly flowing only with milk and honey for thy possessors, **now** stretchest forth the food of life, and the means of salvation to the entire world.'[7] [my emphasis]

What exactly did Bernard mean by this strange statement? In Church doctrine the crucifixion of Christ had already brought about the salvation of all mankind and Bernard, as a senior and influential member of the Church, had apparently dedicated his life to uphold just that doctrine. Could it be that the 'new' means of salvation to which Bernard was referring in these strange terms was the expected discovery of ancient sacred knowledge that lay hidden in some location within the Holy Land? A cache of documents whose hiding place the new abbot was perhaps already aware of?

The Copper Scroll discovered among the other Dead Sea Scrolls at Qumran lists various sites where the treasures of the Temple of Jerusalem were reputedly hidden.[8] In matters of such importance it would seem most unlikely that the only copy of such a document was the scroll found in 1948. Did Bernard of Clairvaux have access to another? Or as a member of Rex Deus did he learn of these secret hiding places as part of the family traditions? It is a matter of record that the first nine Templar knights in Jerusalem, where the Order was founded, spent several years excavating under the Temple Mount.[9] They certainly knew exactly where to dig, for the most persistent esoteric tradition in Europe claims that they discovered treasure, a variety of sacred documents and, according to some accounts, the Ark of the Covenant.[10] One modern author, Prince Michael of Albany, claims that the Templars discovered documentation that contained the fruits of thousands of years of knowledge. He also claims that documents were found by the Templars which disproved the Crucifixion and the Resurrection of Jesus.[11]

The Knights Templar

The true story of the foundation of the knightly order that became known as the Knights Templar is still shrouded in mystery. The dates are disputed and the first reliable account we have of their foundation is dated over seventy years later. That account by Guilliame of Tyre claims that the *Order of the Poor Knights of Christ and the Temple of Solomon* was founded in Jerusalem in 1118 by Hughes de Payen, André de Montbard and seven other knights. The Order was also known as *La Milice du Christ,* and, according to accepted legend, was founded principally to protect the pilgrim routes within the Holy Land.[12] Both of the principal founding members of the Order, Hughes de Payen and André de Montbard, who was also a relative of the Duke of Burgundy as well as the uncle of Bernard of Clairvaux, were vassals of the Count of Champagne.[13]

According to documents found in an archive in the Principality of Seborga in northern Italy, Bernard of Clairvaux founded an abbey there ostensibly to protect some 'great secret'. Among the community under the direction of its abbot Edouard, were two monks who had joined the order with Bernard and his family, namely Gondemar and Rossal. One document in the archive claims that Bernard himself came to the abbey in February 1117 to release Gondemar and Rossal from their vows. The two ex-monks and their seven other companions, Hughes de Payen, André de Montbard, Payen de Montdidier, Geoffroi de St Omer, Archambaud de St-Amand, Geoffroi Bisol and Count Hughes of Champagne were blessed by Bernard before departing for Jerusalem in November 1118. The documents also record that Bernard nominated Hughes de Payen as the first Grand Master of the Poor Militia of Christ and that this position was consecrated by Abbot Edouard of Seborga.[14]

This account, although so far unconfirmed by any independent source, is in line with the fact that Hughes of Champagne was part of the conspiracy that founded the controversial Templar Order. All those involved in founding the Order were linked by a complex web of family relationships within Rex Deus. Hughes de Payen was a member of a cadet branch of the family of Champagne. Furthermore their activities immediately after their foundation belied their stated purpose of defending the pilgrimage routes.

The newly formed Templar Order was granted quarters on the site of the Temple of Solomon, hence their name. The founding members spent nearly nine years excavating under the Temple Mount,[15] apparently under the patronage of the King of Jerusalem. The Templars' excavations were re-explored by Lieutenant Warren of the Royal Engineers in the early years of the twentieth century. The access shaft descends vertically downwards for over eighty feet before its junction with a series of radiating tunnels under the site of the ancient Temple. Warren found various Templar artefacts in the tunnels, a spur, the remnants of a lance, a small Templar cross and a Templar sword. There is, of course, no indication of what the original knightly excavators actually found. However, on a pillar in the north portal of Chartres Cathedral there is an indication of what they may have been seeking, a carving of the Ark of the Covenant being transported on a wheeled wagon (see figure 15).[16] One persistent legend recounts that Hughes de Payen had indeed been chosen by his fellow members of Rex Deus to locate the Ark and bring it back to Europe.[17]

When the Templars had completed their excavations, their return to Europe was swift. At Hughes de Payen's request, King Baldwin II of Jerusalem wrote to Bernard of Clairvaux asking him to intercede with the pope for formal papal recognition of the Order. Bernard was the principal advisor to Pope Honorius II, and his former teacher.[18] Hughes de Payen and his fellow co-founders set sail for Provence, from where they travelled to England and then on to Scotland where he stayed with the St Clairs of Roslin. In Scotland, King David gave the new Order a donation of land at Ballantrodoch that became the headquarters of the Order in Scotland and has since been renamed Temple.

Figure 15

The Order was granted estates not only in Scotland, but also in England, Champagne and Provence. These first donations of land had been long planned for and were followed by the gifts of estates, castles, towns, farms and villages throughout Christian Europe. The Templars were endorsed by both St Bernard and the pope[19] who gave his blessing. The pope commanded the papal legate, Cardinal Matthew d'Albano, to call a council of Church and temporal dignitaries to legalise the new Order and give the knights their first religious rule. The council opened at Troyes on 14th January 1128 and on 31st January the Grand Master, Hughes de Payen, and his fellow knights were called to appear before the council to receive the new 'Rule' that had been written by Bernard of Clairvaux.[20]

Ten years after this pivotal event, Pope Innocent II issued the papal bull *Omne datum optimum* that made the Templars responsible, through their Grand Master, to the pope and the pope alone, thus freeing them from the authority of bishops, archbishops, kings and emperors. This freed the Templars from any interference by prelates or princes and thereby made them the most independent religious Order in the Christian world. It was soon to become the most powerful, both in wealth as well in military power.

When drawing up the Templar's 'Rule' Bernard of Clairvaux laid down a specific requirement on all the knights to make 'obedience to Bethany and the house of Mary and Martha'.[21] This tends to reinforce what many scholars have long believed: that the great Notre Dame cathedrals financed or influenced by the Templars and Cistercians were dedicated not to Mary the mother of Jesus as the Church teaches, but to Mary Magdelene and the son of Jesus instead. In esoteric tradition, Mary Magdelene is 'the symbol of divine wisdom'. And, in the Nazorean tradition, the Magdelene is described as being dressed in black just like a priestess of Isis, wearing Sophia's crown of stars. Her infant child wears the golden crown of royalty.

The Growth of the Templar Order.

By the early 1140s the Knights Templar had acquired land in Portugal and had begun to receive donations on the eastern side of Spain. Soon they had acquired enough land and recruited sufficient members to be able to mount military operations on two fronts, in the Holy Land and the Iberian Peninsula. Grants of land, castles and other property came in so fast in the early years after the Council of Troyes that the Order sometimes had to defer garrisoning some of their new lands for a considerable amount of time owing to a shortage of manpower.

The main focus of Templar activity was always the protection of the kingdom of Jerusalem. All recruits capable of military service were sent to the East as soon as it was possible following their Grand Master's example – Hughes himself, accompanied by 300 knights drawn from the noblest families in Europe who had rushed to become members of the Order, returned to the Holy Land in 1129.[22] When we consider the time it would take to arm and equip these men much less transport them to a rendezvous point within Europe, this massive influx of recruits and their speedy transportation to the Holy Land is yet another example of Rex Deus foresight and long-term planning coming to fruition.

The struggling Cistercian Order that had revived appreciably since Bernard and his companions had joined its ranks also underwent an extraordinary period of expansion. In the lifetime of Bernard of Clairvaux they established over 300 new abbeys and recorded the most rapid expansion of any monastic order before or since. Furthermore, during his lifetime at least, the Cistercians and the Knights Templar were widely regarded as two arms of the same body – one a contemplative monastic arm, the other the strong, swift, military arm of the same organisation.

France, Provence, Champagne, Bar, England, Tuscany and the present area known as the Languedoc/Roussillon became major centres of Templar power and influence within Europe, closely followed by Aragon, Gallicia, Portugal, Scotland, Normandy and the Holy Roman Empire. At the peak of their power their estates, castles and churches stretched from the Baltic to the Mediterranean and from the Atlantic coastline to the Holy Land. They became, to all intents and purposes, the precursor for the multinational conglomerates of today.

One consultant in business management, the American S T Bruno, described the Templars in the following terms:

> 'The fact of the matter is that the Templars ran a "worldwide" system of farms, shipping concerns and financial services. They pressed olives in the Jordan Valley, made wine in France and traded wool in Ireland. Agriculture was, of course, only one activity. They also shipped lumber from Edessa, and carried

pilgrims across the Mediterranean from Lombardy to Acre. They even provided a medieval form of "travellers cheque" to pilgrims and loaned money to kings. Although one might envisage their primary military "product" as singularly focused on the conquest of the Holy Land, the resource branch of the order operated in a number of different markets.'[23]

It is difficult to conceive that, in the medieval era, the organisational skills existed to manage a vast, international, multifaceted enterprise of this nature and keep a standing army in the field at the same time. But the Templars did just that, and yet some of their clerical critics within the modern Church call them 'illiterates'! Bruno claims that for almost 180 years the Templars managed their vast and complex organisation in a manner consistent with some of the most sophisticated and best management practices of the twenty-first century.[24]

A complex organisation of this nature cannot flourish unless the proper financial infrastructure is developed to sustain it[25] so these 'illiterate' warriors added yet another string to their bow. The Templars, who worked in all European currencies and organised the safe transport of gold and money across frontiers to finance their military activities in the Holy Land, soon began to offer financial services to the newly emergent trading classes. They became international bankers, using a device they had learned from the Sufis of Islam, the 'note of hand', to arrange financial transfers from one part of Europe to another. They lent money to merchants, the nobility, princes, prelates, kings and emperors and all their financial dealings were backed by their reputation for probity, accuracy and safety. They soon rose to be the wealthiest financial institution in the Christian world, with all their immense profits devoted towards one aim and one aim only, the defence of the Kingdom of Jerusalem.

The estates, buildings and castles of the Knights Templar, that strange mélange of soldiers, monks and bankers, were scattered all over Europe, many strategically situated near the most important trade and pilgrimage routes. Some are still identifiable by their place names which give a clue to their Templar history. In England there is Temple in Cornwall, Templecombe in Somerset, and the centre of the legal profession, the Inner Temple in London; in Wales, Templeton and Temple Bar in the county of Dyyfed; in Scotland, Temple, previously Ballantrodoch in Midlothian, Temple in Strathclyde, Templehall in Fyfe and Templand in Dumfries/Galloway. France, the country where the Templars owned most of their lands, Doncourt aux Templiers, Templehof et Colmar, Bure-les-Templiers, Moissy-le-Temple and Ivry-le-Temple[26], to name but a few. Portugal, Spain, Germany and many other countries have their quota of names indicating their Templar history.

In effect the Knights Templar became richer than any kingdom in all of Europe. Their military prowess allied to the strategic position of many of their holdings helped to ensure the security of the major trade routes within Europe. In this manner they made a significant contribution to the growing climate of peace and stability that allowed merchants to trade securely and with comparative ease over greater distances than ever before. As a result, Europe began to bloom economically for Templar protection ensured that this new climate of unprecedented commercial confidence and economic growth continued to strengthen the power of the merchant class and ultimately led to the development of capitalism. Furthermore, this stability arose as a direct result of the application by the Templars of a bizarre mix of their strategic planning and sacred gnosis.

The comparison between the impressive achievements of the Templars in their brief 180-year history and those of other orders that were established long before them and who outlasted them by many centuries, is startling. Yet the obvious questions whose answers could explain these differences are generally ignored or brushed under the academic carpet as irrelevant. After their suppression following a contro-versial trial for heresy in the early fourteenth century, their private records may have been stolen or suppressed by the Inquisitors, hidden by the knights themselves or destroyed. Yet, we still do have a valid, if incomplete, guide to their true beliefs in the symbolism they adopted for their own use and the hidden symbolism in the great church buildings they financed or patronised as well as in the churches dedicated to the saints and cults with which they were intimately associated.

Templar Crosses

The first symbol of identification awarded to the Knights Templar at their foundation, was not the familiar *Croix Pattée* (see figure 16) that has since become so intimately associated with the Order that it is generally known as 'the Templar Cross'. The knights first insignia was the Cross of Lorraine, a very different cross indeed.[27] (See figure 17.) This was awarded to the Order by the Patriarch of Jerusalem, yet another relative of Bernard of Clairvaux, his cousin in fact. The *Croix Pattée*[28] did not come into use until some years later.

Pope Eugene III gave the Order yet another familiar cross, the Cross of the Eight Beatitudes[29] (see figure 18) in 1147. This cross was identical in shape to that already in use by the rival order, the Knights of St John of Jerusalem, better known as the Knights Hospitaller. The Knights Hospitaller wore a white cross, the Templars an identically shaped red version. The inner circle of the Templar Order were not content simply to adopt the same cross as their rivals in the Order of St John however, so they used their considerable ingenuity and developed this design still further into a more elaborate, curved form of the Cross of Eight

Figure 16

Figure 17

Figure 18

Figure 19 right

Figure 20 below

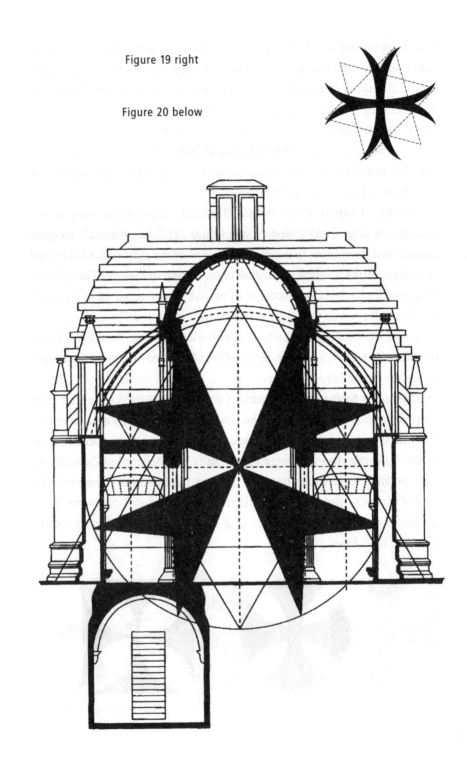

Beatitudes (see figure 19) that demonstrated a mastery of geometry. They then used this new and uniquely Templar Cross as a tool to create all the regular divisions of a circle. It became, in practice, an architectural tool that was used in building design and construction. An example of this can be seen in figure 20 which shows how this cross was used as the basis for the design of the elevation of Rosslyn Chapel.[30] Thus, exoterically this cross became a sign of recognition; esoterically it indicated a mastery of geometry and building techniques.

Another Templar Cross with a distinctly Gnostic meaning is the Discoid Cross or *Croix Céleste*[31] (see figure 21). This distinctly circular design, which was used as the central feature of the dust jacket for one of my earlier works, *Rosslyn, Guardian of the Secrets of the Holy Grail*,[32] and indicates the universal application of sacred gnosis or 'Hidden Wisdom', is a direct allusion to the Gnostic spiritual path followed by the Templars. Each seal of the Order carries somewhere within its design *La Croix Templière Terrestre,* another familiar but 'squared' form of the *Croix Pattée*(see figure 22).

The use of forms of the Templar Cross outlived the Order that used them. One such is the Cross of the Order of Christ that was used by the Portuguese order of that name which grew out of the suppressed Templar Order. Its design loomed large on the sails of Christopher Columbus's ships on their first trans-atlantic voyage in 1492 and also decorated the sails of the ships used by Prince Henry the Navigator. There were many variations on the Templar Cross and I have only been able to list the principal ones here.

Figure 21   Figure 22

Templar Seals

The Templars, being Gnostic initiates, did not concern themselves with the salvation of individual souls, but were mainly concerned with the spiritual and material transformation of entire communities and nations. It has been claimed that their ultimate objective was to restore true Gnostic monotheism to the world, uniting Christianity, Judaism and Islam.[33] Luckily, there is another source of Templar symbolism that gives us clear clues to their Gnostic dualism, the large number of Templar Seals that have survived and given rise to a number of books on this vast field.

A large amount of Templar symbolism and practice reinforce this dualism; the carvings of two brothers behind the Norman almond-shaped shield, the *escarboucle,* that decorated the west front of cathedrals such as Chartres, Rheims and Amiens, for example (see figure 23); the Templar seal of Two Brothers on One Horse (see figure 24); the simple black and white design of their battle standard, the *Beauseant;* the fact that many of their domains were 'twinned'. The dualism of the two knights behind the *escarboucle,* the Two Brothers on One Horse and the

Figure 23 left

Figure 24 above

Figure 25

Figure 26

duality enshrined in the *Beauseant* are held by many to represent Castor and Pollux, possibly the two-faced god Janus and, more credibly, the heresy of 'the Holy Twins', Jesus and Thomas Didymus.[34]

Another Templar seal of unarguably Gnostic provenance is that of the *Abraxus* (see figure 25). This seal, used by the Grand Master as a sign equivalent to the modern usage of 'Top Secret' or 'Highly Confidential' is pure Gnostic symbolism of such a nature that it is totally incapable of any orthodox Christian explanation. It has its roots in ancient Greek Hermeticism. Sometimes used with it is the equally ancient symbol of sacred wisdom, namely the serpent who eats its own tail. The nineteenth-century scholar of esotericism, Magnus Eliphas Levi believed that the Templars classed themselves as: 'the sole repository of the great religious and social secrets ... without exposing them to the corruption of power.'[35] Levi elaborated this further when he wrote:

> 'The successsors of the old Rosicrucians, modifying little by little the austere and hierarchic methods of their precursors in initiation, had become a mystical sect and had united with many of the Templars, the dogma of the two intermingling, as a result of which they regarded themselves as the sole depositories of the secrets intimated by the Gospel according to St John.'[36]

One can be forgiven for wondering if the 'old Rosicrucians' he refers to are not the secretive families of Rex Deus? The British author, Graham Hancock wrote: '... the research that I had conducted into the beliefs and behaviour of this strange group of warrior monks had convinced me that they had tapped into some exceedingly ancient wisdom tradition ...'[37]

Of course, indeed they had, for through their Rex Deus ancestry they had maintained continuous and unbroken contact with the wisdom

Figure 27

traditions of biblical Israel and, before that, of ancient Egypt. Templar seals reflect this, albeit in the guise of seemingly Christian symbolism. Two seals showing the Paschal Lamb carrying a cross look, at first glance at least, as mainstream Christian symbols (see figure 26) – but the cross that is depicted is the long-stemmed cross associated with John the Baptist. Two others show what they believed was the Temple of Solomon (figure 27), which in fact was the Al Aqsa Mosque. This sly reference to the 'Wisdom of Solomon' was meaningful to the Templars in both Gnostic terms and as a celebration of the Order's foundation. Crescent moons, the Star of the Sea and the fleur-de-lys are also recorded and are all associated with ancient wisdom traditions. Thus openly, in plain view, but unrecognised by all except the initiated, the symbols of initiatory wisdom were recorded as the 'seals of approval' on all Templar documents.

Templar Buildings

In the course of their existence, the Knights Templar became great builders, constructing commanderies, fortified farmhouses, barns, workshops, armouries, castles, harbours, prisons, chapels and churches for their own use. Most are relatively plain apart from the occasional decoration around the capitals of pillars. Most of the Templar churches are small, rectangular buildings with an apsidal end at the east. The round churches associated with Templar tradition are relatively rare and are held to have some, as yet, unexplained Kabbalistic significance. The attribution of these buildings to the Order is usually dependant on two factors, archival sources which clearly state their Templar ownership, such as deeds of donation or bills of purchase, and the manner of their construction. Many others have been given an inappropriate Templar attribution on the grounds of their manner of decoration.

The French Templar scholar, J-A Durbec has established what has become the main standard of judgement in these, often hotly disputed, matters. He has listed six signs and seals that can be held to authenticate a decorated Templar building. They are:

1. Carvings of a five-pointed star – *L'etoile.*
2. Carvings of the Templar seal of Two Brothers on One Horse – *Deux frères sur un seul cheval.*
3. A representation of the Templar seal known as the Agnus Dei – *Un agneau pascal, nimbé ou non, tenant une croix pattée au dessus de lui.*
4. A stylised representation of the head of Christ imprinted on a cloth, such as that on the Shroud of Turin or the Veil of Veronica, for example – *the Mandylion*
5. A dove in flight carrying an olive branch in its beak – *une Colombe tenant en son bec une branch d'olivier.*
6. A form of oriental decorated cross known *as the Floriated Cross.* [38]

All of these symbols are taken from standard Church iconography, so any one or even possibly two on their own should not be held as validation of Templar attribution. In those circumstances they need to be experienced as standard Christian symbols. However, when three or more can be found in the any building erected between 1127 and 1307, we can be reasonably certain of that building's Templar origin.

The Cult of St John the Baptist

The origin of the importance of John the Baptist to the Templars may lie in his role as teacher to Jesus and is reinforced by the passage from the Gospel of Thomas where Jesus is quoted as saying: 'Among those born of women, from Adam until John the Baptist, there is no one so superior to John the Baptist that his eyes should not be lowered (before him).'[39]

Throughout the lands once subject to Templar rule, especially in the Languedoc and Provence, there are numerous churches dedicated to St John the Baptist. In Trigance in central Provence, there is an ingenious arrangement that allows a beam of light to illuminate the altar with a golden glow at dawn of the Baptist's feast day. In most of these churches and chapels in southern France, carvings of John the Baptist appear to take precedence, yet there are no contemporary carvings of the

Crucifixion. In many cases not only are these buildings noted for their alchemical symbolism, but also a substantial number are, or have been, home to a Black Madonna, a cult I will describe in a later chapter. This special veneration of the Baptist is certainly not restricted to the south of France, his principal shrine lies far to the north in the city of Amiens.

The largest cathedral in France is to be found in the city of Amiens and has a vault that rises over 140 feet above the floor of the nave. The west front is dominated by two carvings that are a direct reference to the 'Hidden Wisdom' tradition of the initiates of old. The first is a statue of Jesus known as the *Beau Dieu* of Amiens, depicted with his feet resting on a lion and a dragon.[40] So here in the centre of the formal entrance to the cathedral is a representation of Jesus and the *Wouivre,* the initiatory telluric energy of the Druids whose presence can be readily detected by dowsing. The second, a carving of the supreme adept of the Old Testament, King Solomon, can be found immediately below the *Beau Dieu.* The walls surrounding all three of the doors on the west front are decorated with quatrefoils depicting alchemical symbolism, representing by the allegorical means of the transmutation of base metals into gold, the true fruit of the age-old initiatory tradition, the spiritual transformation of base humanity into the pure 'gold' of spiritual enlightenment.[41]

The French mystical writer François Cali claims that in travelling from Chartres to Amiens, one makes an almost imperceptible transition, 'from the love of God to the love of Wisdom – which is in order, number and harmony – which can be equated with God, but which need not be'. [42] The qualities of order, number and harmony are all attributes of the sacred gnosis of the Templars. Amiens cathedral, a wondrous, symphonic blend of space, stone and light, was not only designed to celebrate the Gnostic principle of Sophia or sacred wisdom, but also primarily to house the Knights Templars' most precious relic: the reliquary containing the severed head of John the Baptist. According to the Templar scholar Guy Jourdan of Provence, this relic is *la vrai tête Baphometique Templier* – the true Baphometic head of the Templars.

In the transept, a series of carved and coloured panels give visual reality to the biblical story of John the Baptist. This theme is repeated again on the outer wall of the choir that is decorated with superbly sculpted scenes, in bas-relief, of his life and death, including one where the top of his severed head is being pierced by a knife. The full significance of this piercing is not understood, but its importance to the Templars can be seen in their burial practices. In a Templar church in Bargemon, Provence, part of the floor has been replaced with a transparent perspex sheet, which permits a clear view of the excavated Templar burials in the crypt beneath. A row of skulls and long bones can be seen laid out in military order and each of the skulls is pierced in precisely the manner depicted in the carvings on the walls of the choir at Amiens.

In the ancient Templar lands throughout France, the feast day of St John the Baptist is still celebrated with considerable gusto. Furthermore, the worldwide fraternity of Freeemasons, like their Templar predecessors, also hold two saints in particularly high regard, namely St John the Divine and St John the Baptist. The question we have to consider is how the Templars kept their heretical beliefs secret for so long?

The Ruling Circle

The Order of the Knights Templar was founded by Rex Deus families who were past-masters at the art of dissembling. From the very inception of the Order, the Knights purported to be a devout and militant Christian Order. Indeed it is highly probable that many of the knights and all the serjeants, craftsmen and auxiliary members were, in fact, true Christians. Part of the real strength of the Order derived from the fact that while the founders and the real leaders throughout their brief history were 'heretics' and Gnostics, this was kept secret from the majority who were Catholic to a man.

The French scholars Georges Caggar and Jean Robin claim that: 'The Order of the Temple was indeed constituted of seven "*exterior*" circles dedicated to the minor mysteries, and of three "interior" circles corresponding to the initiation into the great mysteries. The nucleus was composed of seventy Templars . . .'[43]

Which precise minor and major mysteries they refer to, is not made clear, however it is reasonable to assume that they represent the same division into major and minor mysteries that are described in alchemy, with the major mysteries being reserved for adepts of the highest degree. Thus the devout Christian members of the Order belonged to the exterior circles and were never allowed to join the inner circles. They, the ruling élite, were restricted to members of Rex Deus with the possible addition of carefully selected outsiders who had earned and maintained the trust and respect of their initiated leaders. The inner nucleus was at all times drawn exclusively from the ranks of Rex Deus. They were dedicated at all times to the quest for sacred knowledge and, like their Egyptian and Israelite ancestors, they used the fruits of their enlightenment to improve the quality of the lives of the communities within which they operated and to maintain their hold on their true inheritance, the Holy Land.

CHAPTER 10

The Outward Reality of Chartres Cathedral

'The Business of medieval building is not a marvel. Such a flowering of the human spirit is mysterious, but it is not a miracle. The time and the place and the loved one were for once in a while all together.'[1]

P robably the most glorious example of the time, place and 'loved one' coming together all at the same time, is found in Chartres Cathedral. This building is nothing more nor less than a vast reliquary containing a superb statement of the truths that lead man closer to God. A timeless statement of Christian belief, it is a hymn to Gnostic, initiatory spirituality; a melodic symphony in stone that is a visible celebration of truly divine harmony. The countless pilgrims, tourists and visitors who go there, irrespective of their religious faith or lack of it, will leave spiritually uplifted, inspired and transformed. That is the true measure of Chartres Cathedral, revered for centuries as the Golden Book in which inspired sages have inscribed their wisdom as a lasting legacy to all who seek spiritual truth.[2] Napoleon put it succinctly: 'Chartres is no place for an atheist!'

Legend tells how, many centuries before the Roman invasion of Gaul, Druids assembling for sacred ceremonies in a grotto on the sacred mound at Carnuntum between the rivers Eure and Loire, now the city of Chartres, received a divine revelation. A virgin was to arise and she would give birth to a child who would be the salvation of the world. An altar was erected and on it was placed a fire-blackened female figurine of a virgin about to give birth. This carving, described as *Virgini Pariturae* by Julius Caesar,[3] had considerable religious significance for all the surrounding Celtic tribes. With the advent of Christianity, the new religion did as the Romans had done before them, they took over the existing site of worship, sanctified it in the name of their new religion and carried on much as before with the new rites and beliefs merely replacing the old. Thus from the earliest times, the era of the Druids and the Celts, a virgin was held in veneration here.

In 876, two centuries after the area was converted to Christianity, Charles the Bald presented Chartres with an outstandingly precious relic, the Virgin's holy tunic. This generous gift ensured that the cathedral became, from that time on, the most celebrated centre of the cult of the Virgin in northern France. The tunic had been a gift to Charlemagne from the Emperor of Byzantium.[4] This gift assured the future of Chartres as a centre of pilgrimage and set the seal on the rise of the cult of Mariolatory, which brought back into European religious consciousness the concept of the Eternal Feminine which, until then, had been suppressed by the all-male, patriarchal hierarchy in Rome.

The Spread of Education

In the Dark Ages, access to education was strictly controlled by the Church and limited to those who had entered the service of religion and taken holy orders. Even the Emperor Charlemagne could hardly sign his name; kings, nobles and peasants alike were illiterate. Even the clergy had their education severely limited to subjects that had gained the approval of the Church authorities. Knowledge of most of the Greek and Roman classics had been lost. Grammar, rhetoric and a little Neoplatonism were deemed all that was necessary to serve the self-appointed guardians of 'Divinely Revealed Truth' – namely the pope and his advisors. It was not until the eleventh century that this began to change when schools of learning, all centred on abbeys or cathedrals, expanded and became the focus of a growing intellectual life. The most influential of these developed at Chartres Cathedral, where the aesthetics of St Augustine were combined with the newly rediscovered philosophy of Plato to produce a synthesis of theology and cosmology that had a profound effect on the development of Christian symbolism in the twelfth and thirteenth centuries.[5]

The School of Chartres

It was Fulbert, who became bishop in 1007, who made Chartres a great centre of learning as well as a focus of pilgrimage. Under his guidance Chartres became a haven of scholarship that remained unsurpassed until the foundation of the University of Paris. Thus the cathedral school, coupled with its attraction as one of the great pilgrimage churches of northern France, was renowned as a place where, through the intervention of Mary, miracles happened.[6] The curriculum of Fulbert's pupils included the works of Plato, Aristotle, Pythagoras and Cicero as well as biblical texts and the writings of the Christian Fathers. Furthermore, they became familiar with more recent Arabic innovations such as the astrolabe, the first successful device for measuring altitudes. Truly they belonged to the international community of scholars.[7] Fulbert was called 'that venerable Socrates' by his disciples and the twelfth century marked the zenith of the Chartres School. Bernardus of Chartres, Gilbert de la Porée, Thierry of Chartres, and John of Salisbury, were its masters who were celebrated throughout France and attracted pupils from every province and even from abroad.[8]

The school at Chartres marked the pivotal time that separated the Dark Ages from the early roots of the Renaissance, for it was from the time of Bernardus of Chartres and Abelard of Paris that one can date the first important breaching of the dam of ecclesiastically enforced ignorance. It was here that the philosophers of classical Greece were reinstated in the mainstream of European Christian philosophy.[9]

Bernardus said of them: 'If we can see further than they could, it is not because of the strength of our own vision, it is because we are raised up by them and borne at a prodigious height. We are dwarves mounted on the shoulders of giants.'[10]

The knowledge of the Greek Classics, mathematics, science and invention taught at Chartres crept back into European consciousness by a very circuitous route. When the original Nestorian scholars had been expelled from Christian Europe, they sought refuge in lands that were conquered by the forces of Islam centuries later. The religion of Islam held education in high esteem and study was actively encouraged. Not only were the philosophical, literary and mathematical treatises from the past treasured and revered, but so was the exploration of science. Thus, paradoxically, classical learning came not from the Christian tradition but from that beacon of light in the Dark Ages, Moorish Spain. The classics were not translated from the original Greek, but from Arabic by Jewish scholars working in yeshiva under the protection of the tolerant rule of Islam.

How did this knowledge get from Spain to Chartres? The answer may well lie in the Rex Deus connection. We find a strong indication of this when we learn that under the outward guise of teaching the seven liberal arts of *gramatica, dialectica, logica, musica, mathematica, geometrica* and *astronomia*, Fulbert taught the seven steps of initiation based on the ancient Egyptian model, the same initiatory pathway preserved by the twenty-four families of the ma'madot in ancient Israel and the Rex Deus families of Europe.[11] Thus we can see that Bernard de Fontain was not the first Rex Deus member to mask his activities by gaining an important ecclesiastical office and, under the leadership of Fulbert, the mystery school at Chartres practised an heretical initiatory pathway right under the noses of the repressive Church authorities.

If we posed the question, 'Where does civilization come from?' the Neoplatonic school at Chartres would have collectively replied that it comes from the eternal world of 'the Nous' or Divine Mind through the medium of the *animus mundi* or world soul made manifest in the physical world.[12] Thus, the ancient and heretical concept of sacred gnosis was now enshrined in acceptable Christian clothing. One of the finest works associated with the school at Chartres is the *Cosmographia* by Bernardus Sylvester. This work is a portrayal of creativity in the universe, demonstrating how order is brought to the primal chaos from the eternal essence. 'Time' according to Bernardus, 'may seem to be rooted in eternity, and eternity expressed in time. All that is moved is subject to time, but it is from eternity that all contained in the vastness of time is born, and into eternity that it is to be resolved.'[13] In many ways the cathedral of Chartres is an ever-present reminder of that.

Fulbert's Romanesque Cathedral

When fire destroyed the cathedral in 1020, Fulbert set about a rebuilding programme with the aid of the kings and nobles who had acted as financial patrons to his theological school. These included King Robert, the Capetian king of France, most of the Rex Deus nobility of northern France as well as William, Duke of Aquitaine.[14] Fulbert's new Romanesque cathedral was not completed in his lifetime but was dedicated by his successor, Thierry of Chartres, in 1037, eight years after Fulbert died. Now the central personality in the initiation school at Chartres was one of his pupils and another member of the Rex Deus families, Bernardus[15] who continued the initiatory teaching and based it on the work of Jesus' most important disciple, St John the Divine. Thus Rex Deus teaching and tradition began its careful infiltration of European society in a manner that exerted far more real influence than their numbers might suggest.

Fulbert's Romanesque building was as wide and as long as the present-day cathedral that eventually replaced it. In the century following Fulbert's death, the clergy of the diocese planned to improve his cathedral by providing a west front that would reflect the growing importance of this centre of pilgrimage and, when yet another fire destroyed buildings around the west end of the cathedral, Bishop Geoffroy de Lèves embarked on a gamble with history.[16]

Plate 1. Carving of St John the Baptist, North Portal, Chartres Cathedral.
Symbolising his teaching role, uniting the Dragon of Gnosis at his feet with the
'Lamb of God' – i.e. Jesus.

Plate 2, above. Jesus Enthroned in Glory at the Last Judgement with his feet resting on 'The New Jerusalem' – west front of Notre Dame de Paris.

Plate 3, above. Mary, the Seat of Wisdom, with Jesus blessing the World – west front, Notre Dame de Paris.

Plate 4, below. A distinctly female serpent tempting Adam and Eve, west front, Notre Dame de Paris.

Plate 5, above. Signs of the Zodiac above depictions of the approriate labours of the season – west front, Notre Dame de Paris.

Plate 6, below. Central Tympanum of the west front of Amiens Cathedral – illuminated by laser-light to recreate the original medieval colouring.

Plate 7, right. Le Beau Dieu at Amiens – he came to reveal and not to redeem.

Plate 8. Jesus enthroned in glory surrounded by the symbols of the four evangelists – Central Tympanum, West front, Chartres Cathedral.

Plate 9, above. Madonna and Child, west front, Chartres Cathedral.

Plate 10, below. Left, Pythagoras, the first verifiable European initiate – west front, Chartres Cathedral.

Plate 11, above. Jesus enthroned in glory at the Last Judgement, south Portal, Chartres Cathedral.

Plate 12, above. The great rose window of the North Transept, Chartres Cathedral.

Plate 13, left. Notre Dame du Pillar, Chartres Cathedral.

Plates 14 & 15, right. The Tarot Trumps.

1. The Emperor

2. The Pope

5. Strength

6. The Charioteer

3. The Lovers

4. The Hermit

7. Justice

8. The Hanged Man

13. The Moon

14. The Sun

9. Death

10. Prudence

15. Judgment

16. The World

11. The Devil

12. The Tower

Plate 16. The Apprentice Pillar, Rosslyn Chapel.

Plate 17. The Master Mason's Pillar, Rosslyn Chapel.

Plate 18. The stained-glass window depicting Longinus, Rosslyn Chapel.

Plate 19. St Mauritius in a stained-glass window at Rosslyn Chapel.

Plate 20. St Michael's stained-glass window at Rosslyn Chapel.

Plate 21. The window of St George, Rosslyn Chapel.

Plate 22. The original version of the *Virgin of the Rocks*, now in the Louvre Museum, Paris.

Plate 23. The second version of the *Virgin of the Rocks*, with the added symbolism of the long-stemmed cross and halos, now in the National Gallery, London.

Plate 24. *The Crucifixion* by Giovanni Donato Montorfano, Convent of Santa Maria delle Grazie, Milan.

Plate 25. *The Last Supper*, Convent of Santa Maria delle Grazie, Milan.

Below, Detail of Jesus from *The Last Supper* – note the position of his hands.

Plate 26, above. The Tour Magdala, Rennes-le-Château.

Plate 27, below. The Magdalene altar, the church of Rennes-le-Château.

Plate 28. Statue of Mary Magdalene with Alabaster Jar and Skull, Rennes-le-Château.

Plate 29. Statue of Mary with child, Rennes-le-Château. But which Mary and which child? Mary and Jesus or Mary Magdalene and her child?

Plate 30. Joseph and Jesus or Jesus and his son? Rennes-le-Château.

De Lèves decided to build this extension in the new 'Gothic' style that had been developed at Saint-Denis in Paris under the supervision of Abbot Suger. First a new freestanding north-west tower was built, then a similar construction was made in the south-west. Linking these structures, the west front we see today was constructed, containing the magnificent Portail Royal with its three impressive doorways surmounted by Gothic, pointed arches. This new west frontage was some little distance from the main bulk of Fulbert's original Romanesque cathedral and was joined to the original structure by a vestibule. The French scholar Lanore demonstrated in a series of studies published in the *Revue de l'Art Chrétien* that some of the sculptors who created the magnificent carvings of the Portail Royal came to Chartres in 1145 directly from the workshops of Saint-Denis.[17]

These highly skilled artists had some of the greatest movements of the twelfth century to draw on. Their work was an expression of man's recent discovery of his own intellect in the Chartres mystery school. By their participation in exalting the Virgin Mary in the symbolism of the new west front of Chartres Cathedral they made a vibrant contribution to the reinstatement of the principle of the Eternal Feminine that had already appeared in the lyrics and songs of the troubadours of the heretical Languedoc. More importantly, perhaps, they contributed, under the guidance of the Rex Deus families, to one of the most extraordinary features of twelfth-century history: the rediscovery and transformation of pagan myth.[18] American Professor of Mythology, the late Joseph Campbell, described this period as one 'when myth changed its function from maintaining society in unaltered ways to a revolutionary and radical force'.[19]

This radical and revolutionary tendency can be experienced when one views the west front of Chartres Cathedral that houses the three main doors. Hidden in plain sight from all except the initiated are the vital clues and pointers to the fact that behind the wealth of mainstream Christian symbols that adorn the triple doorway in such profusion, the 'hidden hand of heresy' has left a very different message. Replicating in a bizarre way what is recorded in the Gospel: 'For there is nothing hid, except to be made manifest; nor is anything secret, except to come to light.'[20] As we shall see, sculpture was the major art form used by the *Compagnonnage* in France and by the various Masonic guilds and brotherhoods elsewhere, to display their clear and unequivocal Gnostic beliefs.

The west front, that once formed the entrance to Fulbert's eleventh-century cathedral, houses the three main doors. In the centre is the main ceremonial door described by Charpentier as the door of Mystical Faith.[21] Above it, the tympanum is dominated by the figure of Jesus enthroned in glory, barefoot with his right hand raised in blessing and his left clasping a bible (see plate 8). To denote his divine status, Jesus' head is surrounded by a nimbus, or halo, containing a cross. Here we find the first of several clues that something other than Christian dogma is being indicated here, for the cross behind the head of Jesus is a specific Templar cross, *La Croix Céleste*, the Cross of Universal Knowledge or Gnosis. Jesus' divine status is doubly reinforced by the aureole that surrounds him. Surrounding the seated figure of Jesus are the four large and superbly carved symbols of the Evangelists. By the raised right hand of Jesus is a depiction of an angel, representing St Matthew; beneath that is a carving of a winged lion symbolising St Mark. On a level with Jesus' left shoulder is a large sculpted eagle, indicating the divinely blessed initiate St John; and immediately under the eagle is a winged bull representing the fourth Evangelist, St Luke. Above the tympanum in the archivolts there are carved angels, the twenty-four elders of the Apocalypse and the beasts and the elders who 'give glory and honour to Him that sat on the throne, who liveth for ever and ever'. On the lintel below the tympanum are the twelve Apostles, seated in four groups of three and, at each extremity, a single standing figure representing the prophets Enoch and Elijah.

The doorway to the right is the Gate of Birth whose tympanum is dominated by a statue of Mary, the Christian incarnation of the Divine Mother, enthroned with the infant Jesus on her lap in a manner reminiscent of the Black Virgin in the crypt, *Notre Dame Sous Terre*.[22] The seated figure of Mary, Queen of Heaven, is flanked by two angels (see plate 9). Around them, lying within the archivolts or the curves of the arches, following on from the two zodiacal signs of Pisces and Gemini are symbolic representations of *the seven liberal arts* and the sages who brought them back into European consciousness. From the viewer's perspective, reading from right to left across the arch, following on from the two signs of the zodiac are carvings representing dialectics brought by Aristotle; rhetoric by Cicero; geometry by Euclid; arithmetic by Boethius; astronomy by Ptolemy; grammar by Donatus; and music by Pythagoras. (See Plate 10.)

This representation of Pythagoras provides another clue to the hidden symbolism within the west front, for he was not only the philosopher famous for the theory of the 'music of the spheres' but the first clearly identifiable character in European history who was celebrated beyond all doubt as an initiate of the Egyptian Temple mysteries. Thus his carving is a memento of the hidden stream of initiates, a rather bizarre inclusion among the symbolism dedicated purely to Christian doctrine.

Almost diametrically opposed to the figure of Pythagoras, but slightly higher, lies another indication of heretical influence, the carving of two knights behind the *escarboucle*, the almond-shaped Norman shield. A symbol denoting the approval of the heretical Order of the Knights Templar for the hidden messages encoded within the carvings. There are two lintels lying below the tympanum, the upper one shows the presentation at the Temple and the lower represents, reading from left to right, the Annunciation, the Nativity, and the annunciation to the shepherds. The whole doorway, therefore, reflects the Neoplatonic belief of the masters of the mystery school in the unity of all knowledge taught by Jesus, mediated through his mother in the guise of *Sapientia*, the Gnostic Wisdom that comes directly from God.[23] The pre-Christian figure of Pythagoras with his tintinnabulum, represents not only the principle of initiation but also the near-worship of classical learning and literature held by the Chartres masters and their belief that the universe was founded on number, weight and measure.[24]

The third door, that to the left and north of the main portal, called by Louis Charpentier the Gate of the Ages, has, in the tympanum, the symbolic carving of the Ascension of Jesus, flanked by two angels. On the lintel below are angels descending bearing the news that 'the same Jesus, which is taken up from you into heaven shall so come in like manner as you have seen Him go into heaven'.[25] The signs of the zodiac, paired with seasonal activities, decorate the archivolts surrounding the depiction of the Ascension of Jesus. Thus the zodiacal themes and associated activities displayed so prominently on the west fronts of both Notre Dame de Paris and Notre Dame d'Amiens are replicated here at Chartres, not so obviously perhaps, but still in a position of prime importance.

The columns surrounding all three doors that support the Portail Royal are all decorated with elongated carvings of biblical figures that are still in the Romanesque style. These figures were originally grouped in a pattern of 3 – 4 – 5 and 5 – 4 – 3, but of the original twenty-four, only nineteen have survived.[26] The two on the extreme left are attributed to sculptors from the school of Etampes, the group to the far right are now accepted to be the work of sculptors from Saint-Denis, as I mentioned earlier, and those on the central door, which are of far better quality, are attributed to the master-mason of Chartres. These columnar figures representing the kings and queens of Judah, the lineal ancestors of Jesus, are carved in superb detail with their entire design and the folds of their clothes leading the eyes of any observer upwards to faces that display the serenity of true initiates, an outward display of inner peace and tranquillity.

Decorating the capitals of the pillars supporting all three doors in the Portail Royal is a continuous frieze containing thirty-eight scenes from the life of Mary and Jesus. While highly decorative, its charm lies in its overall effect rather than in its detail which has become somewhat indistinct in time with many figures having been deliberately mutilated. The strange order of the scenes is, at first, more than a little confusing. Normally one would tend to read such a continuous frieze from left to right, but not here. It is possible that they were carved in sequence but, for whatever reason, they were not positioned in that manner. The first part of the narrative commences on the central portal and ends on the left. In a similar manner, the second part of the narrative starts again on the central portal and wends its way to the right. The important part, from our perspective, is the last which begins at the depiction of the Last Supper which is to be found on the outer face of the pillar separating the central doorway and that of the Virgin to its left near the south end of the west front. The Last Supper, which is readily identifiable, is followed by a carving of Peter cutting off Malchus' ear. Next to that, but not in chronological order, Judas betrays Jesus with a kiss as a soldier arrests him. Again, bizarrely ordered, comes Jesus' triumphal entry into Jerusalem riding on an ass. Then comes a carving of Jesus' entombment (see figure 28) followed by carvings of the holy women.

This frieze, although in plain sight and in prime position over the main entrance of the cathedral, is easily overlooked. When found, it is hard to read coherently because of the strange and chaotic order in which

Figure 28

it is placed. There is a further important anomaly here for in over 200 figurines depicting the thirty-eight most important scenes from the lives of both Jesus and his Blessed Mother, there is not one representation of the Crucifixion. Yet, this is a Christian cathedral dedicated to the saving grace of Jesus who, according to the Church, died for our sins on the Cross at Calvary! One could be forgiven for wondering if the chaotic ordering of this frieze was neither more nor less than a deliberate ploy to confuse the orthodox and disguise the heresy contained within it.

A heresy that is quietly repeated elsewhere in the cathedral, for while there is also a figure of Jesus on a pier of the central door of the south entrance; another in the tympanum of the door on the right, between Mary and John; he is again depicted between two angels at the door on the left, the Knights door; and there are other scenes from his life at the north door, but nowhere is there a carved representation of a Christ crucified that dates from the thirteenth or fourteenth centuries in the entire cathedral.[27] This astonishing omission is a deliberate reflection of Templar belief. The only representation of the Crucifixion is in one of the twelfth-century stained-glass windows on the west front, namely the window dedicated to the Passion and Resurrection of Jesus.

This startling and blatant omission of any sculpture commemorating the central tenet of Christian dogma is quite deliberate: it is a reflection of Templar 'knowledge' that Jesus came to reveal and not to redeem. The message subtly but distinctly made by the assembled clues and pointers to hidden symbolism on the west front of Chartres Cathedral all indicate one important point – there are secrets encoded here; hidden in plain sight; unrecognised by prying prelates and only capable of being perceived and understood by initiates.

The master masons of Chartres in 1194 were intent on building the finest cathedral in Europe, however they faced certain inescapable limitations. Once the decision had been made to keep the west front of the building, the two towers and the Portail Royal created an immovable baseline from which they had to work. The building of the nave and the aisles would have to spring westwards from it and be constructed upon foundations of the Romanesque basilica with its remarkably wide span in a manner that would still accommodate the crypt of Fulbert's cathedral. At the east end of the new cathedral, the crypt would need to be considerably strengthened by Gothic inserts in order to take the additional weight of the new double ambulatory and its radiating chapels. The building could not be extended any further to the east because of natural geology where the land sloped steeply down to the river Eure. As the west front was already decorated, all their efforts to embellish the façade of the new building would have to go into the north and south fronts of the huge transepts centrally placed between the nave and the choir.[28]

A veritable flood of verbiage has been expended over the years in trying to discern who was the overall architect of the magnificent cathedral of Chartres. Who was the genius who directed the rebuilding of this glorious building and who brought it to completion in the almost unbelievable space of less than thirty-five years? The answer is that, contrary to modern architectural practice, not one individual architect can be identified. Indeed, according to Eric Gill, this Gothic masterpiece was designed by the very builders who were working upon it, with their ideas taking form around the expressed needs of the clergy and the demands of the pilgrimage trade. Decoration was formulated according to the emerging doctrine of the Church at that time. Gill claimed that: 'The only difference between a modern engineer and a medieval builder is that the latter controlled gangs of labourers most of whom shared his enthusiasms and understood his theory (for he had risen from their own ranks) and none of whom was entirely deprived of intellectual responsibility...'[29]

As we move from the west front around to the porch in the north transept, certain anomalies in the design and construction of the building become apparent if we examine it closely. The most obvious is the Gothic construction of pointed arches and buttresses arising from the Romanesque arches of the windows of the crypt, but there is far more to it than that. The Australian architect John James spent several years in

Chartres, studying every accessible stone of the cathedral and his analysis reveals that the building was composed of a series of mismatches that are readily detectable to the discerning eye. Few things at one end of the building match those at the other; few bays between the buttresses are identical to those alongside; windows, piers and buttresses change subtly yet distinctly as does the detail of many of the decorative elements. The flying buttresses of the nave are immensely solid and powerful while those of the choir are light and elegant. This apparently chaotic design is compounded when we study the porches and rose windows of the north and south transepts. James was able to establish that there were thirty building campaigns in the period of construction, conducted by nine identifiably different teams of masons.[30] Yet the miracle is that the end result of this apparently disorganised and random approach is an almost tangible and yet mystical sense of unity.

When we examine the carvings that decorate the porches of the north and south transepts we begin to appreciate the truth of Viollet le Duc's comment that: 'The mass of intelligence, knowledge, acquaintance with effects, practical experience, expended on those two porches of Chartres, would be enough to establish the glory of a whole generation of artists.'[31] It not only establishes the glory of the sculptors concerned, but speaks eloquently of Christian dogma and, in its esoteric content, stresses the direct continuity that exists between the initiatory traditions of Egypt and the teaching of Jesus. Furthermore, there are two glorious examples of carvings of interesting esoteric significance tucked away, almost carelessly, on pillars supporting the main canopy over the north porch. Both could be easily missed and each has its own message to convey.

The first of these is a strange representation of the Ark of the Covenant being transported on a wheeled vehicle (see figure 15, Ch. 9). The Bible recounts how this important religious artefact was carried on poles, so the assumption must be that this carving refers to a far more recent event. This carving, interpreted in conjunction with a long-standing esoteric legend, stimulated Trevor Ravenscroft and me to write in *The Mark of the Beast:*

'The first Knights Templar were quartered in the former stables of King Solomon beside the site of the destroyed Temple. It was here that the Ark of the Covenant had been hidden from the Roman soldiers of Trajan. Hugo de Payne, a close friend and relative of Chretien le Troyes, had been chosen to unearth the Ark and to bring it back to Europe where it was later hidden beneath the crypt of Chartres Cathedral.'[32]

Some years after the publication of those comments, the Masonic historians Christopher Knight and Robert Lomas found evidence that indicates that we may have been correct in our conclusions. They claimed that the Templars went to Jerusalem to retrieve the Ark and also found documents that may replicate some of those found among the Dead Sea Scrolls at Qumran. Knight and Lomas believe that these were hidden at Chartres[33] and other sites under the guardianship of Rex Deus. After the brutal suppression of the Knights Templar these sacred documents were reassembled and moved en masse to Rosslyn Chapel in Scotland, which, they claim, was principally built as the ornate repository for the most sacred documents in the world.[34] Thus there may well be a direct link between two of the most important sacred sites in the European esoteric tradition.

Chartres Cathedral and Rosslyn Chapel were built for the same purpose: exoterically they are both places of Christian worship decorated with mainstream Christian symbolism within which are encoded the secret keys to Gnostic initiation. Behind the outward mask of this symbolism, however, they share another, far more important purpose. They were constructed as secure reliquaries for the most important religious documents in the hidden tradition. The beautiful exteriors of these church buildings disguise their true function; in reality they are mere containers. There is a mystical difference between the container and the contained. It is that which is hidden within them that is most important. Chartres was the original repository, but from the suppression of the Knights Templar down to the present day, that role has been assigned to Rosslyn Chapel.

Further interesting carvings demonstrate the need to be fully observant when examining cathedrals and churches such as Chartres or Rosslyn. Near the bases of other pillars supporting the canopy over the north porch at Chartres are carvings of *La Croix Fleury* enclosed within a circle. These carvings have been there since the early thirteenth century and while comparatively rare, they do occur elsewhere, but always in conjunction with sites under the protection or patronage of one or another of the Rex Deus families. The *Croix Fleury* has since become the emblem of the chivalric Order of the Fleur-de-Lys, a direct lineal derivative of another Rex Deus organisation, the Order of the Croissant founded by King René D'Anjou. Membership of the modern Order of the Fleur-de-Lys is by invitation and is, theoretically, open to anyone of good standing. However, serving officers within the Order must be legitimate descendants of certain clearly defined families, all of which are drawn from the Rex Deus group. So here again, an easily overlooked piece of seemingly innocent symbolism carries a hidden message, that the Rex Deus families advertised their presence to other initiates as early as the thirteenth century.

The north and south transept porches combine together to form a systematic series of complex, interlinked, symbolic themes. The Creation and The Fall are celebrated within the outer archivolts of the central bay of the north porch, with the tympanum portraying the death, Assumption and coronation of the Virgin Mary as Queen of Heaven. This doorway, known for centuries as 'the Portal of the Initiates' is flanked by two rows of larger-than-life-size figures, each consisting of five statues that, in their Christian interpretation, encompass most of the symbolic themes I have mentioned in earlier chapters: the spiritual ancestry of Christianity within Old Testament Judaism and prefiguring the life of Jesus, using types and implied anti-types. Yet those same symbols are capable of another, distinctly different interpretation which is more direct and explicit, one that shows the Egyptian origin of biblical Judaism and, therefore, of Christianity. It demonstrates the continuity of ancient Egyptian initiatory gnosis throughout the era of biblical Israel and shows that Jesus himself was an integral part of this stream of teaching.

The figure on the extreme left of the central doorway represents Melchizadek, the priest king of Jerusalem to whom Abraham gave tithes (see figure 29).[35] Melchizadek carries a chalice containing, according to one of Chartres' most knowledgeable guides, Malcolm Millar, bread and wine.[36] Next to the priest king is the figure of the great patriarch Abraham with his son Isaac in front of him, bound and ready to be sacrificed (see figure 30). A paternal hand rests beneath the chin of Isaac whom Abraham is prepared to sacrifice just as Our Heavenly Father later sacrifices His son Jesus at Golgotha. An angel is carved above Melchizedek's head and Abraham is depicted in such a way that there can be no doubt that he is looking directly at the angel, (see figure 31) who is bringing the patriarch a message from God himself telling him that sacrifice of Isaac is not necessary as Abraham has amply demonstrated his willingness to accept God's will. The prophet Moses stands beside the patriarch, carrying in his arms the tablets of the Law and bearing a staff entwined by a brazen serpent (see figure 32) with which, it is claimed, he healed those bitten by poisonous snakes as a prophesy of Jesus healing the spiritual wounds of mankind by his sacrifice as recounted in the Gospel: 'As Moses lifted up the serpent in the wilderness, even so must the Son of Man be lifted up.'[37] Next to Moses is the figure of his brother Aaron with a lamb and the sacrificial knife, yet another prefiguring of the Lamb of God. Aaron was, of course, the ancestor of the Cohens, the hereditary high priests of the people of Israel. The statue of King David completes the set of figures on the left of the central doorway of the north porch. He is depicted carrying a spear and, some would claim, a crown of thorns, again held to be a prophesy of the redemptive sacrifice of Jesus.[38]

Esoteric interpretation of the same statues tells a somewhat different story however, one that is completely in line with the modern understanding of the true history of the people of Israel from the time of Abraham up to the reign of King David; a story that stresses the continuous, initiatory and Gnostic nature of the spirituality that was

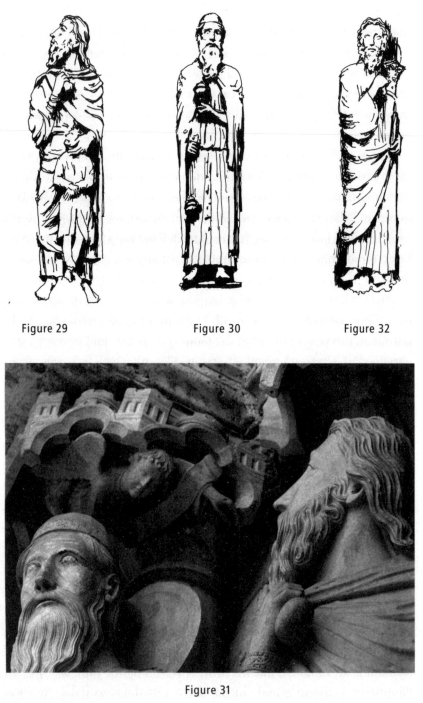

Figure 29   Figure 30   Figure 32

Figure 31

Jesus' true heritage. Melchizedek, far from having bread and wine in his chalice, is shown very clearly to hold in his left hand a chalice with a stone protruding from it. The mystical stone that fell from heaven and that is a symbol of the Holy Grail that we will describe in a later chapter. He, as 'King of Salem' was clearly an Egyptian as that city was a province of Egypt at that time.

The figure of Abraham is interpreted esoterically, in very nearly the same manner as the Church would describe, however the stress put on the importance of God's message sent by means of the angel is somewhat different. From the perspective of the hidden streams of spirituality, the principle of human sacrifice is forbidden forever for Abraham and all his heirs, for all time – and do not forget that Jesus was a devout Jew and a rabbi.

The Old Testament is awash with accounts of God's displeasure at those who ignored this command. The entire Judaic mystical tradition reinforces this point for, as I have mentioned earlier, the prophet Ezekiel declaimed that, 'the Righteous One' will not suffer for someone else's sin. He will not die. It is: 'The man who has sinned who is the one who must die. A son is not to suffer for the sins of his father, nor a father for the sins of his son.'[39] So, in the light of that, what can we make of the supposed sacrifice of the innocent Jewish prophet Jesus the Nazorean for the sins of mankind? It transgresses the ruling given by God to Abraham and contradicts the injunction by Ezekiel.

Once more we are forced to contemplate one of the principal beliefs preserved by the Rex Deus families of the hidden stream of spirituality, 'that Jesus came to reveal and **not** to redeem'. What he came to reveal was an initiatory pathway of great antiquity and supreme power that demands of all its followers a life founded firmly and irrevocably on the principles of Righteousness, Brotherhood, Truth and Justice. The figure of Moses carrying the Pharonic serpent-entwined staff of office is a simple declaration of the fact that he was a true Pharaoh and not a foundling, and that he, like his brother Aaron beside him, was, like all Egyptian royalty, an initiate of the ancient Temple mysteries. Another valid interpretation of the serpent on Moses' staff would have appealed to the masons who carved it, for the serpent can also represent the *Wouivre*, the Druidic term for the earth energies of initiatory power.

The carving of the priest king David that completes the tableau, rounds off this row of carvings that, both individually and collectively, stress the antiquity and power of Egyptian initiatory spirituality and its ongoing and the instrumental role it played in the development of Judaic mysticism and ritual forms of worship. This doorway is aptly named as the Portal of the Initiates, a description that it still carries despite centuries of the Church's repugnance at the initiatory tradition that it still deems to be a heresy.

The line of figures to the right of the Portal of the Initiates comprise, from left to right, the prophet Isaiah, Jeremiah, Simeon, John the Baptist and St Peter. Isaiah who prophesied that 'there shall come forth a rod out of the stem of Jesse'.[40] Jesse was the father of King David and therefore, a direct ancestor of Jesus. Jeremiah, as a prophet of the Passion of Jesus carries a cross. Simeon is depicted bearing the infant Jesus in his arms. When Mary and Joseph brought Jesus to the Temple for the circumcision, Simeon took Jesus in his arms and prophesied the Passion to Mary with the words: 'A sword will pierce your own soul too.'[41]

Next comes the figure of St John the Baptist in camel-hair clothing, his bare feet resting on a dragon symbolising the conquest of evil. In his arms he carries the *Agnus Dei*, the Lamb of God pictured with a cross in his paw representing Jesus' sacrifice at Golgotha; the *oriflame* or elongated flag flying from the cross symbolises Jesus' eventual victory over death. Next to John is the statue of St Peter, clothed in a twelve-stone pectoral symbolising his hereditary priesthood and carrying the Keys to the Kingdom. Beside Peter stands the figure of Elijah passing down his mantle to Elisha as he ascends.

The important figures here, from the point of view of the hidden streams of spirituality are John the Baptist and Elijah. In esoteric terms John, as the teacher or hierophant of Jesus, is the human bridge between the sacred knowledge, or gnosis represented by the winged dragon, and

Jesus, represented by the *Agnus Dei*, a symbol of great significance to the inner circle of the Knights Templar. Furthermore, within the Sufi tradition, Elijah and John the Baptist are conflated into the mythological figure of El Khidir. This ancient mystical pathway, which according to the mythologist and poet Robert Graves, pre-dates Islam by more than a thousand years,[42] claims El Khidir as the source of all divine wisdom. Therefore in these two pivotal figures we can sense a confluence between two of the oldest and most respected initiatory spiritual traditions in the world. This association has complex ramifications, for, as I will detail later, deeper research discloses that El Khidir, the source of the Sufi path, the Babylonian resurrecting god Tammuz and the mythological Christian St George, are simply one and the same figure clothed in differing mythological guise.

The central doorway in the south porch of Chartres Cathedral is dominated by the seated figure of Jesus, his hands raised in blessing displaying an indirect reference to the Crucifixion in the wounds in his palms. This theme is reinforced by angels on either side of Jesus carrying the instruments of his passion. In the lintel beneath is the Last Judgement with the saints and the sinners being divided and en route to their eternal destination. (See plate 11.) It is somewhat strange that this scene, which usually occupies the prime position on the west front of most other cathedrals, is here relegated to a side porch.

The central Trumeau figure is that of Jesus teaching. He is portrayed trampling on both a dragon and a lion, symbolising, in Church tradition, the crushing of the forces of evil and, in the esoteric tradition the source of his sacred gnosis. Two rows, each of six of figures, on either side of the bay represent those twelve Apostles carrying, where appropriate, the instruments of their martyrdom. James the brother of Jesus carries a fullers club; Peter, who carries the keys to the Kingdom, also bears a cross, as does St Andrew. Four others carry swords, namely Simon, Jude, Philip and Thomas. The boyish figure of John carries a cup – a sign of the Holy Grail perhaps; James the Great is identified by the scallop shells associated with the pilgrimage to Santiago of Compostela; and Bartholomew carries a broken knife. Thus in the south porch, while we have acceptable Church teaching being symbolised, yet even here there is a reference to the message that Jesus came to reveal and not to redeem.

CHAPTER 11

The Mystical Interior of Chartres Cathedral

The very first time I ventured through the doorway in the Portail Royal and entered Chartres Cathedral it took some time for my eyes to adjust to the sudden change in light. Outside it was bright sunlight, but once inside I stood as if transfixed. The sudden gloom of the shadow-like interior began to glow with opalescent blue and ruby-tinged colours, which made the massive limestone pillars seem transfused with vibrant energy. The stained-glass windows transformed the sunlight into a shimmering haze of colour that complemented the natural colour of the vast limestone pillars and their purple shadows, creating a distinctly vibrant atmosphere of subtly coloured light.

The stained glass of Chartres does not react like ordinary glass for as the outer daylight passes through each brightly-coloured pane, it is as though the light has been miraculously transformed and the glass itself has become a jewelled and luminous source of splendour. These windows were created by master craftsmen using scientific knowledge, the fruit of true gnosis that had been discovered by the Knights Templar in the Holy Land.[1] Indeed the earliest stained window-glass on record is known to have been created by adepts, masters of the Gnostic tradition, such as the poet Omar Khayam, in Persia at the beginning of the eleventh century.

Louis Charpentier claims that it was first produced at laboratories of such alchemists before the secrets were passed on to other initiates on a long journey that culminated when it was brought to Europe by the nine returning founder members of the Templar Order who passed it on to the Cistercians. This glass was made to neutralise, or filter out, light rays and luminous particles that are harmful to mankind's innate capacity for spiritual activity.[2] This selective filtering of the cosmic rays creates a wavelength of light that harmonises with the natural vibrations of human cellular tissue and maximises the effect of initiatory energy.[3]

The Stained-Glass Windows of Chartres

There are 179 sets of stained glass among the windows of Chartres that, in total, create a surface area of over 2,000 square metres. Over an acre of the most glorious stained glass in the world. The only plain windows in the cathedral are those replacing the stained glass removed by the clergy in the eighteenth century to shed more light on their ministrations at the main altar, and a few that were destroyed during the French Revolution. The majority date from the thirteenth century, except the four earlier windows that escaped the catastrophic fire of 1194.[4] Part of the true miracle of Chartres is that these fragile masterpieces have survived the ravages of time, the Hundred Years War, the French Revolution and two world wars, to entrance and puzzle us today. Yet their original purpose was simple, for as Abbot Suger wrote of the windows in Saint-Denis: 'The pictures in the windows are there, for the sole purpose of showing simple people, who cannot read the Holy Scriptures, what they **must** believe.' But Suger delighted as much in their magical as well as their didactic function, in transforming 'that which is material to that which is immaterial'.[5]

A full description of the stained-glass windows in Chartres Cathedral is far beyond the scope of a work such as this, and for those readers who wish to investigate the marvels of the medieval era more fully I can unhesitatingly recommend any of the many books on this subject published by Malcolm Millar. Malcolm has spent over thirty years of his life studying the cathedral and he is, without doubt, the supreme authority on the stained-glass windows of Chartres in the English-speaking world.

Three great rose windows, one on the west front and one each over the north and south transepts form the major features of the stained-glass windows of Chartres. There are many other, smaller rose windows placed over each pair of long windows, or lancets, in the nave, the two transepts and the choir. Then there are the lancets of the west front and the two transepts, which, when added to all the others make up the staggering total of 179 stained-glass windows in all. All exert their alchemical filtration on the light and thus maximise the initiatory effect of the telluric vibrations within the cathedral.

Sacred geometry plays its part in the design of the windows, especially in that of the great rose windows of the west front and the two transepts. The architect John James was astounded when he analysed the intricate geometrical patterns that form the great west rose. He wrote:

> 'It is a marvellous and fascinating tour de force where five
> separate systems of proportion rhythmically pulse across the
> wheel ... There is a triangle, a square, a hexagon, and a number
> of twelve and twenty-four pointed stars – which seem to have
> been applied in this natural order. There is an octagon that
> grows into eight points repeated three times to form a
> magnificent jewel coruscating through its eyes. The final figure
> is an endless twelve-pointed star, where you can travel along
> each line without ever once repeating yourself until you finally
> return to the beginning.'[6]

This magnificent window, the best known and most admired of its kind in Europe, was installed about 1215. It is set in the west to catch the rays of the setting sun and depicts the themes of the Last Judgement. The central figure is that of Jesus showing the wounds of his passion and crucifixion. He is surrounded by three concentric series of twelve circles in each. The circles of the inner series are at the outer edge of superbly jewelled elliptical forms and display eight angels grouped in pairs with each pair being separated by one of the symbols of the four Evangelists.[7] The middle series of larger circles show the Apostles, again grouped in pairs; and the outer series scenes from the Revelation of St John,[8] the supreme initiate of the true teachings of Jesus.

The rose window of the north transept, (see plate 12) above the Portal of the Initiates that is known as the Rose of France, was donated by Queen Blanche of Castile, the mother of King Louis IX, who was later canonised as St Louis. Blanche of Castile was the regent of France between 1226 and 1236. This window dates from about 1230. Stare at it intensely and its innate sacred geometry makes it appear to rotate. According to Colin Ward: 'This [window] is an exploration of the properties of a square inscribed within a circle and it gives rise to an unseen spiral linking the orifices in the stonework. This is the pattern of growth in nature itself.'[9]

It is not merely sacred geometry at work here for, as Fulcanelli remarked: 'The rose represents by itself, the [alchemical] action of the fire and its duration. That is why the medieval decorators sought to express in their rosaces the movements of matter quickened by elementary fire, as one may see over the north door of the cathedral at Chartres ...'[10]

The main focus of attention in the rose window of the north transept is the Madonna and Child in the centre encircled by a series of four round panels depicting doves representing the Holy Spirit, and a further eight showing angels and thrones. As with the rose in the west front these panels are at the outer extremity of jewelled, tapered designs that draw the eyes inwards towards the figure of the Virgin. In the next series of quadrilateral panels are Mary's ancestors, the twelve Kings of Judah, then, beyond those are quatrefoils emblazoned with gold fleurs-de-lys on a blue background, symbolising the Capetian Kings of France's claimed descent from the ma'madot and, through them, to the Royal House of Egypt. The twelve elliptical designs on the outer ring of this great rose depict twelve minor prophets.[11]

The rose over the south porch was donated by another great Rex Deus patron of the cathedral, Pierre Mauclerk, the Count of Dreux and his wife, Alix de Bretagne, another member of one of the leading houses within the hidden families. The central figure, as befits the rose above the

New Testament themes celebrated in the south portal beneath, is Jesus in his second coming at the Last Judgement. Surrounding him are four pairs of angels, with each pair separated by a symbol of one of the four Evangelists. These, in their turn, are surrounded by the twenty-four elders of the Apocalypse[12] depicted in circles and semi-circles, each carrying medieval musical instruments in their left hands and in their right, 'golden vials full of odours'. [13] Insofar as it can be established, this rose window and the lancets beneath, which display in their bases representations of both Pierre, Alix, their children and the coats of arms of the houses of Dreux and Brittany, was installed between 1224 and 1228. In 1228, Pierre Mauclerk led a revolt against Blanche of Castile and one important contributory factor in this armed quarrel may well have been Blanche's devout Roman Catholicism and the fact that she had therefore turned away from the traditional beliefs of the other members of Rex Deus. Despite this bitter dispute, however, the lancets beneath both the north and the south rose, repay further study as once again we have the strange situation of an heretical message being encoded within acceptable Church symbolism.

Beneath the northern rose in the transept are five important lancet windows. In the central lancet is the figure of St Anne, the mother of the Virgin, suspiciously dark-skinned and wearing a halo that, according to a priest that I guided through the cathedral in 2003, is normally only used for Mary Magdalene.[14] Rex Deus tradition informs us that Mary Magdalene was dark-skinned. According to Raban Maar 776–856, the Archbishop of Mayence whose original treatise on *The Life of Mary Magdalene* was rediscovered at Oxford University in the fifteenth century, Mary Magdalene was of the Hasmonean Royal House of Israel.[15] Furthermore, a later Capetian monarch, Louis XI who ruled France from 1461–83, claimed that the French royal family were descended from the Magdalene.[16] So it is, perhaps, not surprising to find a depiction of the Magdalene somewhat disguised as the acceptable figure of St Anne, occupying centre stage in the five lancets above the Portal of the Initiates. Any further doubt is clarified by the fact that she stands on a shield emblazoned with the fleur-de-lys of the Royal House of France who claim descent from her.

The lancets flanking her on either side are a glowing litany of the royal initiates of the Old Testament. Led by Melchizedek, the King of Righteousness, whose teaching inspired the Kibeiri and their spiritual heirs the Druids and the Essenes. Between Melchizadek and St Anne is Aaron, the brother of Moses, also a member of the Egyptian royal family and an initiate of the Egyptian Temple mysteries. From the viewer's perspective, to St Anne's right stands the direct ancestor of Jesus, namely King David and to complete the litany we have David's son, King Solomon, the builder of the first Temple in Jerusalem; the priest king 'whose wisdom was greater than all the men of the East and greater than all the wisdom of Egypt'.[17] Thus here again, within these five lancets, we have depictions of figures all conforming to Church doctrine and yet each, in their different ways, subtly teaching heresy: one extolling the fact that Jesus was married and founded a dynasty, the other four expounding the wisdom of the initiatory tradition that the Church abhorred.

Mary carrying the Christ child is featured in the central lancet below the south rose and is flanked by four other lancets depicting the four major prophets of the Old Testament, each carrying on their shoulders one of the four Evangelists. Dwarves mounted on the shoulders of giants yet again? Reading from left to right, firstly Jeremiah carries the figure of St Luke, Isaiah bears St Matthew on his shoulders, Ezekiel carries St John the Divine, and, lastly, Daniel carries St Mark. According to Malcolm Millar, this is a beautiful illustration symbolising Jesus' words: 'Think not that I am come to destroy the Law or the prophets: I am not come to destroy, but to fulfil.'[18]

The donor's signature is given by the coats of arms depicted at the bottom of each lancet and each displays the chequerboard design so common among the Rex Deus families. The same design that was used by the Knights Templar in their battle-flag, the *Beauseant* and later used as the basis for the 'hop-scotch' symbol of the Pilgrimage of Initiation and then, centuries after, for the design of the ritual carpet used in the lodges of the worldwide fraternity of Freemasonry.

These designs also provide a link between Chartres Cathedral and another mystical site of great importance to the Rex Deus tradition, Rosslyn Chapel in Scotland where they again occur as donor signatures on stained-glass windows specially commissioned in the late nineteenth century.[19] Around both sides of the south transept are further windows and those to the east are liberally decorated with red crusader crosses most of which are readily identifiable as being Templar.

By some miracle the three main windows beneath the great west rose remained intact after the fire in 1194. These are the only complete twelfth-century windows in the cathedral and are important in at least two major respects. Firstly they impart a deep and abiding respect for the artistry and skill of their creators and, more importantly, as they are undoubtedly the work of artists who had previously been employed at Saint-Denis by Abbot Suger, they give us an insight into his theological beliefs. All three symbolise important aspects of the life and ancestry of Jesus and are completely orthodox in the view of the messages they impart.

To the right is perhaps the most famous, depicting the Tree of Jesse. This grandiose conception is that of Suger himself as it is an exact reproduction of the one he commissioned for Saint-Denis. At the bottom of the window, Jesse lies asleep and from him springs a giant tree formed by the figures of kings and topped by the Virgin Mary. Surmounting it all is the figure of Jesus enthroned in glory surrounded by seven doves representing the Holy Spirit. Each side of this long window is decorated with the prophets who are deemed to be the harbingers of the Messiah throughout the ages. The whole is a beautiful symbolic representation of the prophecy of Isaiah: 'And there shall come forth a rod out of the stem of Jesse and a branch shall grow out of its roots: and the Spirit of the Lord shall rest upon him.'[20] It is not possible to state with any degree of certainty whether or not the other two windows are also reproductions of originals at Saint-Denis, but it is highly likely.[21]

The central window is dominated by a large figure of the Blessed Virgin surrounded by a series of alternating square and circular medallions symbolising various scenes from the life of Jesus. The predominant colours within this window are fiery red and blue. The third window, on the extreme left beneath the rose, is dedicated to the Passion, Crucifixion and Resurrection of Jesus. The windows depicting both the Tree of Jesse and the Passion are composed of an almost supernatural blue that enhances the mystical atmosphere conveyed by their contents.

The Passion window is of vital importance, being commissioned by Suger it is, as it were, almost an import from a theologian and cleric of a far more orthodox variety than those of the Chartres mystery school who commissioned the carvings of the Portail Royal. Thus it is not so strange that this window carries the only direct representation of the Crucifixion that can be dated to within two hundred years of the cathedral's rebuilding. The strict adherence to Church doctrine within these windows that are situated in such a prime position drew the attention away from more questionable forms of symbolism elsewhere within the cathedral. For rarely in an ecclesiastical building of such importance can so much heresy be encoded within mainstream Christian iconography without awakening the unwelcome attentions of the 'thought police' of the Church authorities.

While the three windows in the west front are the last complete surviving twelfth-century windows, there are four panels, dating from about 1180, built into a thirteenth-century window in the south ambulatory. This is the famous *Notre Dame de la Belle Verrière* a truly exquisite window that shows the Virgin, seated with Jesus on her knee, surrounded by angels. Below are panels telling the story of the miracle of changing the water into wine and depicting the three temptations of Jesus. The figures of the Virgin and Child show a strong Byzantine influence. They remind us of Russian or Greek icons, but the colouring demonstrates that wonderful manipulation of blue and ruby luminescence that was the great secret of French glass-makers.[22] In the opinion of Louis Charpentier, *Notre Dame de la Belle Verrière*, like the three twelfth-century windows in the west front, also came from the hands of craftsmen first employed at Saint-Denis.[23]

The vast majority of the other stained-glass windows in the cathedral contain figures that bear no relation to whatever story the window is telling, these are the 'donor figures' that form a type of signature indicating who commissioned them and gave them to the cathedral. Forty-two of these windows were donated by the various craft-guilds of the city of Chartres; forty-four by the royal house and nobility of France[24], mostly members of the Rex Deus group of families, sixteen only from the clergy and fourteen by donors whose name and rank is unknown. Families of chivalric importance include the Montmorencys, the de Montforts, the Courtneys, the Clements – who were marshalls of France – Philippe Count of Boulogne, the Count of Dreux and the King of Castille.[25]

The *Wouivre* and the Mound

The mound upon which the cathedral of Chartres is built was a sacred site long before the advent of Christianity. It was sacred long before the Druids came here and was a centre of pilgrimage in their time and ever since. What drew people here in pagan times? What indicated to the Druids and those who preceded them the sacred nature of this place? It was of course, the *genius loci*, the very spirit of the place, made manifest by a conjunction of sacred signs all indicating the detectable cosmic forces, telluric currents that were named by the Druids as the *Wouivre*.

This spirit of the earth manifested itself sometimes where there were underground waters exerting their magnetic force or where geological faults caused different soils to mix or where, according to the ancients, the gods had made their presence known. Among the latter are some very special sites, Delphi, the Temple Mount in Jerusalem and the Mound at Chartres. These are the places where that most powerful telluric force, the *Spiritus Mundi*, or Spirit of the Earth can be detected. The *Spiritus Mundi* is deemed to be so powerful that it is capable of awakening man to the spiritual life. This has been recognised since Druidic times when the mound was known as the *Hill of the Strong* or the *Hill of the Initiates*. [26]

This current, symbolised by the pillar on which the Virgin of the Pillar stands, is so sacred that no material influence may be allowed to trouble or destroy it; the sacred mound from which it arises must not be polluted in any way. Thus Chartres is the only cathedral in France wherein no king, cardinal or bishop is interred.[27] The Hill remains undefiled like the Temple Mount in Jerusalem, *Virgo Intacta* so to speak, which, in the light of the Druidic goddess Virgini Pariturae and the Blessed Virgin to whom the cathedral is dedicated, is wholly appropriate.

The presence of the *Spiritus Mundi* at Chartres has been recognised since pre-history and it was certainly known to the initiate Fulbert, for his cathedral was built on a series of artificial water-courses designed to enhance its effect. We will never know whether or not these canals were constructed by Fulbert, but his cathedral and the present one that was built on its foundations, take full advantage of their amplifying effect. Blanche Mertz, who has made a detailed investigation of these matters, describes an arrangement of fourteen fan-like streams of such regularity that they must be man-made. She also claims that these fourteen streams are symbolised by the seven doves depicted around the Black Virgin in Fulbert's Romanesque crypt, as each of these doves has two beaks.

The Black Madonna, *Notre-Dame de Sous-Terre*, Our Lady Under the Earth, a modern replica of *the Virgin of the Druids,* takes the place of honour on the altar in the underground chapel in the crypt. Mertz claims that this mystical power point in Chartres is intensified by a large loop in the underground river and then strengthened by the fan-like convergence of the underground watercourses.[28] Within the cathedral above there are several other points of telluric power that have the capacity to raise man to a point of etheric enhancement, to a true 'state of grace', a quality that was recognised, used and amplified by the skills of the craftsmen who created this magnificent building.

The choir itself, with its boundaries so carefully delineated by later master craftsmen, provides a vault of protection for those who sought the benefits of initiation and righteousness. This total, spiritual transformation cannot develop in man just anywhere and Blanche Mertz writes that: '...in the centre of the choir where fourteen subterranean watercourses curiously converge there is a precise point equidistant between the top of the gothic vault and the underground water which gives the individual an impression of weightlessness.'[29]

When I met the gifted French initiate Frederic Lionel in 1997 he informed me that there are other places, apart from the choir, within the confines of Chartres Cathedral at which the detectable levels of energy are those of an initiation point. One lies at the junction of the transept and the nave, which is now inaccessible as a large, solid-silver altar has been placed there. Another lies almost vertically underneath it, in the crypt. Dowsing the crossing points of the transept and the nave, I have found that the energy point that once manifested itself where the altar now stands, appears to have been displaced a short distance to the north-west and arises just beside a huge pillar near the beginning of the north transept.

These 'initiation points' are not the only such points of telluric power that can be detected in the main cathedral, they are simply the most powerful. Another, which is almost on a par with these, can be found immediately in front of the statue Virgin of the Pillar (see plate 13), in the north side of the ambulatory. The Virgin is clothed according to tradition, in heavy, ornate robes formally shaped in a triangle.[30] If one stands in front of the pillar on which she rests, it is possible to detect a tangible level of energy, a place of God-given power where the vibration is so low that it can induce a fainting feeling indicating that this too is a point of spiritual transformation. Another initiatory Black Madonna is in an equivalent position in the south side of the ambulatory, namely *Notre Dame de la Belle Verrière* that I described earlier. The third is, of course, *Notre Dame Sous-Terre*, the Black Madonna in the crypt[31] which, so the guide assures everyone, was once used as an initiation chamber.

The ancient Celtic well within the crypt, the Well of the Strong sinks to the water table thirty-seven metres below the floor of the choir. The main vault of the cathedral rises approximately thirty-seven metres above that same floor level[32] giving visible proof of the masons' credence in the old Hermetic principle of *as above, so below*. It is, of course, no coincidence that the initiation point in the choir is exactly midway between these two extremes; it is a matter of the builders of this mystical place seeking to achieve perfect cosmic balance and harmony

The Labyrinth

Certainly the largest and perhaps the most intriguing esoteric symbol within Chartres Cathedral is the labyrinth (see figure 33). This circular design of black and white flagstones occupies over one third of the floor space of the nave and, sadly, is normally obscured by serried ranks of chairs placed upon it. The guidebook claims that traversing the labyrinth, in bare feet or on one's knees, was a form of penance that earned an indulgence, or the medieval equivalent of 'time off for good behaviour' from the prison of purgatory. It also describes walking the labyrinth as a substitute form of pilgrimage, reaching the centre being the equivalent

Figure 33

of reaching the Holy City of Jerusalem. I, for one, do not find either of these explanations particularly convincing, as several Neolithic labyrinths of an identical pattern have been found and it is simply beyond belief to claim that they were created to gain an indulgence from the pope, much less act as a substitute for a pilgrimage to the Holy City.

The first time that I saw the labyrinth fully exposed to view was when I visited the cathedral in the early 1990s with a colleague, Ray Peake. Later that same evening, en route to the port of Roscoff, we spent some hours at a folk festival in a small Breton town. Partway through the proceedings, the compère announced that it was time for *the Dance* and an odd assortment of musicians took to the stage: one carried a medieval drum; another a snake charmer's flute; the third the strangest set of bagpipes we had ever seen; and, finally, there was a guitarist. The music was haunting, oddly familiar, and yet distinctly foreign. It was Arab music; slow, reedy, rhythmical and, quite literally, entrancing. The mayor and his wife led the dance, standing with arms linked closely so that their sides touched, and they moved in a shuffling, sideways, curving pattern; others joined them until, eventually the entire population of the village, toddling infants, adolescents and ancient grannies, were all in the line. I began to realise that a formal pattern was being created by the dancers, one that replicated the curving, weaving design of the Chartres labyrinth. What we were seeing was, most likely a derivation of a traditional Sufi dance designed to bring about a shift in consciousness.

I later learnt that the labyrinth of Chartres was indeed intended to be taken according to a fixed ritual, as a rhythmic dance. Furthermore, that this dancing traverse of the sacred flagstones was performed unshod so that the feet were in direct contact with the stone which acted like a medieval accumulator for the currents of the earth. In the Middle Ages it was the bishop himself who led the ritual dance through the labyrinth at the equinoctial festivals, when the earth energies were pulsating strongly. The mere act of a group of devout people traversing the labyrinth in this manner acts upon the telluric currents as yet another form of amplification.

Since I first saw it exposed in its entirety, I have 'walked' the labyrinth with three different groups – one daytime walk with a group from the Edgar Cayce Foundation in America, and two evening walks. The two evening walks were remarkable. The first with a large group from the Plymouth Natural Health Centre was by candlelight and was very moving indeed. The second was with a small group of Americans that included a Vietnamese gentleman who traversed the entire course in a Tai Chi walk.

Before and after all three walks, I dowsed the labyrinth and in each case, after the group had finished, the energy at the centre had appreciably increased. Thus it is not hard to believe that those who have reached the centre in the traditional manner and at equinoctial times were changed, for every time I have traversed this mystical pathway I have experienced a strong sense of being spiritually open and a feeling of divine harmony. So, in symbolic terms, there are two different approaches to the 'spiritual journey': one finds its expression in the act of pilgrimage, the other in traversing the labyrinth. In the first, one undertakes a journey through time and space, through the sacred landscape; in the second, one moves ritually, physically and spiritually inwards, towards a still, motionless centre.[33]

The labyrinth is indeed the largest symbolic feature within Chartres Cathedral and one that had special meaning for the cathedral builders. It is not merely a giant symbol, but an instrument designed to bring about a change in consciousness. The trump card of the researchers is that 'the great twelve-fold west rose window not only conforms basically in size to the maze, but when hinged down on to the floor of the nave covers it almost exactly'.[34] Why? Who knows? The medieval masters still guard their secrets well.

It is plain to see from the material recounted in these two chapters that Chartres Cathedral is not merely a vibrant prayer in stone and a monument to medieval Christian belief, but also a hymn to the hidden streams of spirituality, an instruction book of initiation carved in stone that is masked by its outward display of Christian symbolism. Whatever one's personal beliefs, Christian or heretic, the iconography of Chartres will work its transformative magic in a manner pertinent to your strength, weaknesses or spiritual needs.

My colleague, Gordon Strachan, in his book on Chartres, posed two questions, firstly: 'Does the cathedral have its own aura or light body which resonates with ours?' and: 'Is that why the building affects us?'[33] I would respectfully submit that the answer is 'Yes!' on both counts. Over the last few decades, much has been made of the mystery of Chartres' odd alignment. The vast majority of Christian churches and cathedrals are aligned due east. Chartres is not. It is aligned 47 degrees north of east. Furthermore this is not a phenomenon that can be ascribed to Fulbert, the Chartres mystery school or the Knights Templar, for it is an alignment that has been there since the very first Christian building occupied this site. The plans of the various churches and cathedrals that have occupied the sacred mound of Chartres are known and they fit, one inside the other, from those of the earliest times to the present like a set of Russian *Matrioshka* dolls. This alignment is, most probably, the heritage of some ancient Neolithic construction on the site for it is only three degrees different from that of Stonehenge and less than five degrees from the alignment of the summer solstice.[34]

There is, in the western aisle of the south transept, a stone, set slightly aslant from the others, that is distinctly whiter than the grey stones that surround it. Within its bounds is set a small, shining, lightly gilded metal tenon. Each year at noon precisely on 21st June, the summer solstice, a ray of light passes through a deliberately contrived space in the stained-glass window dedicated to Saint Apollinaire that strikes this tenon with absolute precision. Why? I cannot answer except to suggest that this may well have something to do with the mysterious alignment of this cathedral.

CHAPTER 12

The Veneration of the
Black Madonna

The all-pervasive Roman Catholic cult of Mariolatry received its main impetus from the veneration accorded to the Blessed Virgin at Chartres Cathedral, despite the fact that its true origins derive from far more ancient and pagan forms worship of a variety of mother goddesses. The principal Black Madonna venerated in Chartres Cathedral, *Notre Dame Sous-Terre*, is definitely a Christianised variation of the Druidic *Virginibus Pariturae*, described by Caesar in *de Bello Gallico* book IV.[1] This initiatory Black Virgin and its two companions within Chartres Cathedral are not unique, for literally hundreds of others are located in France, Germany, Italy and Switzerland. Many other Black Madonnas can be found in Spain near the pilgrimage routes to St James of Compostela and the most celebrated of these is the one at Montserrat not far from Barcelona, the mountainous site that inspired Wagner's *Parsifal.* Copies of these miracle-working black statues spread right across Europe but, strangely, one does not find statues of the Black Virgin in Poland or in staunchly Roman Catholic Mexico, where Our Lady of Czestakova and our Lady of Guadeloupe are icons.[2]

Statues of the Black Virgin, or the Black Madonna appear to have developed a standardised form of representation during the twelfth century, one that portrays the majestic figure of the Virgin seated on the Hieratic Throne of Wisdom in a manner that is as rigid as dogma. She is the symbol of Wisdom personified. From the late thirteenth century, however, the picture changes and the Madonna is no longer enthroned on the seat of wisdom but is portrayed in a more human manner as a caring mother.[3]

From the mainstream Christian perspective, there is no scriptural passage in the Gospels or any other part of the New Testament that could, by any stretch of the imagination, act as the basis for a cult of the eternal feminine whether or not she is depicted as the embodiment of divine wisdom, the mother of God or as the Queen of Heaven.[4] Certain questions arise, therefore: Why is it that, for many centuries, the sanctuaries consecrated to the Black Virgins have attracted pilgrims without number, be they humble or powerful; peasants or kings – including King Louis IX, King Louis XI and King Philippe le Bel? And: 'Why is the figure of the Queen of Illumination always installed in the most sombre part of any Christian temple, namely the crypt?[5]

Many modern researchers have, like Jacques Huynen, been particularly interested in the esoteric and initiatory aspects of the cult. This led him to focus on its development in the twelfth century and its association with alchemy and the Order later condemned for heresy, the Knights Templar.[6] It is impossible to find credible origins of the cult within mainstream Christian history and while many researchers have tried to find proof that the cult of the Black Virgin began in the fifth or sixth centuries, their results have been meagre and inconclusive. These strange statues did not appear in any significant number until the end of the eleventh century and continued to be erected up to the end of the thirteenth century.[7] Bernardus of Chartres, in his treatise *Liber Miraculorum Sancti Fidis* written between 1013 and 1020, described his journey to Conques in 1013, and he makes no mention of any Black Virgins, which, if they were there, he would have done if for no other reason than to compare them with the celebrated Black Virgin in his own cathedral's crypt. This is a strong indication that the cult was not well developed much before the twelfth century when, as the records disclose, it made notable progress with the active encouragement of the Rex Deus pillar of the Church, Bernard of Clairvaux.[8]

Pre-Christian Origins of the Cult?

The principal sanctuaries dedicated to the Black Virgin are located at sites that were deemed sacred long before the advent of Christianity, and therefore it is apparent that this cult of the Virgin simply replaced a far more ancient form of veneration and had simply transposed the worship of the Earth Mother into Christian practice. They were originally all sited in a crypt, and while many have since been moved for one reason or another, it is almost always to some place of relative obscurity within the church. These crypts associated with the Black Virgins, such as those of Chartres, Saint Quentin and Issoire, act as amplifiers of resonance and telluric powers in a similar manner to the grottos of pre-Christian and more ancient times.[9] The French writer, Marie Durand-Lefèbvre, claims that there is both iconographical and cultic continuity between the pagan goddesses and the Black Virgins, [10] a view confirmed by the author Émile Saillens.[11] The veneration of the Black Madonna is one of the mystical keys to the symbolic language of the Middle Ages and is a medieval manifestation of a tradition that reaches back into pre-history and mankind's mother goddess, the universal symbol of life and spiritual rebirth.[12]

The noted Scottish author, Ean Begg, who first brought the cult to the attention of the English-speaking world, recounts that over and over again in the legends and traditions associated with the Black Madonna, it is claimed that the statue was found in woodlands, or accidentally discovered when animals refused to pass a certain spot. When the statue was taken to the church, it would return miraculously to her original hiding place, where a chapel would then be built in her honour. The cult is also invariably associated with sites distinguished by their healing waters, proximity to extinct volcanoes or the confluences of rivers, all of which manifest telluric power.[13] Begg claims that the theory that these images of the Black Madonna and Child were often based on those of the Egyptian goddess Isis and the Horus Child, is now widely accepted as proven.[14]

The original Egyptian cult of Isis involved initiatory ceremonies and mystery rites of which we know absolutely nothing, for disclosure of the mysteries of the cult to the profane was an offence punishable by death and entry into her temples was forbidden to all except the initiates. Isis was the patroness of navigators who spread her cult all over the Mediterranean basin so that by the second century BCE it was firmly implanted in Sicily and throughout Italy. In Gaul it spread through contact with Alexandrian merchants and it took firm hold in the towns. As the cult developed it became well established throughout North Africa, Spain and Gaul, long before the beginning of the Christian era.[15] Indeed the French historian of the cult, Charles Bigarne, mentions that some statues of Isis carried the same inscription celebrated by the Virgin at Chartres, *the Virgin about to give birth*.[16] Furthermore, all three great goddesses from the east, Isis, Cybele and Diana of the Ephesians, are depicted as black and their cults have had a long history in the West since pre-Roman times.[17]

The story of *Notre Dame de Puy* provides one example of the accepted Egyptian origins of the Black Madonnas, for during the French Revolution in 1794, this very ancient statue was thrown onto a fire and burnt along with numerous other objects and religious artefacts. The chronicles of the time report that as the populace consigned the statue to the flames, the cry went up, '*Death to the Egyptian*'. [18]

Another possible source for an Egyptian attribution to the Black Madonna is through the legendary history of St Sarah, the black Egyptian 'maid' of the Magdalene when she landed at the site that became known as Les Saintes Maries de La Mer in present-day Provence. Veneration of St Sarah gave birth to one particular cult of the Black Virgin particularly venerated by the Gypsies, although some authors prefer to ascribe this privilege to Isis the Egyptian goddess.[19]

Throughout Europe, similar adoptionist techniques were regularly employed to retain older, pagan forms of worship and incorporate them into Catholic ritual and practice. Veneration of the Black Madonna obviously started in this manner, for, as Ean Begg recounts: '… in the Empire of the East, the hyperdulia accorded to Mary, a short step short of the worship of God but superior to the veneration that is offered to the saints, perpetuated the cult of Wisdom and the Great Mother.'[20]

Strangely, the Roman Catholic Church, while it has always been happy to rake in the financial benefits of pilgrimage to these sites, has consistently felt uncomfortable with the cult of the Black Madonna. But why, when Mariolatry plays such an important role in the Roman Catholic faith, is the hierarchy uncomfortable with the intense local, national and sometimes international, veneration of Black Madonnas? Why does the Black Virgin cause the hierarchy so much embarrassment? This ambivalent attitude infects many clergy of all classes throughout Europe. When I started to question the parish priest at Limoux in the Languedoc, about the local Black Virgin, *Notre Dame de Marceillon*, this previously garrulous cleric became suddenly and inexplicably silent. Ean Begg asked a Greek Orthodox priest at Pelion about the colour of an icon of the Black Madonna in his parish, and the priest replied that: 'in Greece they came in all the colours of the rainbow and that this had no significance.'[21]

Bizarrely, art historians who normally analyse coloration in art to the nth degree, express no curiosity about the dark pigmentation of these statues and theologians display even less enthusiasm for the subject. Despite the miracles that continue down to the modern day, discussion of the origins of the strange black coloration of these statues triggers deep-seated concerns about highly sensitive issues such as the pagan origin of much of Christian belief and practice; memories of the heretical Knights Templar and the crusade against the Cathars and other heretical matters. So the obvious black coloration is simply ignored and, if admitted at all, is put down to the effects of centuries of candle smoke or artistic whim.[22]

Jean Tourniac tried to put the whole problem in perspective when he wrote: 'Black Virgins, White Virgins, the first hidden and sealed, the second an illuminatrice. One complements the other and, I hardly need say, both representing the Sacred Feminine of primordial motherhood.'[23]

Most devout and practising Christians, both clergy and laity, who continue to venerate these medieval symbols simply accept that the origins and colour of the Black Virgin poses a mystery for which there is no explanation, but happily continue to venerate her as one that can still work miracles.

The Black Madonna and the Magdalene

Bernard of Clairvaux as a young boy at Fontaine is said to have drunk three drops of milk from the breast of the Black Virgin of Châtillon.[24] Indeed another indication of one probable cause of the Church's discomfort with the cult may arise from words spoken by Bernard. When giving 'The Rule' to the Templars, Bernard laid down a specific require-ment for all the members of the new knighthood to make: 'Obedience to Bethany and the House of Mary and Martha.' [25] In simple words, to swear obedience and loyalty to the dynasty founded by Mary Magdalene and Jesus. Based on these remarks, many scholars have raised the hypothesis that all the great Notre Dame cathedrals built or financed by the Templars were dedicated not to Mary the mother of Jesus, but to Mary Magdalene and the son of Jesus: an idea that, when viewed from the Church's perspective, is plainly heretical.[26]

The subsequent Templar veneration of the Magdalene in the guise of the Black Madonna was widespread and Ean Begg lists over fifty places of veneration of the Black Virgin found in churches dedicated to Mary Magdalene.[27] The early Christian Gnostics accorded the Magdalene special status for they believed she was Jesus' favourite disciple and the one to whom he had transmitted the highest level of gnosis.[28] In the Western esoteric tradition, the Magdalene is 'the symbol of divine wisdom'; in the Nazorean tradition, she is depicted garbed in black like the goddess Isis, wearing Sophia's crown of stars, and her infant wears the golden crown of royalty.[29]

According to the twentieth-century initiate Rudolf Steiner, symbolism can be interpreted at up to at least nine different levels depending on the initiatory status of the viewer and the Black Madonna is a classic example of this. At the simplest, exoteric level she is the mother of Jesus with her child; at the second level, Mary the seat of wisdom is depicted. In esoteric terms, the same symbol can represent the Magdalene and the child of Jesus; at a deeper level, in the Egyptian tradition, the black symbolises wisdom. There is another tradition that ascribes Egyptian origins to the Black Madonnas found within the cult of the Magdalene at Orléans, where the Black Virgin is referred to as St Mary the Egyptian. King Louis XI of France, a notable member of Rex Deus, was one of the most enthusiastic votaries that the Black Virgin cult has ever known and it is well recorded that he repeatedly visited more than twenty of her shrines. In addition, as I have mentioned earlier, he regarded Mary Magdalene as one of the progenitors of the Royal House of France.[30] So it can be claimed that the Templars were venerating the Magdalene as a symbol of the goddess of Divine Wisdom, Sophia, embodied in the form of Isis and the Horus child, thinly disguised as the Blessed Virgin and the infant Jesus.

At yet another level, Isis was venerated as 'the Initiate of Light'[31] or the pure embodiment of enlightenment. In purely pagan terms the Black Virgin can symbolise the Earth Mother or the Egyptian goddess Anna, who was always represented in Egyptian tradition as being black.[32] Was this some form of pagan precursor to the later Christian depiction of a black St Anne in the stained glass of Chartres? Ean Begg, who has dedicated many years of his life to the study of the Black Madonna and the hidden streams of spirituality within Christian Europe, claims that the study of the history of the Black Virgin may reveal a heretical sect with the power to shock and astonish even current post-Christian attitudes.[33] A comment which, when judged in the light of the Rex Deus tradition, is absolutely correct.

A Focus of Pilgrimage

The Templars, to whom St Bernard gave their Rule, are justly renowned for having an incomparable veneration for the Virgin, and each Templar establishment had a representation of the Mother of God in the form of a statue in full majesty, exactly like those of the Black Virgin.[34] The Templars protected pilgrims en route to the shrine of St James of Compostela, a pilgrimage that was actively encouraged by Bernard of Clairvaux. The route was punctuated with Templar commanderies, both Benedictine and Cistercian hostelries and churches dedicated to the Black Virgin. One of the four great French starting points, namely Vézelay, was a strong centre of the cult of the Magdalene and eventually became a

Black Virgin site. It was here that Bernard preached the Second Crusade. At his canonisation, St Bernard was granted the same feast day, 20th August, as St Amadour, the legendary founder of Rocamadour which, incidentally, is the site of perhaps the most powerful and one of the earliest Black Madonnas in France.[35]

The major pilgrimage to St James of Compostela drew floods of pilgrims from all over Europe to Spain. In numerical terms, the pilgrims who followed the *Camiño Santiago*, the route laid out by the Benedictine treatise the *Codex Callextinus*, far outnumbered those whose destination was Rome or Jerusalem. Thus the pilgrimage to Spain and that to the Holy Land brought many thousands of devout pilgrims into contact with the mystical worlds of Islam and Judaism.[36] Contact that was already a regular occurrence in southern Provence and Sicily for parts of southern Provence had been invaded and occupied by the Saracens and had acted as a cultural bridge between the two rival religious cultures. The English mythologist Robert Graves noted that both Provençal and Sicilian Black Virgins were so named in honour of an ancient tradition in which Wisdom is symbolised as Blackness.[37]

The great Muslim mystic and Sufi poet, Mohyiddin ibn Arabi, wrote in his *Treatise on Categories of Initiation*, that: 'For the men who are in the confidence of God, … the face of the Sufi is black like … the Sulamite in the Song of Songs.'[38] The earlier Sufi mystic, Mevlana Jalaluddin Rumi, states that 'in Islamic mysticism, radiant black is the colour of the Divine Light par excellence, a light inaccessible to most'.[39]

Thus, in the veneration of the Black Virgin we can again discern crossover points between the mystical traditions of all three of the world's great monotheistic traditions, namely Christianity, Judaism and Islam. A glorious example of the sublime mystical paradox of divine unity being perceived within apparent diversity. As with the re-entry of the Greek classics into European consciousness through the Chartres mystery school, there were certain monks well versed in both Hebrew and Arabic at the monasteries of Citeaux and at Cluny, who profited from documents coming from Spain. Etienne Harding, the third Abbot of

Citeaux, worked in close collaboration with Talmudic scholars in his compilation of Hebrew texts which he used to update the Latin Bible.[40]

Therefore, Ean Begg was absolutely accurate in stating that: '... those who stress the hidden, initiatory aspect of the Black Virgin cult are quite correct to do so in terms of the opposing orthodoxy of the Middle Ages.'[41] While the apparent heresy that lies behind the Black Virgins is multi-layered and has complex but nonetheless identifiable roots, a great part of the original message conveyed by them has disappeared. Disappeared but not lost, for it is hidden and protected behind another language – that of symbols.[42]

All of these statues act as a receptor and amplifier for the vibrations that descend from God. Telluric vibrations that emanate from the invisible world and that are made manifest in the visible one. Even today these play some mysterious role in the fact that certain statues of the Black Virgin are still associated with miracles.[43] The symbol of the Black Virgin establishes a link between the heart of the believer and the divine presence using the symbolic charge inherent within the statue allied to the telluric power of the site, in its function as mediator. This mystery replicates that which the Bible proposes as one of the functions of the Ark of the Covenant, a mystery that Judaic mysticism sums up in the sacred word for divine wisdom, the *Shekina*.

Thus the Black Virgin is truly a symbol of a vibrant power, total and esoteric. It cannot be apprehended by the intellect, it is too simple, it has to be experienced and thus it can only be apprehended by those who listen with their hearts. For the mystics and initiates and all who are in a true 'state of Grace', the Black Madonnas speak a universal language that permits them to understand the incomprehensible and it is, at the same time, a true conjunction of contraries.[44] It is, perhaps, for this reason that the Black Virgin is honoured on her special feast days in certain sanctuaries by the burning of green candles. In most others she is often clothed in green vestments. The colour green, as explained by the Church, is dependant upon the time in the liturgical year, but to the hidden streams of spirituality it indicates a transformation in the state of consciousness to a higher level. It is, quite simply, the colour of initiation. This is in line with the Kabbalistic tradition of divine mercy when the two columns of the tree of the Sephiroth permit one to see the third column, bringing all into true cosmic balance, and that too is symbolised by the colour green.

Is this green a reflection of the emerald spoken of by the alchemists? Is the light of the green candles the one that pierces the most profound secrets and then illuminates the pathway to initiation? Let us also remember that the green emerald is also the 'stone that fell to earth and rests in the cup' celebrated at Chartres in the carving of Melchizedek and reported in certain of the Grail legends.[45]

CHAPTER 13

The Grail, the Tarot Trumps and the Demise of the Templars

Wolfram von Essenbach, the Templar author of the first complete Grail saga claimed that the Grail is symbolised by a 'stone of light' brought down from heaven by angel hosts.[1] He wrote of the Knights of the Grail: 'By a stone they live, and that stone is pure and precious its name you have never heard? Men call it *Lapis Exulis* ... if you look at this stone ... young you will live for ever. And this stone, all men call the Grail.'

This Grail stone, the source of eternal youth, was also called *Lapis Exulis* by the alchemist Arnold of Villanova, however he also called it the 'Philosopher's Stone' thereby forging an overt link between alchemy and the Grail.[2]

The Grail is described as taking many forms – as a chalice, a cup, the stone that fell from heaven, the stone within the cup or a magical bowl,[3] and all were believed capable of restoring the dead to life or granting the blessed gift of good health to the wounded or the maimed. Pre-Christian Celtic legends describe the Grail as a cauldron with similar magical qualities.[4]

The Grail sagas were transformed into a Christianised version of far older legends by the inspired genius of Wolfram von Essenbach[5] and Chrétien de Troyes. They mixed pagan legend, Celtic folklore, Jewish mysticism, Rex Deus tradition, alchemical and Kabbalistic symbolism to create a magical 'Christian' legend apparently extolling veneration for the holiest relic in Christianity – the cup used by Jesus himself at the last supper and again, reputedly, by Joseph of Arimathea to catch the blood of the Saviour after the Crucifixion. This legend immediately invites disbelief, for Jewish burial practice at the time of the Crucifixion demanded that any man who handled a corpse was under a strict obligation to undergo a prolonged period of purification, which is hardly credible for any devout Jew on the eve of the Passover. Furthermore, Jewish traditions also ensured that the corpse be interred with the entire body and blood together in order to guarantee life in the hereafter. This practice continues among the Hassidim today and poses an absolute and divinely ordained barrier against the taking of blood from any corpse.

Rex Deus and the Grail

Dr Walter Johannes Stein wrote of the group he called 'the Grail Families' nearly fifty years ago, long before the Rex Deus secrets began to be disclosed and over three decades before the publication of Baigent, Leigh and Lincoln's *The Holy Blood and the Holy Grail*. Indeed in the last few pages of his seminal work, *The Ninth Century, World History in the Light of the Holy Grail*, Stein traces the genealogies of the Grail Families from Charlemagne down to the Capetian Kings of France and the Royal House of Flanders and their scion, Godfroi de Bouillion, later Protector of the Holy Sepulchre.[6]

Yet people all over Europe and far beyond had been familiar with Rex Deus legends and stories for centuries, but had been completely oblivious to their true origins. The creation and dissemination of the stories of the search for the Holy Grail, was the masterstroke that immortalised Rex Deus traditions; a literary genre deliberately created to disseminate the true initiatory teachings of Jesus to the general public beyond the narrow confines of the families who were descended from the high priests of the Temple in Jerusalem.

Once again, the trail of heresy brings us back to the conspiring Rex

Deus families in the city of Troyes in the twelfth century. The first Grail romance was circulated around 1190, in the form of an unfinished epic, *Perceval,* or *Le Conte del Graal,* written by a certain Chrétien de Troyes.[7] Chrétien, a relative of Hughes de Payen[8] the first Grand Master of the Templar Order, was a priest who became a noted translator and a writer of considerable repute. Three of his earlier works were dedicated to Marie, Countess of Champagne, the daughter of King Louis VII of France and Eleanor of Aquitaine,[9] and, according to tradition, he intended to dedicate *Le Conte del Graal* to her also. However, Marie retired from public life when her husband Count Henry of Champagne died shortly after returning from the Holy Land and as a result Chrétien was forced to seek a new patron. He chose another leading member of Rex Deus, Phillipe d'Alsace the Count of Flanders the son of a co-founder of the Knights Templar, Payen de Montdidier and a close relative of the early Christian kings of Jerusalem.[10]

The first Grail romance was circulated at a time when Europe was, in modern parlance, a police state, where anyone perceived as being spiritually or religiously different risked being burnt at the stake. For centuries the Rex Deus families had to dissemble simply to survive. Thus, while the Grail sagas describe a long and dangerous quest for that most holy of all relics, encoded within it, in the form of allegory, is a very different message. The Grail romances describe a long and arduous quest wherein Perceval is subjected to repeated temptations and acute physical dangers that, in some respects at least, replicate the well-known perils of prolonged pilgrimage. This was consistent with common knowledge for this was the age of the veneration of holy relics and thus these sagas were, at first, apparently acceptable, but only just, to the hierarchy of the time. Even this grudging acceptance did not last long, however, for the Grail sagas were soon perceived as an allegorical guide to an alchemical quest,[11] a heretical guide to a spiritual pathway in search of enlightenment.

The Real Grail Quest

Chrétien and Wolfram's Grail romances carry coded clues to an heretical belief system that contradicts the monolithic power of the oppressive Church of the medieval era. The king of the Grail castle, the Fisher King, being wounded, imperfectly serves his impoverished realm in a manner similar to those usurpers of the true teachings of Jesus, the hierarchy of the Christian Church, who despoil the lives of those they claim to serve. This wasted kingdom will only be restored when someone pure enough to see the Grail restores the Fisher King to full health. When the true teachings of Jesus triumph over dogma, corruption and distortion, then heaven will be made manifest upon earth.

My first literary collaborator, the late Trevor Ravenscroft, composed his masterwork, *The Cup of Destiny*,[12] to reveal to the younger generation that the Grail romances reveal within their drama and symbolism, signposts to a unique path of intitiation, the true teaching of Jesus. He was not alone in this conclusion, for one of the world's leading mythologists, the late Professor Joseph Campbell, writing of the importance of the Grail, cites a passage from the 'Gospel of Thomas': 'He who drinks from my mouth will become as I am, and I shall be he.'[13] Campbell came to the conclusion that this represented the ultimate form of enlightenment that can arise from a successful Grail quest.[14]

Thus the Grail quest is not what it seems for there is a hidden agenda here, one deliberately designed to conceal an heretical truth from the prying eyes of the clergy. The original Grail sagas of Chrétien and Wolfram are nothing more nor less than coded guides to initiation.[15] As Trevor Ravenscroft wrote:

> Outwardly Parzival can be enjoyed as a medieval romance about the adventures of knights and their ladies against a background canvas of life in the feudal courts; while inwardly it veils a prescribed path to the development of spiritual faculties, the attainment of higher levels of consciousness and further dimensions of time.[16]

Why should any knight, however devout, seek the Holy Grail when, if he genuinely sought a guaranteed pathway to salvation, he merely had to volunteer for duty in the Holy Land? This exercise in Christian virtue guaranteed absolution for all sins, both those already committed and any that might be committed in the future so ensuring a fast-track post-mortem promotion to the ranks of the feathered choir. Knights Templar killed in battle went straight to heaven, bypassing purgatory, so why should they seek the Grail? What was so holy about the Grail? Relics of the various saints abounded in Europe, some were even believed to pertain to Jesus himself. Furthermore, by attending mass and taking communion in any church or cathedral he could, by the miracle of tran-substantiation, get direct access to the actual body and blood of Jesus. Hardly a perilous path to take, if one discounts the mild embarrassment of confession.

Myth and legend have been employed for millennia to carry spiritual allegories and uncomfortable truths into the public consciousness in an apparently acceptable manner. Earlier scholars who have tended to dismiss these as simply 'inspired fiction' suitable only for children, ignore the fact that tribal and national traditions and all forms of religion, including Western Christianity, generate their own mythologies to buttress their belief systems. Thanks to the work of Joseph Campbell and many others, the true value of mythology has been significantly revised.[17] Myths, like symbolism of which they are an important part, can be understood at many levels and, when used with discernment, are a useful signpost to truth. Campbell wrote that: 'Mythology is the penultimate truth, because the ultimate cannot be put into words.'[18] The Indian scholar, Ananda Coomeraswamy claimed that: 'Myth embodies the nearest approach to absolute truth that can be stated in words.'[19] That poetical genius, the late Kathleen Raine, said: 'Fact is not the truth of myth; myth is the truth of fact.'[20]

The name 'Holy Grail' is claimed to be a corruption of the term 'Holy Gradual', with 'gradual' used in the sense of a gradual spiritual ascent or an ascending initiatory way. In the early 1980s another meaning was suggested: the Holy Grail, or *Sangraal,* as it is written in French, is claimed to be a corrupt version of *sang real,* or Holy Blood.[21] This first came to the attention of English-speaking people with the publication of *The Holy Blood and the Holy Grail* in 1981. This was the first book in English that claimed that Jesus had married and founded a dynasty. The book was greeted with howls of protest, claiming 'blasphemy' and 'heresy' on the one hand, and an equally loud chorus of 'brilliant' and 'provocative' on the other. It is still selling like hot cakes.

Stories of the Holy Grail have always evinced a somewhat mixed response. Soon after their first publication, the Grail epics proved to be an irritant to the Roman Catholic Church, an organisation that was always ready to massacre any group of Christians who sought a more direct approach to the divine Word and the Light. It is interesting to note that in the original stories both Perceval and Parzival had the way to the Grail suggested by a holy, lay hermit.[22]

It is, therefore, easy to understand that the Grail sagas in their original form were deemed to be troublesome to the Church hierarchy. They attained such wide public acceptance, however, that suppression was out of the question, so the Church authorities adopted a tried and tested formula that they had perfected with the creation of the Gospels, they put out their own version and ensured that it gained wide circulation. With the aid of a group of monks they created a highly sanitised and censored variation on these stories, written in total conformity with Church doctrine of the time. The new 'official' version became known as the Vulgate Cycle.[23] This, in its turn became the foundation for later writers such as Thomas Mallory whose *Morte d'Arthur* in 1469 sealed the link between the Arthurian legends and the Grail sagas for all time. Holy Mother the Church had solved the problem posed by the heretical message within Chrétien and Wolfram's original works in an effective way that was to endure for centuries and, centuries later, fire the imaginations of such eminent Victorians as Alfred Lord Tennyson and the Pre-Raphaelites.

The heresy inherent within the original sagas was blindingly obvious

to the educated reader, for the hidden code within the stories was not
very subtle. For example, Wolfram von Essenbach said of himself that he
could neither read nor write. He wrote:

> 'I do not know a single letter of the alphabet. Plenty of people
> get their material that way, but this adventurer steers without
> books. Rather than have anyone think this is a book, I would sit
> naked without a towel, the way I would sit in the bath – if I
> didn't forget the fig leaf!'[24]

Trevor Ravenscroft commented upon this passage in the following words:

> 'The clue to the question of the so-called illiteracy of Wolfram
> von Essenbach is in his sly sense of humour within the last
> sentence of this enigmatic passage. ... The fig leaf has always
> been the symbol of the occult initiate who has developed
> supersensible faculties and entered into higher realms of
> consciousness.'[25]

Thus Wolfram's admission of apparent illiteracy was just an oblique way
of saying that he could see into the spiritual world and read the occult
script. He went on to claim that the source for much of his material was
a certain Kyot of Provence whom he met in Toledo, Spain. In the early
thirteenth century when Wolfram was writing, Toledo was a remarkable
city, a true beacon of light where students of the Islamic esoteric tradition
mixed freely with Jewish Kabbalistic scholars and the Rex Deus adherents
of the true teachings of Jesus, who were the principal propagators of the
esoteric stream within Christianity.[26] Links have also been established
between troubadours singing the Grail sagas and certain of the Sufi poets
of Islam who were on the same quest. Indeed, it is within the history of
Sufism that we can find the earliest and most complete record of the
transmission of spiritual knowledge from master to initiate. Their
mystical founder, El Khidir was known as 'the verdant one', green being
held to be the colour of initiation.

The English poet, Robert Graves described the Sufis as: 'An ancient spiritual Freemasonry whose origins have never been traced or dated although the characteristic Sufic signature is found in widely dispersed literature from at least the second millennium BC.'[27]

Sufi teaching in Europe reached its zenith with the Sufi mystery schools of Spain in the ninth century. From these bases, their teaching began slowly to permeate into Christian Europe – a process which gathered great momentum with the formation of the Templar Order. The Templars were in frequent contact with the Sufis, and some of their secret practices, their belief in selfless obedience, for example, may have derived from oriental mysticism. This German Grail romance preached yet another form of heresy, namely religious toleration between Christianity and Islam.[28] In Parzifal, Wolfram identifies the Knights of the Grail as wearing white surcoats with red crosses as did the Knights Templar.

Unlike the majority of their fellow crusaders, the Templars had developed a considerable degree of respect for Islam. Chivalry, for example, was an alien concept that the Knights Templar acquired from the 'heathen' Saracens and brought back to Europe. What we would now call technological advances such as the telescope, the principles of stellar navigation, the financial instrument known as the 'note of hand',[29] considerable advances in medicine and surgery, mouth-to-mouth resuscitation and free access to the world of knowledge and ideas were among the benefits imported from Islam by the Knights of the Holy Grail. Like the Cathars, the Templars had been influenced by Kabbalistic, Sufi and Islamic doctrines, and followed the true initiatory path taught by Jesus and his brother and spiritual heir, James the Just.[30]

The earlier collection of legends about King Arthur, written by Geoffrey of Monmouth in 1136, eighteen years after the foundation of the Knights Templar, and those of the Holy Grail composed some decades later, were separate and distinct entities to begin with, but it took very little time for them to become inextricably mixed. Themes common to both ensured this, for they share similar ideals of chivalry and both genres speak movingly of a spiritual search acted out in a world of brutal reality that was all too familiar to the enthralled listeners and readers. In the opinion of many scholars, both of these traditions – the Arthurian cycle and the Grail search – share a common source that has long since been lost. We know, however, that both were indeed linked by one specific, hidden common source – the teachings and traditions of the hidden, heretical families of the Rex Deus group.

One modern English Grail scholar, Malcolm Godwin, came close to identifying this linkage when he wrote:

> 'The Legend of the Grail, more than any other western myth, has retained the vital magic that marks it as a living legend capable of touching both imagination and the spirit. No other myth is so rich in symbolism, so diverse and often contradictory in meaning. **And at its core there exists a secret which has sustained the mystical appeal of the Grail for the last nine hundred years, while other myths and legends have slipped into oblivion and been forgotten.**'[31] [My emphasis]

The ultimate heresy within the original Grail sagas is that Parzival or Perceval, the leading protagonist who was searching for the Holy Grail, claimed direct descent from Joseph of Arimathea. A bloodline that viewed in the light of Rex Deus' direct descent from the twenty-four high priests of the Temple in Jerusalem is highly significant. This claim had other, far more disturbing implications for the Church hierarchy. Church dogma asserts, with the 'Imperium' of the self-appointed guardians of 'Divinely Revealed Truth', that Jesus appointed Peter as his successor with the words: 'Thou art Peter and on this rock I will build my Church...'[32] Yet, disturbingly from the Church's perspective, Jesus appoints Joseph of Arimathea and not Peter as the guardian of the Grail. Some scholars suggest that this is 'a visible and tangible symbol of an alternative apostolic succession'.[33]

All in all, the Church had good cause to be concerned about the ever-popular stories written by Chrétien de Troyes and Wolfram von Essenbach and, perhaps for this reason, Grail symbolism within church buildings is a comparative rarity. Yet, Grail symbolism abounds and it is not restricted to the beautiful Pre-Raphaelite illustrations that became popular in Victorian times, it is to be found in abundance within yet another manifestation of the Rex Deus propaganda machine that began to impinge on European consciousness many decades after the brutal suppression of the Knights Templar, in the unlikely guise of the tarot trumps.

The End of the Templars

By the beginning of the fourteenth century the power, wealth and influence of the Knights Templar had aroused considerable resentment among certain European monarchs and the hierarchy. King Phillipe IV of France was undergoing prolonged financial difficulties and was heavily in debt to the Order. He had applied to join the Templars as a young man, but had been refused. During one severe riot, seeking sanctuary from the aggrieved mob, he sought refuge in the Paris Temple.[34] Bedazzled by the vast store of treasure he saw there, he began to scheme and plot in order to acquire it for himself, and thereby also cancel his enormous debt to the knightly bankers. His fertile mind soon hit upon a plan that would destroy the Order.

In that age of repression and injustice, the perfect means was readily available for the Inquisition had honed its skills in torture, secret trial and condemnation during its sixty-year-long apprenticeship suppressing the last vestiges of the Cathar heresy.[35] Contact between the Templars and Islam could easily be established and links could also be proved between the Knights and the Cathar heretics.

The King prepared his case with secrecy and skill and the first blow fell on Friday 13th October, 1307. At dawn, Jacques de Molay, the last Grand Master of the Templar Order was arrested along with sixty of his senior knights, simultaneously many other Templars were arrested all over France.[36] However, when the king's agents raided the Paris Temple treasury after the first arrests, the Templar treasure had vanished without trace and the entire Templar fleet had left La Rochelle for an unknown destination. French Masonic ritual indicates that Scotland was designated as the principal place of safekeeping for the missing Templar treasure.[37]

The barbaric finale for the Knights of the Holy Grail took place on an island in the Seine on 14th March, 1314 when the elderly Grand Master, Jacques de Molay, and the Preceptor of Normandy, Geoffroi de Charney, were publicly burnt on a slow fire. Before being burnt, de Molay prophesied the imminent demise of the king and the pope. Both died within the year.[38]

One of the many charges against the Templars was that of idolatry; the worship of an idol called Baphomet. Idries Shah, author of *The Sufis*, claims that Baphomet is a corruption of the Arabic *abufihamet* (pronounced bufhimat) that translates into English as the 'Father of Understanding'. Magnus Eliphas Levi, the nineteenth-century mystical writer, put forward the hypothesis that it should be spelled in reverse TEM. OHP. AB. He then transliterated this as *Templi Hominum Pacis Omnium Abbas* or 'Father of the Temple of Universal Peace Among Men'.[39] The Provençal Templar scholar, Guy Jourdan claims that the reliquary containing the head of St John the Baptist that is kept at Amiens Cathedral is the true Baphometic head of the Templars. Dr Hugh Schonfield, a historian of Early Christianity, who had discovered secret messages encoded within many of the Dead Sea Scrolls by means of the Atbash Cipher, applied this cipher to the name Baphomet, and produced the word *Sophia*, the name of the Gnostic goddess of Wisdom.[40] The veneration of the Black Madonna, by the Templars tends to support this theory.

Reactions to the suppression of the Order varied from place to place. German knights joined the Hospitallers or the Teutonic Knights. In Portugal the Templars were not suppressed but, under royal patronage, changed their name to the Knights of Christ and carried on as a national order of chivalry.[41] In Spain, the Archbishop of Compostela made a vain plea for clemency, writing to the pope begging that the Templars be spared as they were needed to fight against the Moors and recapture Spain for the Roman Catholic cause.[42] In France and England some Templars later joined the Knights Hospitallers, others are recorded as retiring on pension but most simply seemed to vanish.[43] Templar property, with some notable exceptions, was mainly ceded to the rival chivalric order, the Knights Hospitaller.

Being condemned for heresy in medieval Europe was a process that reached far beyond mere death, however horrific that may have been. Such people became 'non-persons', their records were destroyed and the Church tried to erase all record of their beliefs and their power in such a manner that the Inquisition was the only remaining source of information about these 'enemies of the church'. However, despite the premature and brutal death inflicted upon these chivalric children of the Rex Deus line, other means were soon to be devised in order to pass on the true initiatory teachings of Jesus the Nazorean.

The Tarot Trumps

Tarot cards, so popular among both the Gypsy people and so-called 'New Age' fortune-tellers, were deliberately designed with a totally different function in mind – the propagation of heresy. They were originally used by initiates as portable teaching boards, or 'flash cards', to impart spiritual insights of a distinctly subversive nature through their symbolism that displays, quite openly, connections with the original Grail sagas and Rex Deus (see plates 14 & 15). The true origins of these strange cards are shrouded in mystery compounded by the errors of those who mistakenly ascribed them to ancient Egypt and the Temple mysteries.

It is believed that they are oriental in origin and came to Europe some time during the thirteenth century. On arrival, the original eastern pack was deliberately transformed by pervasive and powerful influences directly traceable to the Cathar 'Church of Love', the Knights Templar, Judaic Kabbalistic spirituality and a *soupçon* of Greek Hermeticism.[44] Some even claim that they originated with the Knights Templar and Malcolm Godwin suggests that 'it is possible that the Templars learned their use from their Saracen rivals'.[45] Godwin continues by saying that the Church's traditional hostility to all forms of playing cards arose from the tarot's Rex Deus and Gnostic tendencies. Indeed the hierarchy described the tarot as 'the Devil's Breviary'[46] or as 'the rungs of a ladder leading to hell'. [47]

In one very real sense the Church had good cause to be uneasy for the use of visual symbolism in the form of 'teaching boards' was central to Templar practice and is continued today among the worldwide fraternity of Freemasonry and also in the revived Templar Orders.[48] My good friend and colleague, the Roman Catholic theologian Margaret Starbird describes the tarot trumps as: 'A virtual catechism for the suppressed beliefs of the alternative Christian Church, the "Church of the Holy Grail", whose articles of faith included the partnership of Christ and his bride, the woman whom the Gospels called the Magdalene.'[49]

Margaret Starbird interprets the designs on the cards in the light of biblical references to the House of David and relates them to the medieval heresy of the blood royal – *the sang real* – which she concludes leads us to understand their secret meaning.[50] Margaret continues by claiming that the cards 'are directly and irrefutably related to the *Church of Amor,* the Cathar Church of Love, and the medieval heresy of the Holy Grail'.[51] Despite being completely unaware of the Rex Deus tradition at the time of writing she states unequivocally that the four suits of the handsome, vividly hand-painted fifteenth-century decks produced in Provence and northern Italy, the *Gringonneur* and the *Visconti-Sforza* packs, were both indisputably associated with the medieval heresy surrounding surviving descendants of the Holy Grail.[52] She unwittingly reinforced the validity of the Rex Deus tradition by stating:

> 'The very elaborate cup symbol found on some of the early
> fifteenth-century decks – the Visconti-Sforza (usually dated
> between 1440–80) packs named for the artist's patrons – is very
> similar to numerous medieval images of the Holy Grail. And it
> is precisely the noble families of Provence and northern Italy,
> the allied ducal families of Anjou and Milan, who were
> connected by ties of friendship and even related by blood and
> marriage to the *sang real.* The trump cards in the fifteenth-

century tarot decks belonging to the Visconti family of Milan
appear to be among the earliest in existence.'[53]

Certainly the tarot teaches a form of spirituality that runs contrary to
much of the dogma of the Roman Catholic Church touching as it does
on heretical themes such as reincarnation, renewal or spiritual rebirth
and transformation.[54]

The tarot trumps are a symbolic depiction of a form of Grail quest in
the form of 'flash cards', in which an innocent pilgrim undergoes
initiatory trials, including the traditional symbolic death to the things of
this world and a subsequent resurrection to spiritual gnosis, before he
gains sufficient purity to meet the goddess. The goddess Isis, the seat of
wisdom venerated by the Templars as the Black Madonna, is depicted in
the tarot by the card known as *Temperance*. However, according to
Margaret Starbird, this card would be better named *Prudence* who is
usually portrayed in the seated position, pouring water from one
container to another in order to preserve its purity. Margaret argues that
this represents the spiritual waters of the true teachings of Jesus being
transferred to new containers, suitably disguised of course, to evade the
prying prelates of the Inquisition, as the old vessels, namely those of the
Knights Templar and the Cathar Church, have been destroyed.[55] Perceval,
the hero of Wolfram von Eschenbach's Grail saga, is sometimes represented symbolically on the bottom left of this card as a valley between
two peaks – Perce-a-Val

Parzival is represented by the card known as the Fool. He is a nobody,
a zero which in its turn is symbolised by *l'oeuf*, the egg, yet another
symbol of the potential for spiritual rebirth through the initiatory
pathway to enlightenment. In some early tarot packs, he is shown as a
wandering beggar with a dog at his heels. The dog in medieval English
symbolism stands for its anagram, god, or the presence of God. The Joker
was known as 'the Adept' or 'the Magician' or, alternatively in the earlier
packs, as 'the Juggler'. He was a trickster, in the hermetic tradition, the
subtle and oft-times deceptive, messenger of the gods. It is perhaps

pertinent to note that in the Languedoc and surrounding parts of France, troupes of itinerant jongleurs, or troubadours, were held responsible for transmitting the heretical teachings of the Church of Love, or Catharism, right under the prying eyes of the hierarchy.[56]

The card known as 'the Hermit', not surprisingly, represents the Grail hermit who showed Parzival the way. It has been strongly suggested that this depiction is based upon Peter the Hermit who preached the First Crusade that resulted in the Rex Deus families once more regaining control over their true heritage, the Holy City of Jerusalem. The hermit is usually shown holding an hourglass and depicted standing next to a rock. The inference of this is simply that time is running out for the Church of Rome and its much-vaunted claim to 'Apostolic Succession' through Peter.

One card that appears to be missing from the Grigonneur pack is that of the Papess or female pope. This is in line with certain practices within both early Christianity and the Cathar Church that not merely allowed, but actively encouraged, women to become priests following the traditional role ascribed to Mary Magdalene who was, according to Gnostic tradition, the supreme adept of 'the Way' taught by Jesus.

The Nag Hamadi Library that was discovered in the 1940s provided evidence of Gnostic beliefs that had been suppressed by the Roman Catholic Church for centuries. Among the Gnostics, the Magdalene was referred to as 'the woman who knew the all' because she had been given teachings by Jesus that were not given by him to the other Apostles. In one pack, the *Bempo* deck of 1484, the female pope is depicted carrying a book symbolising 'Wisdom'. Wisdom is always represented in female form following the Greek tradition of Sophia the goddess of wisdom and the Hebraic concept of the Shekina, the bride of Yahweh. Thus she symbolises the personification of the true 'Wisdom of God' and the Torah. The early Christian Gnostics venerated Mary Magdalene, the 'Beloved of Jesus' as Wisdom incarnate.[57]

The card known as the 'Tower' is also a symbolic representation of the Magdalene, referring to the word Magdala which translates as 'Tower'.

The trump card representing 'the Pope', is usually numbered V, a sly reference to Pope Clement V who was responsible for the order suppressing the Knights Templar. 'The Emperor', or King, is numbered as IV, again a distinct if subtle reference to King Phillipe IV of France whose greed and ambition caused him to destroy the Templar Order, the Knights of the Holy Grail.[58]

The bloodline of the Holy Grail, that of the Rex Deus dynasties, is symbolised by the card known as 'the Lovers'. According to Margaret Starbird, the design on this card is an overt reference to the sacred bloodline as the lovers represent the true 'Vine', the descending lineage of the House of David. Above the two dancing lovers are two cupid-like angels aiming their arrows at the young couple. Each angel has a red X marked across their breast, one of the signs used by the Cathars to symbolise enlightenment, a subject that Margaret treats in considerable detail in her earlier work, *The Woman with the Alabaster Jar*.[59]

Another card that refers to the *sang real,* the Davidic bloodline of biblical Israel, may also prove to be of interest to the worldwide fraternity of Freemasonry. The card for 'Strength' displays a woman holding in her arms a broken, Solomonic pillar. The pillars of Boaz and Joachin, described as being erected at the portals of the Temple of Solomon,[60] and Boaz, named after one of King David's ancestors, was held to symbolise strength. Another reference to the royal bloodline here is to be found in the decoration of the capitals of these pillars, they were decorated with lilies, symbolising royal descent from long before the time of David, from the era of Tuthmosis III in Egypt who erected similar free-standing pillars outside the entrance to the Temple of Karnak.

Members of the heretical Order of the Knights Templar are symbolised in two cards, namely the 'Charioteer' and the 'Hanged Man'. The Charioteer is dressed in armour and carries a battle-axe, he has one foot resting on the letter 'I' and the other on the letter 'C', the initials for the Latin form of Jesus Christ, Iesu Christi. In the opinion of Margaret Starbird, this card is a direct reference to the 'treasure' discovered under the Temple Mount by the Knights Templar and also stresses the humanity of Jesus and denies his divinity. The card known as the 'Hanged Man' is yet another symbol denoting the torture of the unjustly persecuted Templars who were subjected to unspeakable tortures to make them confess to the Inquisition.[61] According to other scholars of the tarot, the Fisher King is also depicted by the Hanged Man.

I mentioned earlier the prophecy made by Jacques de Molay just before he was burnt alive. He foretold that within less than one year that Pope Clement V and King Phillipe IV would join him in the afterlife. The tarot card known simply as 'Death' celebrates this prophecy. Death shows the grim reaper in the form of a skeleton carrying a scythe, mounted on a black donkey that is trampling the two figures of the Emperor and the Pope, as depicted on the cards I and II. The card of the 'Devil' depicts the evil one as the Inquisitor. His large ears are straining to catch the whiff of heresy and his chains are ever ready to bind and oppress all the people.

Of the four suits of the tarot, one symbolises the House of Pendragon, a direct reference to the Arthurian legends, and another, the South or the House of the Spear, refers to the St Clair family, to which I shall refer later, as the House of Lothian and Orkney, for the St Clairs were Lords of Roslin in Lothian and also the Earls of Orkney. The St Clairs were one of the leading Rex Deus families whose activities were to make an enormous contribution to passing the true teachings of Jesus to a much wider public. One of the most intriguing ways they did this was by creating a centre of mystical excellence without equal in Europe by building Rosslyn Chapel.

CHAPTER 14

The Mystical Symbolism within Rosslyn Chapel

S even miles south-west of Edinburgh lies Rosslyn Chapel, which has exerted a timeless and mystical appeal to pilgrims of every denomination for over five centuries. This revered place of worship is a temple to the spirituality and mysticism that pervades all of the great religions and yet transcends each one of them. The original plan was to build a great sanctuary in the form of a cross with a high tower in the centre, a collegiate church with 'a provost, six prebendaries and two singing boys'. The foundations of the whole of the planned building were laid in 1446 and were excavated at the end of the eighteenth century, and confirm that the nave was to be about ninety feet in length. However, what gives Rosslyn Chapel its international reputation today is the variety, candour and exuberance of its endless rich profusion of carvings which certainly have no equal anywhere else in the world. Even the most inexperienced eye can tell instantly that the building is unfinished for only the choir, with its strange, barrel-vaulted roof, has been completed.

Earl William St Clair

The chapel was founded by Earl William St Clair, the last Sinclair 'Jarl' of Orkney and hereditary Lord of Rosslyn who also rejoiced in the somewhat odd title of 'Knight of the Cockle and Golden Fleece'. Described by his contemporaries as 'one of the Illuminati', or as 'a nobleman with singular talents' and as 'a man of exceptional talents much given to policy, such as buildings of Castles, Palaces and Churches,' Earl William was the patron of Craft masonry throughout Scotland. It is a matter of record that Earl William was appointed grand master of various orders, the Craft masons and other hard and soft guilds in Scotland in 1441

The care and precision that went into the construction of the chapel fall into the category of what we would now call 'quality assurance' for the Earl exerted absolute and complete power of decision over every aspect of the construction, design and artwork in a manner that was truly unique. The designs for the chapel were first drawn out upon 'Eastland boards' made from Baltic timber, before being approved and then cut in stone. Each carving was also first made in wood and, if approved, then carved in stone. Thus the Earl exerted tight and absolute control over every aspect not only of the construction of the building itself but also all of the decoration within it. The symphonic harmony of design to be found here results, therefore, from an inspired plan originating in the mind of a supremely gifted man combined with a comparatively rapid rate of build which left no time for new or alien influences from any outside source to contaminate the original design.

The absolute secrecy which shrouded the first three centuries of Freemasonry makes it extremely difficult to prove the connections that may relate the Freemasons with the other esoteric movements that first came to public notice at the time of the Renaissance. However the carvings within Rosslyn Chapel give indications of some of these possible links, with the Rosicrucians for example, and there is a wealth of Masonic symbolism that belies the 'official' history of Freemasonry that declares, rather dogmatically, that the craft was only founded in the seventeenth century.

Several of the carvings of angels in the retro-choir depict postures that relate to the initiation rituals of the First Degree of Freemasonry. Near them in a similar position is a beautiful carving of a fallen angel, Lucifer depicted upside down and bound with ropes. This is a symbolic reference to the beginning of chapter two of The Revelation of St John that states:

'And the great dragon was cast out, that old serpent, which is the devil and Satan, and bound for a thousand years.' It also records that, for the 'pure in heart' who tread the spiritual path, Satan is bound and powerless.

The carving of the horned figure of Moses carrying the tablets of 'The Law' to be found in the south aisle may be symbolic of one of the Hebraic rites of early Freemasonry. The head of Hermes Trimegistos on the exterior of the east wall shows the common ancestor of many European esoteric movements, for Hermes is one of the pivotal figures in the mythology which has moulded the Western Esoteric tradition.

> 'If a historian is permitted to express himself in allegorical-mythical terms, we might say that Thoth, the Egyptian god of books, who is actually Hermes Trimegistos, was then entering his hidden realm which endures down to our days: the hermetica, the mysteria, the secrets, are set down in books and nevertheless they remain inaccessible to those of "closed mind": astrologers, alchemists, natural philosophers and poets – and in our time psychologists – are their guardians, the Christian hierarchs and theologians are their – sometimes stern, sometimes mild – adversaries.'[1]

The Exterior

On the outside of the chapel, there are many flying buttresses that are diagnostic of Gothic architecture. One at the extreme east end of the south wall is decorated with incised or carved dividers, or compasses, symbolic of the Masonic Order. Also in one of the window bays at the eastern end of the north wall there is a badly weathered carving reputedly of 'Baphomet' the idol the Templars were accused of worshipping. On the east wall is the carved head of Hermes Trimegistos, mentioned above, and a more humorous carving that speaks volumes about the sardonic and disrespectful way the Craftmasons viewed their clergy, a fox is portrayed dressed as a clergyman and preaching to a flock of geese. The west wall was originally intended to be the inside wall of the never to be completed transept, and on it are the emplacement for the stones of various arches which would have spanned the transept itself. Also present are some of the internal furnishings, an altar emplacement, a piscina and an aumbrey in each arm of the transept. Flanking the more modern baptistery is the obvious outline of the pulpitum doorway. In the western window of the south wall is a rather badly weathered carving of a Templar knight leading a blindfolded man by a cable-tow noose in the manner of modern Masonic First Degree Initiation. This is the first symbolic representation that I have seen that links Freemasonic practice directly with the Knights Templar.

Templar Symbolism

The Templar Order had been suppressed and its members imprisoned and tortured by the Inquisition over a century and a half before Rosslyn Chapel was founded yet clearly recognisable Templar symbolism abounds, half-hidden to all except the initiated, paradoxically in plain sight, yet overlooked by all. In the vault of each bay in the main chapel and arching across the vault of the crypt are carvings of the *Engrailed Cross* of the Sinclairs. At the junction of every cross, subtly, but nonetheless distinctly delineated in each case, and in plain sight for all to see, is the distinctive, splayed cross of the Knights Templar. Not merely the standard *Croix Pattée*, but the more overtly Gnostic 'Cross of Universal Knowledge'. Recently moved into the shelter of the chapel, safe at last from the ravages of the elements to which it had been exposed for centuries, lies a burial stone engraved with the name William de Sinncler. Sir William was the Grand Prior of the Templar order who, according to family tradition, led the Templar Knights in the final charge that put the invading English to flight at the Battle of Bannockburn thereby ensuring Scotland's independence.

One of the diagnostic signs of Templar influence, mentioned in an earlier chapter, is carved beside the third window on the north wall (counting from the east end). To the left of the window is a small pillar above which will be found a Templar seal in the form of 'the *Agnus Dei*'.

The carving depicts the seal being revealed by two hands drawing back a curtain or veil.

In assessing these definitive signs of Templar tradition, we have to proceed with some caution as many buildings have been given completely inappropriate Templar attribution even when they date from the accepted Templar era. Because its foundation is of a much later date, we must examine the deeper meaning that lies behind the symbolism at Rosslyn. However, it is no accident that the heraldic colours of the St Clairs are Argent and Sable, the same as those of the battle flag of the Templar Order. the *Beauseant*. The carving of an angel bearing the Sinclair shield decorated with the Engrailed Cross in the south aisle has something in common with the carving of the Agnus Dei, the repeated motif of two hands. Yet more intertwined Templar and Sinclair symbolism can be seen in the memorial to the fourth Sinclair Earl of Caithness.

The St Clair family motto displayed on this memorial, *Commit Thy Verk To God* is remarkably similar in tone and content to that of the Templars – *Non Nobis Domine. Non Nobis, Sed Nomine Tuo De Gloriam*, that translates to 'Not to our name Lord. Not to our name, but to Yours be all the glory'. On the central pendant boss in the retro-choir is another carving of great importance to the Knights Templar, namely a Madonna and Child. As we have already seen, the Templar Order, mysticism and the veneration of various Black Madonnas linked several of the esoteric streams in medieval Europe. The principle of the Sacred Feminine and her embodiment of Wisdom can be traced back through the goddess Cybele to the ancient Greek concept of Gaia the Earth Mother, and even further back in time to Ishtar, the Sumerian 'Goddess of All Life Giving Power'. In many of the temples dedicated to Ishtar are carved a profusion of roses and rosettes as well as the other symbols always associated with her – the sun, the moon, the five-pointed star and the cornucopia. All symbols that are represented in the carvings of the stone vaulted roof of Rosslyn Chapel.

It is in conjunction with the fascinating character of Earl William

St Clair, the founder of Rosslyn Chapel, that any analysis of the meaning of the spiritual and artistic content of the carvings within this building must be assessed. Considered in isolation they remain mysterious and capable of misinterpretation. For what can we make of carvings in a late medieval Christian church that link nearly every spiritual influence that obtained in the centuries before Rosslyn was built? There are so many referring, directly or obliquely, to the mystery cults of both Christian and pre-Christian times. A series of strange carvings that commemorate the exploits of a distinguished ancestor of the founder can be found dotted randomly throughout the chapel.

Prince Henry St Clair, first Jarl of the Orkneys, known as 'The Holy Sinclair', was one of the most remarkable men among a family rightly renowned for their nobility and insight. Prince Henry commissioned a fleet for at least two voyages that explored the 'New World' over one hundred years before Columbus made his memorable trans-atlantic crossing.[2] To commemorate his ancestor's epic voyage, Earl William commissioned carvings of certain strange plants that had been brought back from America to be placed within the chapel. To the right of the south door on one of the lintels can be seen carvings of aloe cactus, while on the arch of the one of the windows on the south wall there are large carvings of Indian sweet corn or maize, which are repeated several times in other parts of the chapel. Also found carved in various parts of the chapel are depictions of *sassandras*, *albidium*, *trillium grandilorum* and *quercus nigra*, all native American plants which were completely unknown in Europe at the time of the chapel's construction.

The Roof

The imposing barrel-vaulted roof is solid stone and over three feet thick. It is divided into five sections powdered with diaper work. The section of the roof most relevant to the Freemasons and the Templars is carved in massive relief and portrays a profusion of five-pointed stars, yet another of the diagnostic Templar signs, containing within them a cornucopia, a dove, the moon and the orb of the sun. The stars are symbolic of the

Milky Way, the *Via Lactodorum*, an allegorical reference to the initiatory pilgrimage route from St Jacques de Compostela to Rosslyn. The dove in mainstream Church iconography represents the Holy Spirit, yet when represented in this precise form – in full flight and with an olive branch in its beak – and in conjunction with other Templar carvings, is diagnostic of a true Templar building. The sun is usually taken to denote the descending Logos, or Christ himself, but in this instance it may have a different and more pertinent relevance, because the sun is part of the coat of arms of a branch of the St Clair family. In Rex Deus symbolism, the Sun in Splendour when half-hidden in this manner and displaying thirty-two rays denotes the Fisher King, the rightful heir to the Kingdom of Jerusalem.

Yet another example of a shield, held by two hands and displaying the Engrailed Cross of the St Clairs, occurs on one side of a dependant boss that forms the central keystone of the high vaulted roof. According to the Masonic scholars Chris Knight and Robert Lomas, this keystone points directly downwards to the hiding place of the scrolls brought back from Jerusalem by the first Knights Templar that were hidden first at Chartres and later moved here to Rosslyn Chapel.

The South Aisle

In the south aisle, abreast of the main altar, there is a lintel carved with symbolic representations of the 'Seven Deadly Sins'. From left to right one can discern a priest, or perhaps a bishop, warning his followers; then comes a man with a puffed-out chest symbolising the sin of pride; then comes the glutton, drinking. Two men arguing show anger; then the centrepiece – the careless warrior representing sloth. Next comes envy followed by a cadavaric miser carrying his purse to show avarice; and finally come the sinful lovers as a warning against lust. The Devil then makes his appearance, raking the sinners into the gaping jaws of hell. On the obverse face of the same lintel are Seven Virtues. Viewed from left to right one can discern a priest blessing all who follow and they are: two people helping the needy – one clothing the naked, another tending the sick; then a saintly man visiting a prisoner whose face can be seen peeping out of a barred cell window. The act of feeding the hungry comes next, followed by comforting the fatherless and destitute and the final virtue – laying out the dead. The last segment represents their just reward – St Peter with the keys of heaven.

If we then turn and face the east wall, on the lintel facing you there is scrollwork marked by a Latin inscription which translates as 'Wine is strong, a King is stronger, women are even stronger, but truth conquers all'. This quotation from the Book of Esdras refers to the time when Zerubabel used these words to answer a riddle posed in one of King Darius' dreams. He was rewarded by being given the King's permission to return to Jerusalem from exile and rebuild the Temple that had earlier been destroyed by the Babylonian invaders. Directly abutting that lintel is an ornately carved pillar symbolising a legend of great importance to the brotherhood of Freemasonry.

The 'Apprentice' Pillar

Of all the mysteries and legends that originate in Rosslyn Chapel, few can be so well known as that surrounding this, the most puzzling and beautiful of its artistic gems, the Apprentice Pillar. The legend of the murdered apprentice with its overt references to the initiation rituals of both the ancient guild of Craftmasons and its parallels to the older legend of Hiram Abif, master mason at the building of King Solomon's Temple in Jerusalem that has immense spiritual and ritual significance for the world-wide brotherhood of Freemasonry.

> 'The master mason having received from his patron the model of a pillar of exquisite workmanship and design, hesitated to carry it out until he had been to Rome, or some such foreign part, and seen the original. He went abroad, and in his absence an apprentice, having dreamed the finished pillar, at once set to work and carried out the design as it now stands, a perfect marvel of workmanship. The master mason on his return was so stung with envy that he asked who had dared to do it in his

absence. On being told it was his own apprentice, he was so inflamed with rage and passion that he struck him with his mallet, killed him on the spot, and paid the penalty for his rash and cruel act.'[3]

Whatever the truth may be about this bizarre legend, the design and workmanship displayed by the beautiful carving of the Apprentice Pillar (see plate 16) surpass in skill the majority of the other sculptures found within this mystical place. It is alleged that the apprentice himself came from Orkney and that the pillar, for which he gave his life, represents Yggdrasil, the ash tree of Norse mythology, the world ash which binds together heaven, earth and hell. The carvings at the crown of this 'tree', symbolise the twelve constellations of the zodiac. The spiralling branches represent the planets and the roots of the trunk dig deeply into the elements of the earth. At the bottom of the pillar the dragons of Neifelheim can be seen gnawing at the roots of the tree to rob it of its fruitfulness. The pillar itself represents a kind of transformation of an ancient pagan conception into a Christian version of The Tree of Life. Thus to the curious admixture of Celtic, Greek, Kabbalistic and medieval Christian symbolism, we have to add Norse influences as well!

The carved head of the so-called 'murdered apprentice' high in the south-west corner of the clerestory wall (see figure 34) has, for centuries, looked fixedly down not on the pillar of his own creation but, surprisingly on the subtly designed and serene pillar carved by the allegedly murderous master mason himself. Indeed, above the beautifully carved Master Masons Pillar (see plate 17), looking outward into the main body of the chapel there is a carving of the master mason's head with his face contorted in the manner of one recently hung by the neck. Closer examination of the carving through a telescopic lens tells quite a different story, for when viewed in this manner, the master is clearly laughing. Some years ago when a colleague was taking casts of all the carvings prior to the commencement of the restoration project that is still in progress, he found evidence that the face of the apprentice had once had a beard that had since been chipped off. Now, medieval apprentices were not

Figure 34

allowed to have beards! It is highly likely that the juxtaposition of the carving of the master mason and his so-called apprentice once symbolised the heresy of the Holy Twins. As this would undoubtedly have been cause for Inquisitorial prosecution, something had to go, so the apprentice had to say farewell to his whiskers.

The Retro-Choir

In the central bay of the retro-choir, or Lady Chapel, there is an intricately carved, large, pendant boss hanging from the roof. The carvings around this boss depict the story of the birth of Jesus. On one side there is a carving of the Madonna and Child, on the other are the three Magi and the shepherds. Nearby on one of the ribbed arches running from the north wall is possibly the oldest and most complete version of 'The Dance Macabre' or 'The Dance of Death' to be seen anywhere in Europe. All walks of life are represented in this eerie procession, sixteen pairs of figures in all, giving vivid illustration to the fact that the only absolute certainty in life is death itself. The east wall of the retro-choir is particularly crowded with intricate carvings, and even the undersides of the canopies for the now vanished statues are carved with complex window designs. Tucked away, almost unnoticed among this plethora of sculptures is a representation of the death mask of King Robert the Bruce, the last sovereign commander of the Knights Templar.

The three pillars separating the retro-choir from the main chapel are the Apprentice Pillar, the Master Mason's Pillar, and a third plain fluted pillar between them – the Journeyman's Pillar. The capitals are decorated with carvings of angels playing medieval instruments. One eighteenth-century historian who was an expert on the Freemasonry of his time, claimed that each true lodge should be supported by three grand pillars of deep symbolic significance. One symbolising 'Wisdom' (The Mason's Pillar), the second portraying 'Strength' (The Journeyman's Pillar) and the third 'Beauty' (The Apprentice Pillar). Accordingly each pillar represents not only the named quality, but also its significance and its function. Wisdom constructs, Strength supports and Beauty adorns. Furthermore Wisdom is ordained to discover, Strength is made to bear and Beauty is made to attract. Each of the three pillars must be built upon the same rock or foundation, and that rock is called Truth and Justice. This tripartite concept of the ideal foundation finds echoes in the qualities aspired to by the true initiate:

> 'He who is as wise as a Perfect Master will not be easily injured by his own actions. Hath a person the strength which a Senior Warden represents he will bear and overcome every obstacle in life. He who is adorned like a Junior Warden with humility of spirit approaches nearer to the similitude of God than others.'[4]

Thus, in the construction and care which have been lavished upon these three magnificent pillars, we have, enshrined in stone, symbolism of the esoteric, spiritual insight and wisdom upon which this chapel was founded.

The Crypt

In the south-east corner of the chapel, steps lead down to the crypt, or lower chapel. Recently refurbished in order to make them safe, until recently they were incredibly well-worn, demonstrating that very many pilgrims had visited Rosslyn Chapel in the ninety or one hundred years between its completion and the Reformation when the veneration of relics and the pilgrimages associated with them ceased in Protestant countries. The exact reasons for this pilgrimage are, as yet, unclear, but it is possible that Templar knights had deposited some holy relic of ancient veneration here – a Black Madonna perhaps? Or, as this site has been a place of spiritual significance since well before the Christian era, there may have been an older tradition that was a source of spiritual benefit to the many pilgrims who were drawn here in such numbers.

As I continued with my ten-year investigation of Rosslyn Chapel, I continually found references to a strange pilgrimage that originated in Spain and culminated at Rosslyn. It was referred to as 'The Pilgrimage of Initiation' or 'The Alchemist's Pilgrimage'. It was only later that I began to discern the significance of this, and that I shall describe later.

There are certain working drawings on the north wall of the crypt that have not been precisely dated, however, they are of an architectural nature and we do know that this area was used as a workshop during the construction of the main chapel. Two stones are to be found alongside the north wall and both are imports from outside the confines of the chapel, one a Templar gravestone of the thirteenth century, the second a much later, seventeenth-century Guild-Stone entitled 'The King of Terrors'. At the eastern end of the crypt is a small altar decorated with the Engrailed Cross of the St Clair family. This pattern is repeated in the roof in such a way as to display the *Croix Pattée* of the Templars at each intersection of the Engrailed Cross.

If one mounts the steps into the main chapel, you come first to the window in the south wall framed by carvings of the maize plants I mentioned earlier. On the east side of the next window, one figure is carved into the plinth that had previously supported some piece of statuary. A large bearded, robed man is shown holding a cup or chalice in both hands; whether this is a standard piece of mainstream Church symbolism or a reference to the heretical search for the Holy Grail is unclear. However, this is one of the few carvings in the entire chapel that shows signs of being subjected to violence. Look closely at the columnar frame to the right of this figure and clear marks can be seen that indicates that this carving has been struck with some sharp or hard implement. On a corbel by the third window is a carving of Moses, horned and carrying the tablets of stone. This a startlingly similar depiction of Moses, complete with horns, to the great statue carved by Michelangelo.

Pausing by the south door, if you cast your eyes to the left a small pillar can be seen carved into the wall. Carved above the capital of this are a group of figures and on their right is St Veronica holding the veil on which is depicted the face of Christ. This is a representation of 'The Mandylion' or 'The Veil of Veronica', yet another of the diagnostic signs of Templar influence. To those who recall the charge of idol worship of a head levelled against the Templars this has particular significance.

The North Wall

Moving across to the left of the north, or 'bachelor's door' there is a narrow pillar and on its capital there is a small carving of the Crucifixion, so small and relatively insignificant it could easily be missed. Yet, this is the only symbol of the redemptive act at Golgotha that is the foundation for the entire religion of Christianity that can be found in the chapel! If you then turn, and with your back to the north door, observe the capitals of the pillars immediately in front of you, on the left can be seen representations of the angels rolling back the stone from the tomb of Christ, and on the right the two Marys and, most bizarrely, John the Baptist facing each other across the Crucifixion.

Close against the west wall of the north aisle we can see the 'Caithness' memorial. It is in memory of George, the grandson of the founder and the last of the St Clairs to be in possession of all St Clair lands of Caithness, Sutherland, Fife and Rosslyn. At the King's request, George left his lands to be divided among his three older sons, thereby reducing the potential threat to the Crown posed by so powerful a family. This was the second major sub-division of the Sinclair lands. Earl William himself had previously divided his estate into three portions, the Islands, lands north of the Forth and those south of that river. Had these divisions not occurred, the St Clairs would have been more powerful than any other family in Scotland.

Close by the Caithness memorial, lying parallel to the north wall on a special plinth, is the burial stone of Sir William de Sinncler, Grand Prior of the Templar Order that I mentioned earlier. On the stone are incised the outline of his sword, the Floriated Cross of the Templars and Sir William's name going up the calvary steps. Standing with your back to the Caithness memorial, the pillar on your right has carved above the capital a depiction of the prodigal son feeding the swine. The window at this level in the north wall shows two important carvings, on the left is the devil in a state of anger because the couple beside him have turned away and are looking at an angel holding the cross, while below the window on the stringcourse is a beautiful carving of The Green Man (see figure 35). Lining this aisle, and also against the wall in the south aisle, is a continuous stone bench. This is the origin of one of the most misunderstood sayings in the English language – 'The weak must go to the wall'. Far from expressing callous indifference to the fate of the weak, this originates from Church practice in the days when the congregation stood.

Figure 35

When the chapel was crowded, on feast days, saints days and times of celebration or invocation, to protect the elderly, the infirm and the weak, the cry went up, 'The weak must go to the wall'. There they would find air and support from the stone bench, thus far from being callous, this instruction was one of compassion and care.

The Victorian Stained-Glass Windows

Important symbolism within Rosslyn Chapel is not restricted to the medieval carvings: superb stained-glass windows installed in the later years of the Victorian era show that sacred symbolism is an on-going art. The designs of these windows, however, pose a puzzling question: Why should two Roman soldiers and the patron saint of England be celebrated within the mystical confines of Rosslyn Chapel? Or, more intriguingly, why the symbolic reference to Mary Magdalene provided by the amethyst coloured halo of Christ to be found in the window of the crypt? One thing is certain, the Victorian stained-glass windows of Rosslyn were designed and commissioned by initiates with deep mystical insight who knew that, sooner or later, their true significance would be recognised!

The first is of St Longinus (see plate 18) about whom a story grew that permeated all of Christendom. This startling legend came to represent, in all its mystery, the hidden stream of spiritual knowledge that continued from Christ himself throughout the ages, despite intermittent persecution by the hierarchy.

> 'In the final chapters of the Gospel of St John it is told how a soldier pierced the side of Christ with a spear. The name of this soldier was Gaius Cassius Longinus ... It was said that for a moment in time he had held the destiny of the whole of mankind in his hands. The spear with which he had pierced the side of Christ became one of the great treasures of Christendom and a unique legend attached itself to this weapon in which one of the nails from the cross was later inserted.

The legend grew around it, gaining in strength with the passing of the centuries, that whoever possessed it and understood the powers it served, held the destiny of the world in his hands for good or evil.'[5]

The spear, like all the other artefacts that touched the body and blood of Christ at Golgotha, was accorded miraculous and mythical powers and was firmly believed to be incorruptible. The illustrious list of all who held it over many centuries, serves as a pointer to those who were believed to possess spiritual knowledge, power and insight.

Another of the stained-glass windows shows St Mauritius (see plate 19), the Christian commander of the Theban legion, whose legionaries were also Christian. It is a matter of record that Mauritius and all his men refused to worship the pagan gods of Rome when commanded to do so by the emperor. Roman law in these matters was both brutal and swift: Mauritius was decapitated in front of his troops. Their response was remarkable. Divesting themselves of their weapons, they knelt as a body, bared their necks for the sword and willingly submitted themselves to the slaughter.

The figure of St Michael the Archangel is displayed in solitary splendour in the window of the south clerestory (see plate 20). He was, of course, the patron saint of the warrior Knights Templar. St Michael, who was likened to God, was not only described as the 'Prince of the Heavenly Hosts' but also as the Guardian Saint of ancient Israel. He was believed to hold the secret of 'The Word' by which God created heaven and earth. The parallels here between 'The Word' of creation itself and the secret 'Masonic Word' are self-evident.

In the window immediately opposite St Michael, between the two windows showing the Roman soldier saints, is a figure that at first glance, one would hardly expect in a Scottish chapel. The saint depicted is the patron saint of England, St George (see plate 21). Why is there a window dedicated to the patron saint of Scotland's traditional enemy? Perhaps it is because St George is another warrior saint whose chivalric principles would commend him as an example to the chivalrous Order of the Knights Templar. According to Pope Gelasius (494 AD), St George 'was a Saint, venerated by man, but whose acts were known only to God'. However, closer examination of the legends surrounding St George link him closely to St Michael in his origins and begin to give us a basis upon which we can cast new light on many of my earlier comments. The earliest known mythological personage on whom St George is supposedly based is Tammuz. I have previously mentioned the apparently bizarre connections between the Sufis and their supposed enemies the Templars, Tammuz may provide further evidence of this, for most modern authorities now believe that El Khidir, the mystical founder of the Sufis, Tammuz and St George are one and the same person portrayed in varying mythological guises.

Tammuz has been described as the spouse, son or brother of the goddess Ishtar and is known as 'the Lord of Life and Death'. A title which has deep Masonic overtones but which pre-dates the reputed history of the Masonic movement by several millennia. One account tells that when Adam was sent to the Gates of Heaven, Tammuz offered him the bread and water of eternal life, which Adam refused, thus losing his immortality. It is interesting to note that St George is depicted as standing upon a rose-coloured board decorated with roses or rosettes. The link with Ishtar is thus made explicit.

In contrast, Saints Longinus and Mauritius are shown standing on a black and white chessboard. The so-called 'Chequerboard of Joy' which symbolises both the Templar battle flag, the *Beauseant*, and the mystical 'hopscotch' symbol of the 'Pilgrimage of Initiation' from Santiago of Compostela to Rosslyn. In the design of both these windows it is depicted in the exact manner in which it is used in Masonic lodges, as part of the floor design upon which people stand for ceremonies and rituals. The inclusion of this specific design in these two windows is no accident, nor is it a product of artistic licence, it is quite deliberate and significant.

The Green Men

Throughout the chapel, carvings of 'The Green Man' proliferate. This figure is, of course, well represented in other medieval churches, but in the confines of Rosslyn there are over 120, and we are still counting. In the vast expanse of Chartres Cathedral, there are only eighty-six. So why so many in the restricted confines of Rosslyn? Is this one of the direct linkages of the Grail impulse with its original Celtic roots in the legendary exploits of Cuchullin who was allegedly 'raised from the dead' by St Patrick?

Running around almost the entire wall of the chapel is a string course depicting various forms of vegetation. The symbolism of the string course is multi-layered and dualistic: to separate good from evil or the negative from the positive are the two most common themes. Below the window near the south door on that string course is a carving of one of the 'Green Men'. His eyes are carved in such a manner that they seem to follow the visitor around the chapel as they move. There is foliage coming out of his mouth, representing the fruits of fertility. Green Men abound, many are situated elsewhere on the string course, others are scattered throughout the interior of the chapel. They peep out from every point, heads jutting from the foliage, sometimes half-hidden in the vegetal designs around the capitals of the pillars, sometimes solitary, on other occasions in groups, even on the tip of dependant bosses. There are so many that like Robin Hood's merry men, they seem to be everywhere.

I now realise that there is a reason for the inclusion of so many Green Men, and, like all the other carving in Rosslyn Chapel, they too have to be understood and experienced at several different levels. They refer us back directly to Tammuz and the origins of this seminal stream of spirituality.

'The May Queen followed in a cart, or chariot, drawn by young men and women. Her partner, or 'consort', the Green Man, descendant of Dumuzi, Tammuz and Attis, also called 'the Green One' was clothed in leaves. In some parts of Europe the couple were 'married'. So May Day celebrated the sacred marriage and the ritual and re-generation of life ... The face of the Green Man gazes out from the midst of carved foliage on Gothic cathedral screens, pulpits, vaulted naves and choir stalls ... invoking the more ancient knowledge of the relationship of the goddess to her son, incarnate through him as the life on earth.'[6]

The association of the Green Man and the Masons was delineated by William Anderson:

'Even if one were to regard him at the lowest level, as a mascot of the Masons, his presence in so many regions and over so long a period indicates that he had a particular meaning for them. Did he sum up for them the energy they had to transform, the energy of both living nature and of the past stored in the collective unconsciousness? Did he, at the same time, express the spirit of inspiration, the genius hidden in created things?' [7]

This could be of considerable significance in that it links Freemasonry with the earliest known system of Initiation, that of Zoroaster. The whole idea of death and resurrection flows like a river through the mystical symbolism of all the religious traditions. They are repeated in the symbolic death and resurrection of Tammuz, a 'Widow's Son' which is held to be symbolic of autumn and spring. This theme is repeated in the story of Hiram Abif; it is implied in that of the 'Murdered Apprentice' at Rosslyn; it is explicit in the folklore of 'The Green Man'. All of these are intertwined with the pantheistic mysticism so apparent in the carvings at Rosslyn. All, from Tammuz right down to the Masons, who built this mystical chapel, depict, celebrate and sustain the glories of God's creation.

A Strange and Mysterious Pilgrimage

I remarked earlier on the deeply worn steps leading to the crypt. There is much evidence that demonstrates that Rosslyn was, for some inexplicable reason, the final destination for pilgrims who had made the arduous journey from Santiago of Compostela. The majority of such pilgrims, who arrived here at the conclusion of their pious journey, were 'normal' pilgrims, drawn to this mystical site to venerate some important relic which is as yet undiscovered. However, a significant proportion of the pilgrims would have had a deeper, esoteric purpose. They would be completing a *Pilgrimage of Initiation* that linked Spain, the seat of Sufi learning in Europe, with the new focal point of Masonry and Rex Deus thinking at Rosslyn Chapel.

There are a plethora of clues indicating a long, unbroken initiatory line of transmission of spiritual wisdom and truth from the earliest years of the Sumerian civilization, down through biblical times, the Arab conquest of Spain, medieval Christianity, the Templar Order, the Masonic guilds and on into Freemasonry and Rosicrucianism, all encoded within the complex carvings within Rosslyn Chapel. Our guidelines in any attempt to research and understand the cultural influences inherent in the carvings and design of the chapel must be the tangible artefacts that remain, interpreted according to our present level of conscious and complex intellectual ability and our growing understanding of the hidden streams of spirituality.

CHAPTER 15

The Continuing Initiatory Stream

T he brutal suppression of the Knights Templar created a hiatus in the initiatory activities of the Rex Deus families, but it did not end them. Initiation continued within the families in secret and they now began to pass on their initiatory teachings in a manner that they made discreetly available to carefully selected novices from outside the ranks of the families. The question is, therefore, 'How did these new novices gain enlightenment in an era of repression?' The heirs to the spiritual traditions of the Knights Templar devised a method to pass on their sacred knowledge by means that ultimately led to the creation of Freemasonry, Rosicrucianism, the Invisible College, and the Royal Society in England. That method was the Pilgrimage of Initiation.[1]

The pilgrimage to the shrine of St James of Compostela was known as the *Shell Pilgrimage*, yet when working with Trevor Ravenscroft, and again when studying Rosslyn Chapel, I came across repeated references to another mysterious pilgrimage known as the *Alchemist's Pilgrimage* or *the Pilgrimage of Initiation.*[2] This pilgrimage was not undertaken to Jerusalem, the place where Jesus met his end, nor to Rome, the city of St Peter and St Paul, but, just like the Shell Pilgrimage, to an obscure and relatively inaccessible corner of north-west Spain. To a shrine dedicated to James the Great, son of Zebedee, and James the Less, also known as James the Just, and the brother of Jesus.

Using this new process of initiation, the Rex Deus families were able to exert an enormous influence on the people who brought about the Italian Renaissance. As a result, a relatively small group of spiritual initiates transformed the thinking, art, commerce, social and religious systems of a continent, and made a significant contribution to the creation of an intellectual climate within which science, democracy and intellectual freedom could flourish.

> 'Nearly all the major intellectual figures of the period –
> including many of the founding fathers of modern science
> down to Newton's day – were deeply invested in ... esoteric
> traditions, as if they believed there might lay hidden in these
> buried sources, secrets of human nature and the universe that
> were nowhere else to be found.'[3]

Most of the intellectuals, artists and philosophers of the Renaissance were members of organisations that were the true heirs of the Knights Templar and operated at horrendous risk under the ever watchful gaze of repressive Church authorities.[4] The Renaissance stimulated major advances in European culture, in art, religion, architecture, philosophy, literature, democracy, freedom and science – all deeply influenced by the hidden streams of spirituality. In reconciling the ideals of spirituality and intellectual endeavour, we need to remember that, unlike the Church who attempted to limit and control all access to knowledge, to the Gnostics and medieval Craftmasons, *Ars sina scienta nihil est* – 'Art without knowledge is nothing'. In this context, 'gnosis', or spiritual knowledge is the quality to which they refer. The name Roslin in the Gallic language, for example, reinforces this concept for it translates as 'Ancient knowledge handed down through the generations'. [5]

The idea of a pilgrimage of initiation using sacred sites believed to be the chakras of the earth, dated back to an ancient Egyptian practice involving eight sacred sites. The number eight was of considerable magical significance to the Egyptians and also occurs frequently in European esoteric symbolism. There are eight points on the Templar Cross, the eight-sided figure, or octagon was the basis for much sacred

Templar architecture and eight is the symbolic number for spiritual resurrection. Preparation took place at the Temple of Buhen in the southern part of Egypt and then the ascending degrees of initiation were awarded to suitable candidates at seven Temples regarded as the chakras of the earth in Egyptian religious thinking.[6]

Trevor Ravenscroft suggested that in the pre-Christian era, Celtic pilgrims who worshipped the Earth goddess had journeyed from Iberia to Scotland via seven Druidic, planetary oracles, corresponding to the chakras of the earth.[7] The sequence of these sites corresponds to that of the planets in our solar system – the Moon, Mercury, Venus, the Sun, Mars, Jupiter and Saturn. Trevor learned from his teacher, Dr Walter Johannes Stein, that the Romans had adopted these sacred sites for their temples and when Christianity became established, it followed suit and built churches and cathedrals on them. I discovered that all these churches and cathedrals – Rosslyn, Amiens, Notre Dame de Paris, Chartres, Orleans and Toulouse – were situated on different routes to the seventh site, Santiago de Compostela. Yet Trevor was convinced that pilgrims travelled from Compostela to Rosslyn, calling at each of the other sites in turn. Two significant questions arise from that concept: Why did the pilgrims travel this route in the reverse order to the pilgrimage ordained by the Church? And was there any way of confirming the validity of this intriguing theory?

The idea that the seven Earth chakras arcing across western Europe from northern Spain to Scotland had been used for a prolonged pilgrimage in pre-Christian times, was confirmed by another English author Philip Heselton:[8]

> 'There seem to be strong parallels between energy in the body and energy in the landscape and ... If the earth is a living being its energy flows and sacred centres correspond to the meridians and acupuncture points in the human body ... Some have taken the parallels between the human body and the Earth much further and have postulated "chakra" points on the

Earth's surface which have specific effects in landscape terms appropriate to the nature of the corresponding chakra. The heart chakra, for example, has been seen in terms of a river curving around a conical hill with a church. They are often referred to as "landscape temples". ... Various axes have been suggested incorporating the seven chakras. One is supposed to run from France up to Scotland.'[9]

An American student of anthropology, Elyn Aviva, wrote a PhD thesis on her own journey to Compostela that confirms the concept of the pilgrimage of initiation. In her thesis, she recalls that as she rested in the shade of Leon Cathedral, another, and somewhat elderly pilgrim, limped towards her and wished her good day. She enquired if he was a *Peregrino a Santiago?* He responded: 'No! I walk the *Camiño de las Estrellas*, the Milky Way, not the *Camiño de Santiago*. The Milky Way is the true and ancient path of spiritual death and rebirth. The *Camiño* was just a Christian attempt to camouflage the true way.' [10]

The ancient centre of spiritual death and rebirth was the Druidic moon oracle situated on the site of Santiago de Compostela. Elyn enquired, 'How could I find the "True Way"?' He said that the true way led along a path under the vault of the Milky Way and passed through churches marked by certain carvings of mystical birds and animals. Were these the symbols of the seven degrees of initiation perhaps? The limping pilgrim continued his explanation: 'The ancients left carvings on the churches, but it is hard to read them because the initiation rites were secret and carried on by word of mouth, and that he and others were trying to reconstruct them.'[11]

Elyn was confused by this encounter at first, for she was travelling the *Camiño* out of intellectual curiosity and not as an act of Christian devotion. Yet, in time, she came to realise that she was not simply on a physical or intellectual journey to Compostela but was instead treading a powerful and pervasive esoteric, spiritual pathway that spiritually transformed her as she progressed. In her thesis she wondered if: 'Perhaps those who travel the *Camiño* are impacted with faint echoes of ancient worship, faint images of archetypical power.' Her final sentence delineates a great spiritual truth: 'I do not know what road I travel, except that there are many hidden beneath the one – and, perhaps beneath the many is the One.'[12]

The Path to Enlightenment

Initiation on any valid spiritual pathway is a form of ritualised mystical experience whereby a master guides the novice so that he develops and enhances the use of his organs of spiritual perception. These chakras are awakened in order from the base upwards to the crown. This specific order of the awakening of the chakras may explain why, in the Pilgrimage of Initiation, the direction of travel is a complete reversal of the normal, orthodox pilgrimage to Compostela. Thus after a period of prayerful preparation at Cintra in Portugal – a city where not only is there a pillar that is the mirror image of the Apprentice Pillar at Rosslyn but also a place analogous to the preparatory temple at Buhen in the Egyptian pilgrimage – the novice travels to Santiago de Compostela for his initiation into the first degree, which symbolises the awakening of the base chakra that connects us with the earth. The symbol of the first degree, the Raven, [13] represents the messenger of the mystery cults who had learned to express spiritual concepts in images that can be understood, albeit at different levels, by both the laity and the initiated.

If the concept of a Celtic pilgrimage of initiation has any validity, then it must be possible to relate it historically to known centres of worship in pre-Christian times. As the Druids were priests within an oral culture, this must, at best, be an indirect process entirely dependant on the Roman and later Christian habit of adopting ancient and revered sacred sites to their own use. It has been established by archaeologists that there was a significant Roman town on the site of Compostela. The Cathedral of Santiago has also been thoroughly excavated, and numerous pre-Christian burials were found under the nave and the remains of a Roman temple was discovered under the south transept.[14] These temple remains abut directly upon the ninth-century foundations of the basilica, adding credibility to the idea of Druidic, Roman and then Christian use of the same sacred site. Altar slabs dedicated to pagan deities that had previously been venerated here, had their original pre-Christian inscriptions chipped off before being incorporated into the so-called *Apostles Altar* in the cathedral.[15] The prime objective of the approved Christian pilgrimage, the alleged tomb of the Apostle James the Great was discovered between 813 and 818 AD but, paradoxically it was the Muslim writer, Ibd Dihya, who first recorded that Christian pilgrims were visiting the tomb of St James in 844 AD.[16] The list of the great and the good of European Christendom who visited the shrine is impressive and includes Louis VII of France, St Francis of Assisi, King Robert the Bruce of Scotland and Earl William St Clair, the founder of Rosslyn.

At the Cathedral of Santiago, the great initiates Melchizedek, Abraham, David and Moses are sculpted above the south door and the façade adjoining it. However, from the point of view of the initiatory pilgrimage, it is the interior and its iconography, enhanced by the tangible feeling of spirituality and telluric energy that are the most significant factors. The spiritual impact is immediate as soon as one enters the heavy main doors that divide the ornate Baroque granite exterior from the medieval carvings of the arches of the *Pórtico de la Gloria* that separates the entry porch from the main body of the cathedral. This superb creation was designed and executed by the medieval genius Master Mateo, and has been described as 'the finest monument of medieval sculpture' and, according to Street, [17] 'one of the glories of Christian art' or as 'resembling a giant triptych in which religious feeling is expressed as ingeniously and sublimely as the artistic ideal of the time was capable of'.

The central column of finely carved marble is crowned by a capital that rests just above the seated figure of the Apostle St James. He grips the top of a tau-shaped staff with his left hand while in his right he holds a tablet bearing an inscription in Latin, *Misil me Dominus* – 'the Lord sent me'. The central pillar is a superbly executed, three-dimensional carving of the *Tree of Jesse* with David and Solomon discernible among the branches. The majority of pilgrims stop and place their fingers in five well-worn hollows that are clearly visible at shoulder height in the leafy ornamentation of the central pillar. On the interior side, at the base of this column there is a bust of Master Mateo kneeling and facing the High Altar, prayerfully and perpetually offering his work directly to God. Devout pilgrims traditionally knock their heads against the sculptured forehead of Mateo's bust, and for this reason the sculpture bears the Galician name *O sancto dos croques; croques* means to 'bang one's head'.[18]

Passing through the arches of Mateo's masterpiece, one enters a cathedral that is a glorious amalgam of the best of the Romanesque, Gothic and Baroque architectural eras. The vast interior of this enormous edifice is, however, nearly completely unspoilt and in almost its original condition. Soft light floods the nave, emphasising the size and grandeur of the whole, but in the galleries and lateral aisles, however, the light and atmosphere is more subdued, in a manner that is more attuned to the prayerful, meditative attitude of the pilgrims. The imposing and over-ornate Baroque decoration of the main altar is the cynosure of all eyes, in more ways than one for this lies directly beneath a representation of the all-seeing eye of God, the old Egyptian design, but Christianised by being embossed centrally in an equilateral triangle, symbolising the Holy Trinity. Directly below the altar is the Romanesque crypt containing the Apostle's sepulchre, which is entered from the ambulatory.

The *Codex Callextinus*, the *Liber Sancti Jacobi* or Book of St. James, was the medieval guidebook and primer for pilgrims en route to Compostela. Two copies of the original survive to this day and one is housed in the cathedral archives. The nearby Chapel of the Relics holds an artefact that is of overwhelming significance to all who follow the hidden streams of spirituality. This is an ornate jewelled and gilt reliquary in the form of an ornate silver bust with an enamelled face, that was designed and created to hold a very sacred relic indeed, the head of St James the Less, the brother of the Lord and the first Bishop of Jerusalem. None other than James the Just, for whose sake, according to Jesus, 'the heaven and the earth came into existence'.[19] The cathedral guidebook describes this reliquary as: 'The most important silver bust is that of St James the Lesser. The cranium of this saint, the younger brother of St

James the Greater, was brought from Jerusalem to Braga in the 12th century.[20]

James the Less described as the **brother** of James the Great. But the New Testament, a scriptural source that even the Catholic hierarchy dare not question, describes James the Less as *the Lord's brother*.[21] Thus literature published by the Church, backed up by the New Testament, implies that the Virgin Mary, mother of God, was also the mother of the sons of Zebedee. Did she marry again and have further children after the death of Joseph?

This reliquary and its contents are described in the guidebook as being second in importance only to the remains of St James the Great. It is salutary to note that the skull of James the Just is pierced in the area of the temple in precisely the same manner as the skull of St John the Baptist that is preserved in Amiens Cathedral and the Templar skulls buried in the crypt at Bargemon in Provence.

The crypt at Santiago of Compostela, or as it now known, the Lower Church or the Old Cathedral, dates from the late eleventh or early twelfth century and is dedicated to James the Just. It contains sculptures of both King David and King Solomon and three thick pillars, one of which is adorned with a figure of St James the brother of Jesus. When I first suggested, some years ago, that under the guise of the Church-sanctioned pilgrimage there might well lie another, I little realised that I might be describing a physical as well as a spiritual reality. When devout Catholic pilgrims were praying in the main cathedral above and venerating the earthly remains of St James the Great, *Santiago Matamoros* – St James the Moor Slayer – pilgrims drawn from the heretical hidden streams of spirituality were venerating that vitally important figure in Gnostic belief, James the Just, in the crypt beneath their feet. Heresy being practiced right under the noses of the clergy. The Hermetic principle still applies, 'as above, so below'. Is this so surprising when above the cathedral itself, over the triumphal arch which crowns the roof, there is a bell arch crowned by the Agnus Dei, a symbol so intimately connected with the heretical Templar Order that it is known as the *Templar Seal*.

As with her descriptions of the energies detectable at Chartres, Blanche Mertz suggests that the telluric powers found at Santiago reflect the watercourses that lie under the cathedral. She states that:

> 'These water inflows are made conspicuous in the paving of the side corridors ... by 14 wide inlays of black marble. During the decade of the 1960s there were large excavations under the cathedral of Santiago de Compostela, and what did they find? These old inflow channels had been dug by human hands ... today, at Compostela the channels are dry! ... As a consequence of these works executed between 1948 and 1968, the subterranean water passages, programmed by the constructors, were cut. ... It is often said that there are no more miracles at Santiago de Compostela.'[22]

As these watercourses were made by human hands it follows that the creation of these underground streams was both conscious and deliberate. Either they were designed to imbue the cathedral with powerful energies, or they were created in order to enhance known and therefore pre-existing telluric forces. These watercourses give shape and physical form to the concept of 'the hidden streams of spirituality'.

As a somewhat heretical pilgrim to the Cathedral of Santiago, I followed tradition and placed my fingers in the five well-worn hollows on the Tree of Jesse in the Pórtico de la Gloria and was immediately over-whelmed with emotion. I also experienced a discernable physical reaction, a buzzing in my fingers, light-headedness and a tendency to sway. I have never claimed to have particularly well-developed gifts in detecting telluric energies and, in the light of Blanche Mertz's comments cited above, was distinctly surprised for a strong and tangible energy was readily detected. If the telluric powers within the cathedral have indeed visibly diminished as a result of the diversion of the underground water-courses, then what was it like before then? How much initiatory power was manifest in this sacred place during the medieval era of the pilgrimage of initiation?

The Initiatory Path

When the novice had been initiated into the mysteries of the first degree he became open to receive the messenger of the mystery cults. After a variable period of probation and further learning, the new initiate would then be instructed to travel from Compostela to Toulouse for initiation into the second degree, which took place in the crypt of the church built on the site of the Mercury Oracle. Mercury, of course, was the Latin name for the Greek god Hermes, known as the winged messenger of the gods.

At Toulouse, initiation ceremonies would take place that would result in the opening of the sacral or abdominal chakra. The second degree, known as that of the Occultist, is represented by the peacock, [23] whose many-splendoured plumage symbolises the student's newly acquired powers of moral imagination.

Hermes is known as *the master of secrecy* and, according to some scholars, is equated with Moses, with Jesus and with St John the Divine. This is not so surprising as it may seem at first, for the medieval Sufi Master Suhrawardi declared that the sages of most religions in the ancient world had all preached the same, true doctrine.[24] Originally this teaching had been revealed by the gods on Mount Olympus, and given to Hermes who was their messenger. In the Egyptian tradition, the religious foundation of both Judaism and Christianity, the same divine teaching had been transmitted to mankind through the words of Thoth, the god of knowledge. To the philosophers of ancient Greece, Thoth and Hermes were simply the same divine entity in differing mythological guise. Suhrawardi also identified Hermes with the prophet Idris in the Koran and the prophet Enoch in the Bible. Hermes is also linked with the Druids, for one of the teachers of Pythagoras was the Druid Abaris. It is known that Pythagoras was initiated into both the Hermetic mysteries and the teachings of the Persian Magi. Therefore, it is reasonable to deduce that the fundamental spiritual teachings of all of these strands were compatible.

At Rosslyn Chapel, Hermes faces the source of light and energy that is transmitted through him to the spirit of all who enter that holy place.

This is in keeping with Hermes' reputation as the transmitter of light, which he does, paradoxically, by veiling it, for secrets cannot be kept in the light or else they are soon revealed; the invisible only becomes visible through concealment. There is a bizarre justification for just this apparently contradictory principle in the Gospel according to St Matthew: 'The light of the body is the eye; if therefore thine eye be single, thy whole body shall be full of light.'[25]

The phrase 'if therefore thine eye be single' almost certainly refers to the opening of the third eye and that of 'thy whole body shall be full of light' symbolises the state of illumination. Suhrawardi, known as *the sheik al-Ishraq* or the *Master of Illumination*, experienced God in terms of light. In Arabic, Ishraq is the first light of dawn and is also a common term for enlightenment; Jesus was described as *the Light of the World;* Earl William St Clair as *one of the illuminati.* The result of receiving the divine message from Hermes is that known as enlightenment.

The second-degree ceremonies took place in the crypt of the church of *Notre Dame la Dalbade,* Our Lady in White, in Toulouse. The first church to be built on this site was constructed in 541, and was rebuilt at least once prior to the erection of the present place of worship. The church built between 1180 and 1200 was the first completely Gothic building in Toulouse and replaced an earlier Romanesque edifice. The date of construction places this building firmly in the Templar era, while its Gothic architecture and its dedication both link it to the Order. On 27th February 1442, a fire in this quarter of Toulouse destroyed the Gothic church, several nearby houses and claimed many lives. The church stands near the *Hotel des Chevaliers* that was once the property of the Knights Hospitallers who inherited most of the vast Templar properties in France. The land on which the church stands and various nearby properties were donated by Raymond Rater of Toulouse to the Templar Order in a charter dated between 1128 and 1132.[26] Thus the church is not merely on the site of the old Roman Temple of Mercury, but was originally the property of the Knights Templar. The present building, built of typical Toulousian narrow bricks, was consecrated on 1st November 1455. It is a church of stunning simplicity and harmony. The high vault rises above a clerestory that is supported by a colonnade of pillars, each adorned with the heraldic symbol of the *Cross of Universal Knowledge,* the Gnostic,initiatory symbol of the Knights Templar.

The knight was the symbol of the third and Warrior degree of the Pilgrimage of Initiation and knighthood was bestowed to those who attained it.[27] This degree was awarded to those who were initiated into the mysteries of the Druidic Venus Oracle in the crypt of Orleans Cathedral. Orleans, like Chartres, was part of the tribal lands of the Carnutes. The Druidic Venus Oracle, dedicated to light and the *morning star,* was situated at Cenabum, part of the Roman district of Civitas Aurelianorum, which corresponded roughly with the ninth-century county of Orleans.

The Cathedral of Orleans has been substantially altered since its original Gothic construction, but modified though it may be, it is truly magnificent in its own right for the west front contains some of the most impressive and delicate church architecture I have ever seen. It is visually stunning and has more in common with the designs one finds in delicate cake decoration than with medieval architecture. The prophet St John the Baptist is commemorated by a superb life-size statue in the ambulatory where he is depicted in the baptising position, with a scallop shell in his hand, thus linking the Catholic pilgrimage to Compostela with the Johannite heresy.

Substantial remains of a Roman temple still abut the north side of the present cathedral and it is plain that the building is constructed on the site of this pagan temple. In the crypt, vestiges of an earlier Christian church can be seen which indicate that this site, along with all the others we have investigated, has been continually used for worship since pagan times. While at Compostela, stones originally dedicated to a pagan deity were used to construct a Christian altar; in the crypt of Orleans there stands a huge font made from ancient stones that still carry inscriptions dedicated to the goddess Venus, which were found on this site. Therefore, it is reasonable to assume that the Roman temple remains that abut against the foundations of the present cathedral are the ruins of a temple dedicated to Venus. That is not, however, the only peculiarity of this great cathedral.

There is a strange and fascinating legend current in Orleans that demonstrates the divine approval of the work of the Gnostic craftsmen whose knowledge of sacred geometry and skill in masonry gave rise to this glorious example of church architecture. It is recorded that at the service of consecration for the cathedral, the bishop fell ill, and before the clergy could devise an alternative way to consecrate the cathedral, Almighty God himself took a hand. According to the guidebook, at this point, the glowing finger of God reached down from the clouds and gently touched each part of the cathedral as an act of truly 'Divine' consecration.[28] Needless to say, there are no consecration marks visible on any part of the cathedral, for how could mere man commemorate what God himself had done?

When initiates had been prepared for further advancement along the path of enlightenment, they would visit the site of the heart chakra and undergo their initiation in the mystical underground chamber of *la Vierge de Sous-Terre* in the crypt of Chartres Cathedral, the ancient site of the Druidic Sun Oracle. I have described Chartres Cathedral in some detail earlier, and it was there that they were accorded the degree of the Lion.

The swan[29] symbolises the fourth degree, for it was believed that the swansong was the sign of the death of self and awakening of a profound inner realisation of the divine presence within the human breast. The first four degrees – the Raven, the Occultist, the Warrior, and the Lion, according to Trevor Ravenscroft, represented the spiritual transformation of toil.[30] The fifth and sixth degrees resulted from the spiritualisation of suffering. Initiation for the fifth degree took place in the crypt beneath the Cathedral of Notre Dame de Paris, erected on the site of the Druidic Oracle of Mars. According to Grail symbolism, the fifth degree was symbolised by the pelican, depicted as a bird pecking its own breast in order to feed its young.[31] This symbol was used by the Knights Templar and in Church iconography is symbolic of the sacrifice of Jesus at Golgotha, furthermore, in another heretical reference it is held to represent an alchemical distilling flask. [32] Carvings at Notre Dame de Paris stimulated Fulcanelli to speak of the grading of the alchemical planets cited in Chapter 8 and which he developed further with the following quotation:

> 'Consider now that the virtues of the planets do not ascend, but descend. Experience itself teaches us that Mars can easily be converted into Venus, but not Venus into Mars – Venus being a lower sphere. Similarly Jupiter is easily transmuted into Mercury, because Jupiter is higher than Mercury ... Saturn is the highest, the Moon the lowest. The Sun mixes with all of them but is never improved by the inferior ones. Further you will note that there is a great correspondence between Saturn and the Moon, with the Sun midway between them. There is also a correspondence between Mercury and Jupiter and between Mars and Venus. In the midst of all is the Sun.'[33]

This ascending grading of the planets may well explain why the pilgrimage of initiation ascends from the Moon Oracle at Santiago, to the Mercury Oracle at Toulouse, then via the Venus Oracle at Orleans to the Sun Oracle at Chartres and so on through Paris – the Mars Oracle; Amiens – the Jupiter Oracle; and on to the Saturn Oracle at Rosslyn. Initiation at the Mars Oracle led to the awakening of the brow chakra, or *third eye*. With the awakening of this chakra, the initiate would be prepared for induction into the sublime mysteries of the Jupiter Oracle and, thereby, be initiated into sixth degree; symbolised by the eagle.[34] This initiation took place in the Cathedral of Amiens.

The feeling of space and light that pervades the interior of this glorious example of Rayonnante Gothic architecture is heightened by the simple, severe lines of arches that lead the eyes ever-upwards to the glorious rib vaulting that suggests that Almighty God himself supports the heavy stone roof with his fingers. The vast majority of the windows are clear or lightly coloured, thus adding to an all-pervading sense of light. The rose window in the north transept is based upon an intriguing design of a five-pointed star, the same symbol that adorned the Babylonian temples of Ishtar and many ancient Egyptian temples as well as forming part of the insignia of the hidden streams of spirituality.

One superbly coloured bas-relief sculpture can be seen on the south-western wall of the transept. It depicts pilgrims en route to Santiago de Compostela and the intricate detail of their colourful costumes, their facial expressions and the scallop shells they wore so proudly as badges of their devotion to the Apostle are all beautifully shown in this master-piece of the medieval sculptor's art.

The French mystical writer François Cali remarked that if one passes from Chartres to Amiens, an intriguing direction in the light of the pilgrimage of initiation, one progresses imperceptibly 'from the love of God to the love of Wisdom – which in order, number and harmony can be equated with God, but which need not be'. Order, number and harmony are all attributes of the gnosis revered by the Templars.

The guidebook recounts how the present beautiful building was erected on the site of its predecessor that was destroyed by fire in 1218, to provide a suitable resting place for the reliquary containing the head of John the Baptist brought to Amiens from Constantinople by Walter de Sarton in 1206. Esoterically speaking, John the Baptist and Jesus the Nazorean, who were born at the opposing poles of the year, form a duality that is held to symbolise our two natures, mortal and immortal, like Castor and Pollux.[35]

The cathedral, as I explained earlier, exhibits sufficient esoteric symbolism to link it intimately with the Knights Templar and the Children of Solomon, but, from the perspective of the theory of the Druidic pilgrimage of initiation what of its Druidic connections? The answer can be found in the Amiens museum where, on a plinth in a room in the lower basement, there stands an intricately carved pillar from the time of the Roman occupation. It was discovered in the grounds of the cathedral and originated from a Roman temple that had previously occupied the site. The pillar is clearly dedicated to Jupiter.

The Pilgrimage of Initiation was undoubtedly reserved for the spiritual élite of the period. Those privileged enough to undertake it were spiritually gifted men indeed, and those who were selected to attain the highest degrees of initiation must have been men of exceptional talent, humility and dedication. We have no idea who might have attained the seventh and highest degree, I can only suggest that, like those awarded the gift of entry into the exclusive *Order of the Golden Fleece*, they were not only limited in number, but also men of the highest rank and ability. The true giants of the early Renaissance perhaps? There were only twenty-four men of supreme talent in the Order of the Golden Fleece, including Earl William St Clair. This chivalric order may have been the outward face of the Rex Deus families or, perhaps, it was formed by that secretive, select few who had finally achieved the highest degree of initiation, the Kings of the Grail. The crown was the royal symbol of the King of the Grail.[36]

The crown is surely the most appropriate symbol for this degree, for the enlightenment which flows from the opening of the crown chakra is the supreme fulfilment of the Grail search. This peak of mystical illumination, was awarded at the seventh site on the long and arduous pilgrimage of initiation, Rosslyn Chapel, the ancient and revered site of the Saturn Oracle itself. The initiation ceremony took place in the hidden chamber under Rosslyn Chapel – the Omphalos or spiritual umbilicus of the world.

CHAPTER 16

Heretical Symbolism in Renaissance Paintings

The Rex Deus families had chosen a highly effective means to spread their heretical message, for the Grail sagas continued to fire the imagination of countless generations of readers and the tarot is used far more today than it was in medieval times. These were not the only forms of symbolism used by the hidden streams of spirituality. With the changing times and the emergence of the great merchant families, the economic balance of power shifted dramatically and the Church lost its monopoly on commissioning paintings and sculpture. Artistic patronage passed from the dogmatic control of the hierarchy to the newly rich merchant classes and the increasingly powerful nobility of northern Italy. As a result, the families' heretical message began to be enshrined in great works of art.

The Renaissance

A leading Rex Deus member, René d'Anjou, titular King of Jerusalem, Count of Provence and a correspondent of Earl William St Clair of Roslin, was one major figure who acted as a human catalyst to the emerging Renaissance. René's friendship with the Sforza counts of Milan led to a prolonged and productive association with their principal allies, the Medicis of Florence. René's influence was pivotal in persuading Cosimo de' Medici to embark on a series of projects that were to transform Western culture. Cosimo despatched agents all over southern

Europe to seek out ancient manuscripts lying disregarded in the monastic libraries of Christian Europe[1] and, after the Reconquista of Spain, in the Muslim libraries of Granada and Toledo they discovered a vast amount of classical Greek texts.[2] In 1444, Cosimo founded Christian Europe's first public library, the Library of San Marco in Florence.[3] Renewed and reinvigorated by these events, the study of the classical literature, philosophy and science of ancient Greece flourished and became the foundation for an insatiable spirit of enquiry that triggered the new artistic and intellectual renaissance.

In the light of its historic attempts to control the spread of knowledge, the papacy viewed this outburst of creative activity and intellectual freedom with suspicion and distrust and resorted to intrigue and violence aimed directly at the Rex Deus nobility in the north. Galezzeo Maria Sforza was assassinated in 1476 as the result of one papal plot, and the Pazzi conspiracy cost Guliano de' Medici his life in 1478.[4] Despite these attempts to halt and reverse this newly awakened spirit of intellectual enquiry and diminish the power of the Italian nobility, within a short time Lorenzo de' Medici consolidated his family's power in Florence. The court of Lorenzo the Magnificent was soon filled with scholars imbued with the mysticism of ancient Egypt and the philosophical wisdom of classical Greece. Literature, philosophy and science were all highly esteemed at court and became the inspiration for artists such as Boticelli, Michelangelo, Veroccio and Ghirlandaio, who all worked under the generous patronage of Lorenzo.[5]

Leonardo da Vinci

Amid the welter of talented writers, philosophers, sculptors and creative artists whose work spawned the Renaissance, one, above all others, stands out as a true genius – Leonardo da Vinci. A widely read man, steeped in philosophy who translated works of Euclid, Vitruvius, Pliny, Ptolomy, Celsius, as well as a wide range of Arab authors; a sculptor of incomparable talent and an artist of pure genius, he was, without doubt, the prototype for the term 'Renaissance Man'. A multi-talented, visionary intellectual who was blessed with insatiable curiosity, he foresaw the machine age and technologies that only came to fruition in the nineteenth and twentieth centuries. Renowned as a designer of military machines and intensely curious about the workings of the human body, this avid dissector of corpses attained levels of scientific, anatomical and medical knowledge that remained unequalled for centuries to come.[6] Well known for possessing, 'a somewhat heretical turn of mind', his towering genius allied to the apparently unassailable power of his patrons somehow protected him from prosecution by the Inquisition.

In his paintings, Leonardo da Vinci ceaselessly pursued both the visible form and the symbols that reveal the invisible and the cosmos. One of the great English twentieth-century art historians, Edgar Wind remarked that: '… a deliberate obliqueness in the use of metaphor has spread over some of the greatest Renaissance paintings. They were designed for initiates, hence they require an initiation.'[7] This approach is most appropriate in any consideration of the works of Leonardo da Vinci or his gifted contemporaries for, in a manner reminiscent of the way heretical symbolism is encoded within mainstream Catholic iconography, many of these famous works teach subtle forms of heresy under the outward guise of acceptable Catholic, devotional paintings.[8]

Truly great art is ambivalent at many interlinking levels; to portray a three-dimensional scene on a two-dimensional plane surface, is unreal to start with; the illusion of distance created by the use of perspective is yet another lie that yet conveys a reality. Furthermore each era imposes constraints upon the artist born of the fashions and techniques current at the time. The true artist uses this ambivalence and distortion of reality to make us view the familiar and yet perceive it in a more profound manner. When it comes to sacred subjects, especially those created during earlier centuries, it is also hard to discern whether we are being affected more by the insight of the artist or by that of the patron. During the Renaissance, however, the instructions of the patron were paramount because they were detailed precisely in the contracts drawn up before work even commenced. Thus the intentions of the patrons concerned are a matter of record that can be compared with the finished artistic work. But, with paintings by Leonardo da Vinci, we also have to allow for his profound spiritual insight, technical skill and outright genius.

It was Duke Ludovico Sforza who brought Leonardo from Florence to Milan. Duke Ludovico was known as Il Moro, some say because of his dark complexion, but true initiates have another, more intriguing explanation. The works of Pliny give us an insight into this for he describes the mulberry tree, *morus*, as the wisest of trees, *morus sapientissima arborum*,[9] because it develops its bloom very slowly then matures so fast that it bursts forth with dramatic vigour. Thus the nickname el Moro was a reflection of Ludovico's consummate statecraft and skill and not just a trite remark on his swarthy appearance.[10]

Ludovico brought Leonardo to Milan to create a mounted statue commemorating the first Sforza duke of Milan, a work that was never completed. However, during his prolonged stay in that city, Leonardo created three paintings that are still regarded by the Roman Catholic Church as supreme examples of Christian devotional art. There are two different versions of *The Virgin of the Rocks* both of which, at first glance, fit neatly into the mainstream of Marian devotion and yet secretly celebrate what the Church describes as the Johannite Heresy. The third painting is the most commonly reproduced work of art in the Western world, the painting known as *L'Ultima Cena*, or *The Last Supper*. This huge fresco covers an entire wall in the refectory of the Convent of Santa Maria della Grazie in Milan and portrays Jesus and the disciples having supper on the eve of his arrest. It is the most well known item of Christian iconography in the world and reproductions, both large and small decorate churches, chapels, schools, offices and private homes of Christians of every denomination. To the devout it is a reminder of the very first communion service and the belief that Jesus died for us as our saviour. Yet, when seen by an initiate, it teaches heresies that flatly contradict some of Christianity's most cherished doctrines.

The Virgin of the Rocks

There are two versions of the painting known as *The Virgin of the Rocks*, by Leonardo da Vinci. The first was commissioned by the confraternity of San Fancesco Grande in Milan as the centrepiece above the altar in one of the confraternity's chapels. The exact size was specified in the contract drawn up before work began, which also gave precise instructions for the positioning of the figures within it. The central figure of the Virgin is portrayed within a dark grotto, seated with her right arm and hand around the shoulder of a baby boy. Her left hand is outstretched protectively over the head of another small child seated in front of her and to her left. An angel sits slightly behind this child, looking adoringly at him. The angel, Uriel, is somewhat effeminate in appearance and, as Edgar Wind has written: 'Perhaps it should also be mentioned here that in alchemy the Hermaphrodite called *Rebis* represents the apex of transmutations; which accounts for his regular appearance in alchemical books, in Paracelsus, 'Trismosin' or 'Basil Valentinus.'[11] So Wind, citing the great alchemists of the late Middle Ages and the Renaissance, equates the angel Uriel with the highest form of initiate. The child with the Virgin's hand on his shoulder is kneeling with his hands clasped in a prayerful attitude looking at the other, who has his fingers raised in blessing. The angelic figure of Uriel is pointing directly at the figure of the baby beside the Virgin. This version now hangs in the Louvre Museum in Paris (see plate 22). The second painting now hangs in the National Gallery in London (see plate 23). King Francis I of France, who conquered Milan, invited Leonardo in 1515 to spend his declining years in France. The king was of the Rex Deus line and it was he who commissioned Leonardo to paint the second version of *The Virgin of the Rocks*. It is broadly speaking the same as the first painting with minor but, nonetheless, important differences of posture and emphasis.

When we first see these paintings most people assume, quite naturally, that the child with the Virgin's arm around his shoulders in such a natural, protective and maternal manner, is Jesus. To their surprise, Jesus appears to be praying to John the Baptist who in his turn appears to be blessing the Son of God. However, the details in the contract tell a very different story for it specifies that the child beside the Virgin is not Jesus but John the Baptist, while the smaller child beside the angel and giving the blessing, is Jesus. It is therefore reasonable to speculate that the priest responsible for drawing up the detailed and highly specific contract may have been a secret follower of the Johannite Heresy, despite his priestly status. Leonardo followed the contractual instructions to the letter and, as a direct result, the painting was wide open for misinterpretation on a grand scale. The paintings seemingly indicate that John the Baptist was of a higher degree of holiness and importance than Jesus. The only time the paintings would not be seen in this 'heretical' light was when a priest was present to explain it.

Some considerable time after the second painting was completed, this apparently heretical confusion over the identities of the children became clear, so steps were taken to clarify the matter. An unknown artist was commissioned to make additions to the work that now hangs in London; distinctive halos for each child were added and the traditional identifying symbol of a long-stemmed cross was given to the baby John the Baptist.

No one can be absolutely sure whether these two paintings are simply glorious examples of Renaissance art depicting the central principles of the Johannite Heresy or, at a more subtle level, yet more hidden references to the heresy of the holy twins: two depictions of the even more heretical concept of the two holy infants. If the latter is the case, and it may well be at one level, then it should be remembered that some forty years earlier this same heresy had been celebrated in Scotland, at Rosslyn Chapel (see Chapter 14).

L'Ultima Cena – The Last Supper

The vast fresco of *The Last Supper* occupies almost an entire wall in the rebuilt refectory of the Convent of Santa Maria della Grazie in Milan. It is a miracle that it has survived for over five hundred years, for the building was bombed in the Second World War and the painting itself has been discernibly deteriorating since its completion. Leonardo, for all his talents, had not been trained in fresco painting and adopted a technique that allowed him to work far more slowly than normal fresco work would have permitted. Unfortunately the means he adopted did not prove to be particularly stable or lasting. Over the centuries various attempts have been made to preserve the work and within the last few years a massive and effective restoration project has now been completed.

The ambivalence inherent in all truly great art is immediately apparent on first viewing *The Last Supper in situ* (see plate 25). The lower borders of the painting are at, or above, the shoulder level of the viewer and yet Leonardo's use of the art of perspective subtly distorts visual reality in a manner that is so inspired that the average viewer is not aware that he or she is intentionally being misled. The majority of the painting is well above eyelevel, yet the viewer is persuaded that his head is almost on a par with that of the central figure of Jesus. Furthermore, one is apparently looking down onto the surface of the dining table and yet, through an act of unperceived distortion, can see through the window at the rear of the supper-room and observe the horizon just below the midpoint of the windows. This window clearly shows that it is bright daylight outside. Yet this is supposed to represent 'the Last Supper' the ritual meal on the eve of Passover which only took place after dusk.

The figure of Jesus with his hands and arms outstretched, is the central figure of the painting and he is flanked on either side by two groups, each consisting of three disciples. Reading from the viewer's left to right are the figures of: Bartholomew, James the Just and Andrew. All three are looking intently toward Jesus. The next trio is dominated by the leaning figure of Peter, whose left hand rests upon the shoulder of John, the beloved disciple, whose head is bent towards Peter in a listening attitude while in front of both of them is the half-turned figure of Judas. Jesus in isolation holds centre stage. Next to him is Thomas, his twin brother, with upraised index finger of his right hand gesturing at Jesus angrily. Half in front of Thomas is James the Great, depicted almost as Jesus' double, and next, half-leaning over him and looking sorrowful is Philip. The last three disciples have Matthew and Thaddeus, facing away from Jesus, but all gesturing emphatically and vigorously in his direction in a disturbed manner, and the twelve are completed by Simon who is sitting end-on to the table facing towards Jesus but slightly averted in the direction of Thaddeus. There is obviously some form of dispute in progress and according to tradition it depicts the moment when Jesus has just said: "'One among you will betray me." They were very sad and began to say to him, one after another, "Surely, not I lord?" Jesus replied "The one who has dipped his hand into the bowl with me will betray me.'"[12]

Yet, paradoxically Judas, who supposedly betrayed Jesus is not within comfortable reaching distance of the bowl in front of Jesus. The question then arises: Was this the only subject at the Last Supper that could have caused the dispute depicted in the painting? I submit that there was another and that was the matter of who was to be in charge after Jesus had died, for this episode is given just as much prominence in the Gospel accounts of the Last Supper. I suggest that this dispute is the subject of the painting. Peter's almost secretive conversational pose, whispering in the ear of John, is counterbalanced by the appearance of his right hand appearing from behind Judas, clutching a knife pointing straight at James the Just. It is as if he is saying to John, 'No, it is not me who is to be the new leader, but him!' A truth that the Church considers as an extreme form of heresy; one that puts into question their claim to apostolic succession and supreme spiritual authority.

Leonardo's ability to make the smallest detail count is shown by the figure of Judas, clutching a well-filled leather purse in his right hand, who has just knocked over a container of salt that has spilled across the table. The differing hand gestures used by the disciples are also extremely important, but deserve a far more detailed discussion than I can give them in this work.

Most recent works have focused their attention on the figure of St John who, according to Baigent, Leigh and Lincoln in *The Holy Blood and the Holy Grail*, is not a man at all, but the figure of Mary Magdalene. This conclusion was accepted without question by Picknett and Prince in *The Templar Revelation*. Although this might be remotely possible, in my view it is highly unlikely. The most probable explanation for this distinctly effeminate figure is similar to that given for the equally ambivalent sexuality portrayed by the figure of the archangel Uriel in *The Virgin of the Rocks*. In esoteric tradition, the truly enlightened initiate becomes a Hermaphrodite, that unique balance between the primal Adam and the Eve of mankind's legendary origins. John, the 'Beloved Disciple' is widely accepted as the supreme Christian initiate to whom Jesus passed his secret teachings and, along with John the Baptist another biblical figure painted frequently by Leonardo, was revered by the Rex Deus families, the Knights Templar and the Cathars.

The Last Supper occupies virtually the entire expanse of the wall of the refectory of Santa Maria della Grazie. In a sort of entrance hall at the other end of the refectory and facing the painting of the Last Supper is another fresco, *The Crucifixion* by Giovanni Donato Montofano (see plate 24). This was completed before Leonardo started painting and he knew, therefore, the relative positions of both paintings and their subject matter. The theological bridge that unites the subject matter of both of them is the institution of the sacrament of Holy Communion. *The Last Supper* does show bread and wine, but the bread is ordinary leavened bread and none of it appears to be broken. The plates, rolls of bread and the wine glasses are placed in a highly formalised manner that bears no recognisable relationship to the diners at the table. Yet while this was an apparently ritualised and sacramental pattern that was acceptable to the Church hierarchy, I sense, instinctively, that something is going on here that would only be recognised by the initiated. Everything on the table is undisturbed, with the exception of the spill of salt near Judas' elbow. Wine glasses are there aplenty, yet there is nothing remotely resembling a chalice that would have been the obvious symbolic representation of the communion cup; the chalice used at the Last Supper and later, according to legend, by Joseph of Arimathea to collect Jesus' blood at the deposition from the Cross.

Jesus looks as if he is being remonstrated at by Thomas, James the Great and a worried Philip. The most likely dispute that could have provoked this animated discussion can be read in the Gospels and is over the future leadership after Jesus' death. Peter's denial of the role ascribed to him by the Church has been mentioned and the symbolism used to depict John tells us that he is to be the main carrier of the teachings revealed by Jesus. The twin-like figures of Jesus and James the Great are a direct reference to another heresy, that of the Holy Twins or the two Jesuses that are referred to in at least two other paintings by Leonardo. While all about him seems chaotic, the central figure of Jesus sits passively, with open arms, left hand facing upwards, right hand palm down.

Similar hand positions occur in another painting, Raphael's fresco known as *The School of Athens* in the Vatican. In this work Plato is depicted gesturing heavenwards with his palm up, while Aristotle is shown with his palm facing downwards towards the earth. It has been suggested that these gestures symbolise the balance of analytical and intuitive thought, the perfect blend of the temporal and the spiritual. A similar explanation is offered for the use of the same hand gestures by Sufi initiates of the Mevlevi Order when they perform their ritual 'dance', or turning. The whirling dervish turns on the same spot with his right hand held up in the air, palm upwards and his left hand extended, palm downwards. Their left foot never leaves the ground and the dervish is said to be 'at the still point of the turning world' – in perfect harmony and spiritual balance. Perhaps this may give us a clue to the position of Jesus as depicted in *The Last Supper*. He is the perfect point of stillness and calm amidst the turbulent gestures of his disciples; the perfect point of balance between the material and the spiritual word. This is yet another depiction of supreme enlightenment in which the higher and lower energies of heaven and earth are imperfect harmony. Moreover, if Jesus drew his arms upwards and brought them parallel to his chest, right hand above the left without altering the disposition of his fingers, he would be making the sign of the *Dieu Garde* which is an important sign within first degree initiation in Freemasonry.

CHAPTER 17

The Controversial Craft of Freemasonry

The secrecy of the craft of Freemasonry, allied to the paucity of records documenting its early years, makes the task of accurately tracing its true origins extremely difficult. This problem is exacerbated by the fact that while it is sometimes useful to refer to the fraternity as a worldwide brotherhood it is in reality a varied collection of differing orders and jurisdictions each practising their own rituals, which sometimes differ widely from one another. However, these seemingly disparate brotherhoods do appear to have a common root and the aims and objectives of every one of them display a startling similarity, and the manner of teaching within each is again pretty much the same.

The craft claims quite correctly to be a fraternity founded upon the principles of true brotherhood, charity and truth, one that aspires to attain standards of morality and spirituality taught by means of allegory and ritual. I mentioned in the chapter on Rosslyn Chapel a quotation by Gedricke, an eighteenth-century Masonic historian, in which he states that a true lodge is to be supported by three pillars each based on a foundation of Truth and Justice. The initiatory manner of teaching through allegory and ritual has strong parallels with the Rex Deus tradition from which it originates and the craft's purpose to help each member to perfect himself so that they can serve society at large carries strong echoes of the ethos of the Knights Templar and even earlier Egyptian initiatory principles. It also carries with it, strong echoes of the

Sons of Zadok, the Essenes whose purpose was to create an élite within the élite who would then act as an example to all of Israel so that Israel would become a 'light unto the Gentiles'.

The manner of instruction is simple, using the symbolism of the tools of the earlier Craftmasons, such as the square, rule, plumb line, mallet and chisels, the new initiate is encouraged to apply these tools and work on the rough stone of his own being. This allegorical system of moral improvement is intended to re-shape the candidate into the perfect ashlar of enlightenment so that he can build the Temple of God on earth in a spiritual form. The rituals describe in detail how these tools are to be used to knock off the rough edges of the 'stone' and create an improved and highly moral human being. They also used *momento mori* symbols of the mortality of man that were carved upon their gravestones to demonstrate their loyalty unto death. Thus the ongoing process of initiation into the degrees of Freemasonry replicates in different allegorical terms, the alchemical process of transmuting the base metal of humanity into the pure gold of spiritual enlightenment. Indeed the seventeenth degree is quite explicit about this analogy.[1]

Early Development

After the suppression of the Templar Order, the rapid disappearance of so many Knights was seemingly inexplicable until fairly recently. It now seems that as they fled they used a previously unknown and secret organisation as a vehicle for their escape. Describing this, the American writer John Robinson gives a plausible explanation for the secret rituals and greetings of the Freemasons and claims, credibly, that Freemasonry was formed as an escape route for Templar Knights fleeing from persecution.[2] His work tends to confirm the conclusion that there were the links between the Templar Order in Scotland and early Freemasonry. Indeed, the St Clairs of Roslin were senior members of the Rex Deus group and also the hereditary Grand Masters of all the hard and soft guilds in Scotland. They acted as judges of all disputes arising from guild activities at courts held at Kilwininng. It has been suggested that under the leadership of the St Clairs, suitable candidates from the operative craft guilds were selected and given instruction in the branches of sacred knowledge; subjects included science, geometry, history and philosophy.[3] As a result, Scotland, and Midlothian in particular, became a beacon of enlightenment. This new fraternity of speculative 'free' masons founded charitable institutions for the relief of poverty. Prince Michael of Albany claims that these were the first charitable foundations in Britain that were outside the direct and stultifying control of the Church.[4]

King James VI of Scotland was initiated as a speculative Freemason at the Lodge of Perth and Scone in 1601.[5] He later became King James I of England and needed political allies as a counterweight against the influence of the English aristocracy. He found these new allies among influential members of certain trade and craft guilds in England and introduced them to the idea of Freemasonry.[6] In Scotland, the hereditary Grand Mastership of the Masonic guilds remained in the Sinclair family until St Andrew's Day 1736 when the then hereditary Grand Master, yet another Sir William St Clair of Rosslyn, resigned his 'Hereditary Patronage and Protectorship of the Masonic Craft' to effect the erection of 'The Grand Lodge of Ancient, Free and Accepted Masons of Scotland'. Needless to say, he immediately became the first elected Grand Master in which position he served with distinction.

The almost impenetrable degree of secrecy that shrouds the early centuries of Freemasonry make it difficult to establish with any precision the full spectrum of esoteric influences that helped to form the fraternity. While circumstances obviously varied from country to country, nonetheless the traditions of Rex Deus and the Knights Templar formed the main impetus behind the foundation of the Order that developed in differing ways in the various countries where it took root. In Scotland it was, and has remained, particularly democratic and continues to admit working people in large numbers. In that country the tradition of preserving sacred knowledge through the use of ritual and allegory was already well established and was used as a basis for the development of further levels of considerable complexity and sophistication. This led eventually to the establishment of what later became known as Scottish Rite Freemasonry and the degrees known as 'The Royal Arch'. In true Scots democratic tradition, Scottish Rite Freemasonry was established using the fundamental principles first given form in the declaration of Arbroath in 1310.[7]

In Europe, Freemasonry developed an innate anti-clerical and anti-Catholic bias while keeping close ties with its founding brethren in Scotland. In the rite of Strict Observance, for example, it is recorded that speculative Masons from operative lodges of the French Compagnonnage visited the lodge in Aberdeen in 1361 and formally instituted a relationship that lasted for centuries. In France, as in Scotland, particular pains were taken to preserve the esoteric teaching as accurately as possible.

In England, on the other hand, where the Church of England was an integral part of the political Establishment, anti-clerical bias was not so much in evidence and, eventually, English Freemasonry became very much part of the Church/State Establishment. Despite this, one indication of the loyalty of seventeenth-century Masons to their Templar precursors can be found in the translation of Heinrich Cornelius Agrippa's *Of Occult Philosophy*, which was published in English in 1651. The original Latin version contained a phrase that reads 'the detestable heresy of the Templars'; in the English translation this became 'the detestable heresy of old churchmen'.

Freemasonry spread across the English Channel with English diplomats and then received a massive boost when the exiled Stuart King James II arrived in France accompanied by a large entourage.[8] The Masonic movements in France that derived from the Compagnonnage were thus considerably strengthened by the new Jacobite arrivals and Masonry began to spread throughout the continent.[9] The Masonic principles of fraternity, loyalty, democracy and public service influenced the creation of the lodges of the Carbonari in Italy which became the foundation of Italian nationalism.[10] In Germany there was close liaison between the new Freemasonic lodges and the Rosicrucians. In Spain, Freemasonry gave rise to another Order, the Alumbrados Illuminati. Meanwhile in France, the Stuart King's first port of call, the craft seemed to draw solely on Scottish exiles and their rivals implanted under the aegis of the Grand Lodge in London. The French people themselves, however, appeared to take little interest in an organisation that claimed descent from simple Craftmasons. That was soon to change dramatically due to the actions of one remarkable man.

Chevalier Ramsey

Andrew Michael Ramsey (1681–1743) was a graduate of Edinburgh University who became involved in the religious disputes that tore Scotland apart during the first ten years of the eighteenth century. In 1710 he fled to France, converted to Roman Catholicism and took a variety of posts under the patronage of the Duc de Château-Thierry before working for the Prince de Turenne.[11] In return for these services he was made a knight of the Order of St Lazarus, becoming thereby Chevalier Ramsey, a name remembered by all Masonic historians. Ramsey travelled to Rome in 1724 to act as tutor to Prince Edward Charles Stuart and to aid his efforts to regain the British throne. Returning to Paris, Ramsey was now deemed to have authority and credibility of the highest order, not only because of his university degree, but also as tutor to Bonnie Prince Charlie, his one-time membership of the Royal Society and his position as Grand Chancellor of the Paris Grand Lodge. He announced to the waiting world that far from having its origins among the unlettered masons of the medieval era, Freemasonry was founded by a consortorium of the kings, princes, knights and nobility of the crusades.

In a speech delivered at the Masonic Lodge of St Thomas in Paris on 21st March 1737, Ramsay's first words were: 'Our ancestors, the Crusaders, gathered together from all parts of Christendom in the Holy Land, desired thus to reunite into one sole Fraternity the individuals of all nations…'[12]

This able Scots orator was quite open about the role of the Eternal Feminine and its connection to the fraternity and mentioned the goddesses Isis and Minerva by name. He claimed that the original members of the brotherhood were not simple workers in stone, but men of nobility who had vowed to rebuild the Temple of God on earth in the Holy Land. He went on to state that lodges were established all over Europe when the Crusaders returned home, but that these early lodges were neglected in all countries save one, Scotland. There the Lord Steward of Scotland became the first Grand Master of the Lodge at Kilwinning in 1286.[13] Thus, according to Ramsey, Scotland was the only country that could legitimately claim to have maintained an unbroken line of continuation of Freemasonry from the time of the Crusades until the present.[14]

Ramsey's oration was published in a journal called the *Almanac des Cocus* in 1741. The French had originally been extremely reluctant to join an organisation that appeared to derive from manual workers such as the Craftmasons, but a fraternity that was the true heir of the medieval chivalric orders, now that was a very different matter. A tidal wave of Masonic enthusiasm swept through France attracting everyone with any pretensions to chivalry, romance and spiritual brotherhood.[15] Ramsey's clear statement of Freemasonry's Scottish roots resulted in one French Masonic system that had been heavily influenced by the Stuarts, gaining the appropriate name of 'Scottish Rite Freemasonry'.[16] Scottish Masonic traditions led to the creation of the Royal Arch and Rosicrucian degrees of American Freemasonry and tend to explain the high moral force and spiritual insight of their initiates. Their lasting legacy to the world was the Constitution of the United States of America which has become the legal foundation for the treasured Western principles of freedom, democracy and the rights of man.[17]

Ritual links with the True Founders

There is a certain degree of correspondence between the Rex Deus oath of secrecy and certain Masonic oaths. The Rex Deus oath of swearing secrecy 'lest my tongue be cut out' has a direct correlation with the oath of secrecy taken within the first degree of Freemasonry which, if breached, incurs the penalty of 'my tongue torn out by the root'. A second part of the Rex Deus oath incurs the penalty of 'lest my heart be torn or cut out of my chest' and, in the Masonic second degree, we read 'under no less a penalty than to have my left breast cut open, my heart torn there from…'. Another replication can be found: the Rex Deus threat 'lest my eyes be plucked out' occurs in the ritual of the degree of 'The Knight of the White Eagle'.[18]

The English Masonic authors Knight and Lomas did considerable research into Masonic ritual that has long since fallen into disuse. In the library of an earlier Masonic scholar, Dimitrije Mitronovic who lived and worked in London in the early part of the twentieth century, they were able to establish links between certain Masonic rituals, Rex Deus history and the Knights Templar. Many of these rituals had been purged at a time when English Freemasonry and the Establishment of which it was an integral part wished to shed all trace of the craft's earlier links with the Stuart cause. Mitronovic's library contained one book by J S Ward, *Freemasonry and the Ancient Gods,* and recorded in this rare work is the ritual for the fourth degree, that of the 'Secret Master'. This degree is concerned with mourning someone who remains anonymous.[19] In the ceremony for this degree, the lodge is hung with black and is lit by the light of eighty-one candles, while the jewel for the degree is inscribed with a simple 'Z' and is held to represent Zadok. This ritual commemorates the time when building work on the Temple in Jerusalem was brought to a halt as the result of a tragedy. Knight and Lomas claim that the Zadok to which the ritual refers has at least two levels of meaning: firstly to Zadok the high priest at Solomon's Temple and secondly to 'the Zadok', the teacher of Righteousness namely James the Just, the brother of Jesus.

From the Dead Sea Scrolls we discover that a group of esotericists known as 'the sons of Zadok' played a significant, if not the major part in the collection of these scrolls. They were reputedly the hereditary descendants of the original Zadok of Solomon's Temple and were also known as 'the Righteous Seed' or 'the Sons of the Dawn'. These titles reinforce the concept of hereditary transmission of holiness so central to Judaic belief at that time and also to the religious tradition that spiritual resurrection to a new life always took place at dawn by the light of the morning star. In Freemasonry today, in the third degree, candidates are ritually resurrected, or 'raised extended' by the light of the morning star.[20]

Freemasonic tradition has another direct parallel with Rex Deus history in that Hiram Abif was killed by a blow to the temple immediately prior to the completion of Solomon's Temple. About one thousand years later, James the Just was murdered by being thrown down from the Temple ramparts and killed by a blow to the temple delivered by a fuller's club. James the Just was very popular and work on the Temple came to an abrupt halt as a mark of respect. Knight and Lomas were drawn to the inescapable conclusion that the long-standing and revered traditions in Freemasonry in respect of the death of Hiram Abif are allegorical accounts of the death of James the brother of Jesus. If this is so, and it is highly plausible, whenever Freemasons ritually re-enact the death of Hiram Abif, they are in fact celebrating not only the legendary origins of their craft, but also its true source, the families of Rex Deus.[21]

Another lost or suppressed degree, that of the 'Perfect Master', commemorates the discovery and reburial of the corpse of Hiram Abif. The ritual states that Solomon ordered Adoniram to build a tomb for the Master Hiram Abif that was completed in nine days. The tomb took the form of an obelisk of black and white marble. For this ritual the lodge is hung in green and lit by sixteen candles and the tomb is set between two pillars supporting a square lintel engraved with the letter 'J'. In this manner the parallels between the demise of Hiram and James the Just are made crystal clear. The reference within Rosslyn Chapel to the rebuilding of the Temple by Zerubabel after the Babylonian exile, is commemorated by the fifteenth degree, that of 'the Knight of the Sword and the Knight of the East'. This degree celebrates the rebuilding of the Temple and for this seventy candles illuminate the lodge, one for each year of the Babylonian captivity.[22]

Yet another degree, that of 'the Knight of the East and West', claims that it was first created during the crusades in 1118, when eleven knights took vows of secrecy, friendship and discretion in front of the patriarch of

Jerusalem. When Knight and Lomas discovered this they were surprised to find that eleven knights were mentioned and not merely the nine who founded the Knights Templar. The additional two were Count Foulk D'Anjou and Count Hughes I of Champagne. The officer presiding over the enactment of this rite is addressed as the 'Most Equitable Sovereign Prince Master' who is aided and supported by the 'High Priest'. The two Masonic authors deduced that 'the most Equitable Sovereign Master' was based on King Baudouin II of Jerusalem and I would suggest that the High Priest was originally the patriarch of Jerusalem, the cousin of Bernard of Clairvaux. The ritual itself features a large bible with seven seals and a floor cloth showing a white bearded man with a golden girdle around his waist. The man has a halo and a two-edged sword issuing from his mouth. He is surrounded by seven candlesticks, thus the sacred principle of sevenfoldedness that pervades the symbolism of the Revelation of St John and Templar tradition is made explicit.[23]

To reinforce my earlier statement that Freemasonry was created as an act of deliberate policy by Rex Deus, we need to consider stronger indications than those mentioned above. Knight and Lomas found yet another suppressed ritual that makes this explicit. In the degree of 'the Grand Master' the evidence for a Rex Deus foundation is frankly overwhelming. It describes the appalling barbarity of the destruction of Herod's Temple in Jerusalem by the Romans in 70 CE. The grief of the brethren is described and also their intention to found yet another temple, which, unlike its predecessors, would be a spiritual temple. The ritual describes how the brethren who survived the slaughter divided themselves into a number of lodges before scattering throughout the known world. It states that one of these lodges came to Scotland and became based at Kilwinning. This lodge was entrusted with the records of their Order and built an abbey there in 1140 to house them.[24] In this manner, Masonic ritual records the outline of the Rex Deus story. Thus we have one degree commemorating the Rex Deus diaspora and another celebrating the foundation of the Knights Templar.

The multifaceted and complex symbolism of the worldwide brotherhood of Freemasonry hides its Rex Deus and Templar secrets in a manner that is analogous to that used by Earl William St Clair encoding his arcane secrets among the multiplicity of carvings within Rosslyn Chapel. The plain message of heresy is hidden, yet explicitly displayed, unnoticed by all except the initiates.[25] The question arises: Are these the only hiding places used by the secretive families to encode their message in a manner that is still accessible to modern man?

Epilogue

The use of symbolism to express mankind's sense of the sacred and the numinous is as old as humanity itself. With the rise of Christianity it began to be expressed in a highly formalised and recognisable manner right across Christian Europe. However, despite the Church's repressive attitude, other belief systems persisted and they, in their turn, began to encode symbolic references to their 'heretical' beliefs within the officially sanctioned system devised by the hierarchy. In a brief work such as this, it has only been possible to describe the broad outlines of this complex and multi-layered process and indicate some of the principal sites where hidden symbolism can be detected. The interpretations I have given are necessarily brief and only begin to scratch the surface of a profound and complex subject.

Harold Bayley, an American author and researcher, wrote a fascinating two-volume book, *The Lost Language of Symbolism*, dedicated entirely to the heretical messages encoded in the watermarks used by medieval paper makers. For example, the company that manufactures bank notes for the Bank of England was founded by a Cathar family who fled to England to escape the unwelcome attentions of the Inquisition[1] and my good friend and colleague Margaret Starbird, describes how heretical watermarks were devised by the Cathars of the Languedoc to act as a system of transmission of their forbidden faith. They include numerous allusions to the Holy Grail and the *sang real*.[2] Harold Bayley states that despite the Albigensian Crusade and the sixty years of suffering imposed by the Inquisition, the Cathar heresy survived for several centuries, spreading right across Europe as the survivors fled from the warm embrace of the stake and sought refuge in northern Italy, France, Holland and England.[3] The concept of heresy encoded within watermarks on paper raises the surreal notion of official documents issued by the papacy, dogmatic statements of belief, papal bulls and encyclicals, being written and distributed on paper encoded secretly with a different message, one that flatly contradicts the Church's official pronouncements recorded upon them. The mind boggles.

The hidden streams of spirituality did not cease their efforts with the dawn of the Renaissance, the coming of the Enlightenment or the advent of the twentieth century; they still continued their efforts to transmit their initiatory message unabated. I have mentioned the beautiful stained-glass windows erected at Rosslyn Chapel during the later years of the Victorian era. They were not an aberration, but formed part of a countrywide campaign instituted by British Freemasons that, under the guise of restoration, made significant additions to the hidden symbolism encoded in many churches and cathedrals throughout Britain. Nor was relatively modern heretical activity restricted to the British Isles, the French department of the Languedoc was once more to be the centre of spiritually subversive activity, but this time as the result of the bizarre and inexplicable antics of an obscure Roman Catholic priest.

In the last decade of the nineteenth century, a brilliant young Roman Catholic priest, Bérenger Saunière committed some misdemeanour and, as a result, was banished to the impoverished and unimportant parish of Rennes-le-Château. This small and insignificant hilltop village in the Languedoc possessed neither running water nor even a proper access road. The only way in or out of the village was by the dirt track that wound its weary way up the steep hill from the nearby town of Couiza. Saunière was as impoverished as his parishioners and his miserly stipend is a matter of record. In 1891, he even had to borrow a small sum of money from a nearby priest, his confidant and mentor, the Abbé Boudet of Rennes-les-Bains, in order to begin a modest restoration of the extremely dilapidated parish church.

The parish records disclose that at this time, between 1885 and 1891, Saunière's stipend amounted to the equivalent of a mere £6 sterling per annum. Yet those same records also reveal that by 1894, his annual outlay on postage considerably exceeded his stipend. It has been estimated that between 1896 and his death in 1917 this seemingly poor parish priest spent the almost unbelievable sum of 200,000 gold francs which would equate with several million pounds at today's values.[4] A considerable proportion of this was spent on the restoration and redecoration of the church, but Saunière also paid for the construction of a modern road to improve access to the village and defrayed the costs of installing running water for the benefit of the entire community. He built a substantial house, the Villa Bethania and a strange tower, the Tour Magdala, in which he housed his considerable library. For his own comfort and amusement he built an orangery alongside the Tour Magdala and installed a small zoo in the garden of the Villa Bethania. The villagers were far from neglected for, in addition to the new water supply and the improved road, he also gave them sumptuous banquets. In fact his life became more like that of an oriental potentate than the austere regime usually expected of a rural parish priest.

His free-spending lifestyle did not go unnoticed and after several unsuccessful attempts to discover the source of Saunière's wealth, the local bishop suspended him. Saunière was not officially reinstated until his death. The parish priest's death was as unexpected and mysterious as his life and, when his will was read, it was discovered that he had died penniless, for he had transferred all his money to his housekeeper, Marie Dernarnaud, some time before his demise. All these events might well have passed unnoticed by the world at large had the English author and TV presenter Henry Lincoln not chosen to spend his holiday in France in the late 1960s.

Henry stumbled upon the mystery when reading a book, *Le Trésor Maudit* by the French author Gérard de Sède. Intrigued he started to investigate. The result was a television programme, *The Lost Treasure of Jerusalem*, broadcast by the BBC in 1972 as part of the *Chronicle* series. The story told was fascinating in the extreme and, as Henry is one of the world's most accomplished storytellers, the programme was an astounding success. Another followed in 1974, *The Priest, the Painter and*

Devil. By now the story had grown to epic proportions, for explanations for the possible sources of Saunière's wealth included such possibilities as the treasure of the Knights Templar, the Cathar treasure, blackmail and the heinous ecclesiastical crime of selling 'indulgences'.

Five years later yet another TV programme hit the screens in Britain, *The Shadow of the Templars* was broadcast in 1979. The story was elaborated into a book that was published in 1981, written by Henry in collaboration with Michael Baigent and Richard Leigh, *The Holy Blood and the Holy Grail*. The book's publication caused an uproar and was greeted with comments such as 'a brilliant piece of detective work' or 'a book that will infuriate many ecclesiastical authorities' and, more commonly, as simply 'blasphemous'. It went straight onto the bestseller list and was rapidly translated into many languages.

Much of the substance of *The Holy Blood and the Holy Grail* has now been shown to be highly flawed. The authors were fed false information and a fantasy deliberately created by a certain Philippe de Cherisey and Pierre Plantard. This piece of imaginative fabrication had been cleverly interwoven with some historically valid facts that, in truth, were irrelevant to the story of Bérenger Saunière. Nonetheless, the once obscure hilltop village of Rennes-le-Château is now firmly on the map for the small army of tourists who traverse Europe every year in search of the arcane and the esoteric. Over twenty thousand people a year visit the village and the foreign invasion has ensured that the population is now leavened with a considerable proportion of English, Spanish and German residents whose obsessional interest in the mystery, real or imagined, has drawn them there. The fact is that even when all the obfuscation, fantasy and exaggeration are stripped from the story, two real mysteries still remain, 'Where did Bérenger Saunière obtain the vast sums of money that he disbursed?' and, perhaps more importantly from our point of view, 'What was he trying to tell us with the strange symbolism that abounds in Rennes-le-Château?'

The symbolism at Rennes-le-Château is not restricted to the church, the sculptures or the paintings; it also includes the names of the buildings and their biblical references. The Tour Magdala, for example, (see plate 26) bears a startling resemblance to the tarot trump known as the Tower. More importantly it is, of course, a direct reference to Mary Magdalene. The Villa Bethania also echoes the same theme, but this time with overtones of Bernard of Clairvaux's instruction to his followers to swear 'allegiance to the House of Bethany', yet another allusion to Mary of Magdala. The church is dedicated to the Magdalene but it is important to note that this dedication was made centuries before Saunière's arrival. A large statue of Mary Magdalene can be found within the church, complete with alabaster jar and human skull (see plate 28) and she is featured again in the painting on the main altar (see plate 27).

The entrance to the church is surmounted by the strange inscription *Terribilis est locus iste*, which Henry Lincoln translated as 'this place is terrible'. My own translation is 'this place is awesome'. Immediately on entering, there is a holy water stoup on your left supported by the strange demonic figure of Asmodeus, the legendary guardian of the secrets of King Solomon's Temple. Above it is a complex statue, four ladies in flowing robes each making one of the four parts of the sign of the cross. Beneath them is the inscription in French that translates to 'in this sign you will conquer'. However, it has also been suggested that these ladies, while making the sign of the cross, are also making signs of considerable importance to initiates of the first degree of Freemasonry, which include the sign of fidelity and signs for 'having one's throat cut' and being dis-emboweled. However, this may be coincidence of course, although it has been alleged that Bérenger Saunière was indeed a Freemason.

The interior of the church is decorated with garish colours that come as a surprise having seen its rather plain exterior. The statue of the Magdalene is accompanied by similar brightly coloured statues of St Anthony of Padua and of St Roche, a saint whose image is extremely common throughout the Languedoc and Provence. In common with most Roman Catholic churches, the one at Rennes-le-Château contains panels depicting the stations of the Cross, the main difference here is their bizarre colouration. However, the panel showing the fourteenth station is worthy of further study. It shows the body of Jesus being carried near a tomb in a scene that is set by moonlight. Is Saunière trying to imply that Jesus was buried many hours later than the Gospel accounts would indicate? Or, is he subtly confirming the story recounted in 'The Lost Gospel according to St Peter' which tells that the guards reported, 'And as they declared what things they had seen, again they see three men come forth from the tomb, and two of them supporting one ...'[5] Is it possible that this station of the Cross confirms this account and thus symbolises the old tradition that states that Jesus survived the Crucifixion?

Flanking the main altar are two statues: the one on the left of the altar when viewed from the nave is of Joseph with a child in his arms (see plate 29); on the opposite side is a statue of the Madonna and child (see plate 30). Depictions of Joseph are rare; those showing Joseph and Jesus together are rarer still. These two images are capable of several interpretations depending entirely on the insight and beliefs of the person who is viewing them. Firstly, according to Church teaching, they undoubtedly represent both parents of the Holy Family with the infant Jesus. However, from another perspective, the question arises: Do they depict the heresy of the Holy Twins? Do they also represent the ancestors of the Desposyni; Jesus with one of his children and his wife, Mary Magdalene with the other? None of these interpretations are mutually exclusive. Like all the other places that abound with sacred symbolism that is capable of interpretation at so many levels, Rennes-le-Château remains a challenge, a place of puzzlement and wonder.

Discoveries at Amiens

Over the last few decades the French government has spent millions cleaning up the exteriors of some of its finest cathedrals and at Chartres, Notre Dame de Paris and Amiens this process is still underway. When cleaning the west front of Amiens Cathedral, traces of the original medieval colouration was found and recorded. This highly professional approach was then used by an unnamed, creative genius with an innate talent for modern technology. Visit Amiens between 15th June and 30th September and every evening at dusk a crowd gathers in respectful and expectant silence. As night falls, the interior of the church is lit to show off the wondrous Great Rose window on the west front. Then, through the miracle of modern technology, small booths equipped with lasers perform their silent miracle and the highly detailed carvings that adorn the west front are illuminated individually in the precise colours they bore in the Middle Ages. The show lasts about an hour. It is totally free and, despite the fact that I have seen it three times, I am still in awe at it.

In this literate and technologically advanced century we are used to being constantly bombarded with coloured images through the medium of television, yet the impact of this demonstration is mind-blowing. What must have been the effect of these superb examples of church symbolism on medieval man? The people at that time were largely illiterate and did not travel very far, yet every church and each of the great cathedrals was a riot of brilliantly coloured, superb carvings. The impact must have been enormous and, in this instance at least, I doubt if familiarity bred contempt. No wonder the church had such a grip on its flock.

The Wheel Comes Full Circle.

I first came into contact with a member of the Rex Deus families a little over ten years ago and have spent much of the intervening time researching, trying to establish the truth or falsehood of the information he gave me. This search soon became inextricably mixed with my main interest, Templar history. I first saw the laser-light show at Amiens some three years ago when en route to Italy to give a talk on 'The Myth and Reality of the Knights Templar' to colleagues in Varese in northern Italy. The venue was the Castello Lombardo, a name which meant nothing to me at first. This fifteenth-century castle was, until fairly recently, part of the extensive estates of the Visconti family. The day before the talk I visited a local church at Sacre Monte and there spied a coat of arms carved on the outer wall of the building. It displayed obvious Rex Deus symbolism and my interest was immediately aroused. Inside the church was one of the

CRACKING THE SYMBOL CODE

largest and most vulgarly decorated Black Madonnas I have ever seen. That was not all; a ceiling in a side chapel was adorned with some of the most sublimely painted heretical symbolism I have ever laid eyes on. It was all there, the Magdalene in all her glory, complete with child. Lilies all over the place so that, to the initiated, the story of the dynasty of Jesus was plain to see but to the average lay person, there was simply a delightful depiction of scenes from the Gospel stories.

When I gave my talk, a colleague took a photograph that shows this geriatric old scribe outlined against the background of a large painted coat of arms of the Visconti family depicting a serpent with a baby in its mouth, the perennial sign of sacred gnosis. Yet, according to the published version of Visconti family traditions, the designs on their coat of arms was stolen from one on a shield carried by a Saracen warrior killed by one of their ancestors during the crusades. At that time in the Holy Land, the laws of Islam strictly forbade all depictions of both human and animal forms. The story is a classic in the art of dissembling and camouflage. Heretical deception has not gone away, it is still all around us. It can be found in the iconography of parish churches, cathedrals and in art galleries. In churches built on sites of ancient sacred significance. It is not there simply to be explained, but to be experienced for its transformative magic is as potent today as when it was first created.

This important point was made obvious to me in a very pleasing manner. Readers who had enjoyed one of my previous works, *Rosslyn: Guardian of the Secrets of the Holy Grail*, wrote and told me of the trans-formative experiences they had enjoyed when they recreated the pilgrimage of initiation described in that work. Europe abounds with sacred sites of great beauty, all plentifully adorned with sacred symbolism that was created to instruct, inform, inspire and transform all who sought its magic. To quote the Master – 'Seek and Ye shall find. Knock and it shall be opened unto you.'

Source Notes

Section 1

1 Bronowski, Jacob, *The Ascent of Man*, p 31
2 Clark, Kenneth, *Civilisation*, p 3
3 Baldock, John, *The Elements of Christian Symbolism*, p 11
4 Wilson, Colin, *The Occult*, p 38
5 Wilson, Colin *The Occult*, p 73

Chapter 1

1 Wilson, Colin, *The Occult*, p 35
2 Bronowski, Jacob, *The Ascent of Man*, p 50
3 Bronowski, Jacob, *The Ascent of Man*, p 54
4 Eliade, Mircea, *Shamanism*, p 19
5 Devereux, Paul, *Places of Power*, p 11
6 Baring, Anne & Cashford, Jules, *The Myth of the Goddess*, p 3
7 Baring, Anne & Cashford, Jules, *The Myth of the Goddess*, p 6
8 Baring, Anne & Cashford, Jules, *The Myth of the Goddess*, p 6
9 Campbell, Prof. Joseph, *The Way of Animal Powers*, p 68
10 Baring, Anne & Cashford, Jules, *The Myth of the Goddess*, p 42
11 Ravenscroft & Wallace-Murphy, *The Mark of the Beast*, p 43
12 Ravenscroft & Wallace-Murphy, *The Mark of the Beast*, p 44
13 Jaynes, Julian, *The Origin of Consciousness in the Breakdown of the Bicameral Mind*, pp 83–94
14 Baring, Anne & Cashford, Jules, *The Myth of the Goddess*, p 43
15 Baring, Anne & Cashford, Jules, *The Myth of the Goddess*, pp 176–77

Chapter 2

1 West, John Anthony, *Serpent in the Sky*, p 1
2 Rohl, David, *Legend – the Genesis of Civilization*, p 310
3 Rice, M, *Egypt's Making: The Origins of Ancient Egypt 5000-2000 BC*, p 33
4 Kantor, H J, 'The Relative Chronology of Egypt and its Foreign Correlations Before the Late Bronze Age' published in *Chronologies in Old World Archaeology*; p 6
5 Rohl, David, *Legend – The Genesis of Civilization*, p 316
6 Derry, D E, *The Dynastic Race in Egypt*, pp 80–5
7 Frankfort, H, *Kingship of the Gods*, p 101
8 Weighall, A E P, *Travels in the Upper Egyptian Desert*
9 Winkler H, *Rock Drawings of Southern Upper Egypt*
10 Rohl, David, *Legend – The Genesis of Civilization*, p 274
11 Rohl, David, *Legend – The Genesis of Civilization*, p 316
12 Rohl, David, *Legend – The Genesis of Civilization*, p 265
13 Bauval, Robert & Hancock, Graham, *Keeper of Genesis*, p 203
14 Bauval, Robert & Hancock, Graham, *Keeper of Genesis*, p 193
15 Goyon, G: *Le Secret des Batisseurs des Grandes Pyramides: Kheops*
16 Bauval, Robert & Hancock, Graham, *Keeper of Genesis*, p 154.
17 Aristotle, *De Caelo II*
18 Proclus Diodachus (5th cent. AD) *Commentaries on the Timaeus*
19 Bauval, Robert & Hancock, Graham, *Keeper of Genesis*, p 154
20 Wilson, Colin, *From Atlantis to the Sphinx*, p 21
21 Schwaller de Lubicz, R A, *Le Temple de l'Homme*, also cited by Robert and Deborah Lawlor in their introduction to

Schwaller de Lubicz's *Symbol and the Symbolic*, p 8

22 Bauval, Robert & Hancock, Graham, *Keeper of Genesis*, p 228

23 Reymond, E A E, *Mythical Origins of the Egyptian Temple* p 273

24 VandenBroeck, André, *Al-Kemi*

25 Wilson, Colin, *From Atlantis to the Sphinx*, p 32

26 The Lawlors' Introduction to Schwaller de Lubicz's, *Symbol and the Symbolic*, p 9

27 Schwaller de Lubicz, René, *Sacred Science*, p 120

28 Wilson, Colin, *From Atlantis to the Sphinx*, p14

29 Pauwels, Louis and Bergier, Jacques, *The Dawn of Magic*, p 247

30 Rohl, David, *Legend the Genesis of Civilization*, p 381

31 Rohl, David, *Legend the Genesis of Civilization*, p 381

32 Schwaller de Lubicz, R A, *Sacred Science*, p 83

33 Wilson, Colin, *From Atlantis to the Sphinx*, p 81

34 Bauval, Robert & Gilbert, Adrian, *The Orion Mystery*, p 58

35 Edwards, I E S, *The Pyramids of Egypt*, p 150

36 Bauval, Robert & Gilbert, Adrian, *The Orion*, p 63.

37 Bauval, Robert & Gilbert, Adrian, *The Orion Mystery*, p 63

38 Edwards, I E S, *The Pyramids of Egypt*, p 151

39 Faulkner, R O, *The Ancient Egyptian Pyramid Texts*, p v

Chapter 3

1 Baldock, John, *The Elements of Christian Symbolism*, p 12

2 Baldock, John, *The Elements of Christian Symbolism*, p 13–14

3 Baldock, John, *The Elements of Christian Symbolism*, p 14

4 Epstein, I, *Judaism*, p 83

5 Lane Fox, Robin, *The Unauthorised Version*, Penguin, p 53

6 Cohn-Sherbok, Dan, *A Concise Encyclopedia of Judaism*, pp 43–4

7 Cantor, Norman, *The Sacred Chain*, p 29

8 Genesis, Ch 20, v 12

9 Rachi – *Pentatuque selon Rachi, La Genèse*, p 251

10 Genesis, Ch 11, v 27

11 Genesis, Ch 11, v 29

12 Genesis Ch 17, v 5 & v 15

13 Genesis, Ch 17, v 4

14 *Sepher Hajashar*, Ch 26

15 Genesis. Ch 21, v 21

16 Genesis Ch 12, v 15

17 'Have you seen the old man and woman who brought a foundling from the street and now claim him as their son?' The Babylonian Talmud, 1952.

18 The Koran, (The Prophets) Sura 21. 72 also cited by Osman, Ahmed, *Out of Egypt*, p 12

19 Genesis Ch 14, v 19

20 The term is used repeatedly by both characters in Genesis Ch 14

21 Freud, S, *Moses and Monotheism*

22 Sellin, E, *Moses and His Significance for Israelite-Jewish History*

23 Genesis Ch 17, v 10

24 *Encyclopaedia Brittannica*, 1956, Vol. 5, p 721P

25 Genesis, Ch 22, v 2

26 Genesis Ch 22, v 18

27 Exodus, Ch 2, vs 1–10

28 Freud, S, *Moses and Monotheism*

29 Sabbah, M & R, *Les Secrets de L'Exode*

30 Sabbah, M & R, *Les Secrets de L'Exode*

31 Sabbah, M & R, *Les Secrets de L'Exode*, p 6 & Freud, *Moses and Monotheism,* pp 96 & 123 (French edition)

32 The Journal *Imago*, 1, 1912, pp 346–7

33 Feather, R, *The Copper Scroll Decoded*, p 34 also confirmed by Joseph Popper-Linkeus *in Der Sohn des Konigs von Egypten. Phantasieen eines Realisten*, Carl Resiner, 1899.

34 Cotterell, M, *The Tutenkhamun Prophecies*, Headline, p 335

35 Freud, S, *Moses and Monotheism*

36 Osman, Ahmed, *Moses, Pharoah of Egypt*

37 Freud S, *Moses and Monotheism*

38 Cited by Feather, R, *The Copper Scroll Decoded*, p 36

39 Deuteronomy Ch 5, vs 6–9

40 Petrie, F, *The Religion of Ancient Egypt*

41 Sabbah, M & R, *Les Secrets de L'Exode*, p 99

42 Osman, Ahmed, *Moses, Pharoah of Egypt*, pp 172–3

43 Faulkner, R O, *The Ancient Egyptian Book of the Dead*, p 29

44 Exodus, Ch 20, vs 13, 15, 16

45 Psalms, Psalm 104, v 24

46 Geddes & Grosset, *Ancient Egypt Myth and History*, p 268

47 D'Olivet A F (1768–1825), *La Langue Hébraïque Restituée*

48 Sabbah, M & R, *Les Secrets de l'Exode*

49 Sabbah, M & R, *Les Secrets de l'Exode*

50 Sabbah, M & R, *Les Secrets de l'Exode*

51 Exodus, Ch 13, vs 21–22

52 Exodus Ch 33, vs 9–11

53 Psalm 99, v 7

54 Allegro, J M, *The Dead Sea Scrolls and the Christian Myth*, p 173

55 Ecclesiasticus Ch 24, v 4

56 Allegro, J M, *The Dead Sea Scrolls and the Christian Myth*, p 174.

57 The Wisdom of Solomon, Ch 10, v 17

58 Proverbs Ch 9, v 1

59 Armstrong, K, *A History of God*, p 82

60 Ussishkin, D, 'King Solomon's Palaces', *Biblical Archaeologist* 35, 1973

61 1 Kings, Ch 6, v 19

62 1 Kings Ch 6, v 26

63 2 Chronicles, Ch 3, vs 15–17.

64 1 Kings, Ch 4, vs 29–30

65 2 Chronicles Ch 1, v 10

66 Aristobulus, Fragment 5 (cited in Eusebius, *Prneparatio Evangelica* 13.12.11

67 Armstrong, K, *A History of God*, p 79

68 Eisenman, Robert, *James the Brother of Jesus*, p 133

69 Ezekiel, Ch 18, vs 17–21

70 Zohar 59b on "Noah"

Chapter 4

1 The Gospel According to St Luke, Ch 2, vs 1–5

2 The Gospel According to St Matthew, Ch 1, v 18

3 The Gospel According to St Luke, Ch 2, v 15

4 The Gospel According to St Matthew, Ch 2, v 11

5 The Gospel According to St Matthew, Ch 2, v 13

6 The Gospel According to St Matthew, Ch 2, v 16

7 The Gospel According to St Matthew, Ch 2, v 14

8 The Gospel According to St Luke, Ch 2, v 47

9 The Gospel According to St Matthew, Ch 3, v 17

10 Matthew Ch 5, v 43; Ch 19, v 19; Ch 22, v 39: Mark Ch 12, v 31; & Luke Ch 10, v 27

11 Paul's Epistle to the Romans Ch 13, v 9; Paul's Epistle to the Galatians, Ch 5, v 14; & the Epistle of James, Ch 2, v 8

12 The Gospel According to St Matthew, Ch 16, vs 18 & 19

13 The Gospel According to St Matthew, Ch 21, vs 8–13; The Gospel According to St Mark Ch 11, vs 8–17; The Gospel According to St Luke, Ch 19, vs 36–46 and (omitting the Temple incident) the Gospel According to St John, Ch 11, vs 11–19

14 The Gospel According to St Matthew, Ch 26, vs 26–28, also in Mark, Ch 14, vs 22–24 & Luke, Ch 22, vs 19 & 20

15 The Gospel According to St Matthew, Ch 26, vs 51–68; Mark Ch 14, vs 46–65; Ch 22, vs 54 & 66; & John Ch 18, vs 12–24

16 The Gospel of Matthew, Ch 27, vs 11–26; Mark Ch 15, vs 1–15; Luke Ch 23, vs 1–25

17 Johnson, Paul, *A History of Christianity*, p 10

18 Strabo, *Geographica*, 16. 2. 46

19 Richardson, Peter, *Herod, King of the Jews and Friend of the Romans,* pp 184–5

20 Josephus, *War,* Book 1. 4. 22 & *Antiquities* 16, 1, 47

21 Josephus, *War* 1. 4. 24 & *Antiquities* 16. 1. 47

22 Josephus, *Antiquities*, 15. 2. 59–65

23 Macrobius, *Saturnalia*, 2.4.1

24 Josephus, *War*, 1. 6. 48–55 & *Antiquities* 17. 1. 49–67

25 Gospel according to St Matthew, Ch 1, v 22

26 Josephus, *Antiquities*, book XVIII, Ch 1,

vs 2–6

27 Armstrong, Karen, *A History of Jerusalem*, p 121

28 Josephus, *Antiquities*, Book XVIII, Ch 1, v 5

29 Josephus, *Antiquities*, Book xviii, v 6

30 Epstein, I, *Judaism*, p 112

31 Johnson, Paul, *A History of Christianity*, pp 15–16

32 Josephus, *Antiquities*, Book xviii, v 6

33 Epstein, I, *Judaism*, p 105

34 Johnson, Paul, *A History of Christianity*, p 15

35 Vermes, *Jesus the Jew*, p 79

36 Armstrong, Karen, *A History of Jerusalem*, p 116

37 Eisenman, Robert, *James the Brother of Jesus*, p 200

38 Eisenman, Robert, *James the Brother of Jesus*, p 133

39 Ezekiel, Ch 18, vs 17–21

40 Josephus, *Antiquities*, book XVII, Ch X, 9; *Wars* Book II, Ch V, 1

41 Josephus, *Antiquities*, book XVII, Ch X, 10; *Wars* Book II, Ch V, 2.

42 Eisenman, Robert, *James the Brother of Jesus*, p xxi

43 Josephus, *War*, 1.1.

44 Powell, Mark Allen, *The Jesus Debate*, p 30

45 Fox, Robin Lane, *The Unauthorised Version*, p 31

46 Koester, Helmut, *Ancient Christian Gospels*, p 305

47 Seymour, P A H, *The Birth of Christ*, p 145

48 Schonfield, Hugh, *The Essene Odyssey*, p 59

49 Schonfield, Hugh, *The Essene Odyssey*, p 59

50 Johnson, Paul, *A History of Christianity*, pp 19–20

51 The Gospel according to St John, Ch 1, v 21

52 Crossan, John Dominic, *Jesus a Revolutionary Biography*, p 34

53 Taylor, Joan E, *The Immerser, John the Baptist in Second Temple Judaism*, p 278

54 Wilson, A N, *Jesus*, p xvi

55 Burton, Mack, *The Lost Gospel*, p 2

56 Wilson, A N, *Jesus*, p 4

57 Armstrong, Karen, *A History of Jerusalem*, p 145

58 The Gospel of Thomas, 108

59 Smith, Morton, *The Secret Gospel*

60 The Gospel according to St Matthew, Ch 10, vs 5–6

61 The Gospel according to St Matthew, Ch 29, v 19

62 St Matthew, Ch 21, vs 1–11; St Mark, Ch 11, vs 1–11; St Luke, Ch 19, vs 28–44; St John, Ch 12, vs 12–19

63 Gospel according to St John, Ch 12, v 13

64 Maccabees, Ch 13, vs 50–51

65 St Matthew, Ch 21, v 12; St Mark Ch 11, v 15; St Luke, Ch 19, v 45

66 Philo of Alexandria, *De Legatione ad Gaium*, 301; Epstein, I, *Judaism*, p 106; Wilson, A N, *Paul the Mind of the Apostle*, p 56

67 Epstein, *Judaism*, p 107

68 Tacitus *Annals* XV, 44

69 From the Gospel of Thomas, v 12, as translated in *The Nag-Hamadi Library*, James Robinson ed

70 *Pseudo-Clementine recognitions*, 1, 43

71 Epiphanius, *Against Heresies*, 78.7.7.

72 Acts of the Apostles, Ch 12, v 17

73 Eisenman, Robert, *James the Brother of Jesus*, p xx

74 The Gospel according to St. Matthew, Ch13, v 55

75 Eusabius, Ecclesiastical History, 2, 234–5; Epiphanius, *Against Heresies*, 78, 14,1–2

76 In a series on St Paul broadcast on BBC Radio 4

77 Wilson, A N, *Jesus*, p 101

78 Hassnain, Fida, *A search for the Historical Jesus*, p 84

79 The Gospel according to St John, Ch2, vs 1–5

80 Hassnain, Fida, *A Search for the Historical Jesus*, p 84

81 The Gospel according to St John, Ch 11, vs 20 & 28–29

82 The Gospel according to St Luke, Ch 10, v 39

83 Published by Bear & Co

84 The Gospel according to Matthew, Ch 26, v 7 also described in Gospel of Mark, Ch 14, v 3

85 Starbird, *opus cit*, p 36

86 Leviticus, Ch 19, v 18

Chapter 5

1 Acts of the Apostles, Ch 7, v 59; Ch 8, vs 1–8; Ch 9, vs 1–2

2 Galatians, Ch1, v 17

3 Acts, Ch 24, v 14

4 Acts, Ch 11

5 Eisenman, Robert, *The Dead Sea Scrolls and the First Christians*, p 146

6 The Community Rule, viii, 20ff

7 Paul's Epistle to the Galatians, Ch 2, vs 11–13

8 Galatians, Ch 2, vs 15–16

9 The Gospel According to St Matthew, Ch 26, v 64

10 Paul's Epistle to Titus, Ch 2, v 13

11 Paul's Epistle to the Romans, Ch 5, vs 6 & 8, Ch 14, v 9 & Paul's Epistle to the Corinthians, Ch 15, v 3

12 Ezekiel, Ch 18, vs 17–21

13 Paul's Second epistle to the Corinthians, Ch 3, v 1

14 Johnson, Paul, *A History of Christianity*, p 41

15 Acts, Ch 16, v 1

16 Acts, Ch 24, v 24

17 Paul's First Epistle to the Corinthians, Ch 9, vs 1–2

18 Paul's First Epistle to Timothy, Ch 2, v 7

19 Cited by Laurence Gardner in *The Bloodline of the Holy Grail*, p 154

20 Paul's Epistle to the Galatians, Ch 5, vs 1–4

21 Paul's First Epistle to the Corinthians, Ch 9, vs 24–26

22 Robert Eisenman devotes an entire chapter to Paul's attack on James citing a variety of sources – Chapter 16, *James the Brother of Jesus*. See also the *Pseudo-Clementine Recognitions*

23 A glossed-over account of this can be read in Acts, Ch 21 v 33

24 Acts, Ch 23, vs 20–21

25 Acts, Ch 23, vs 23–24

26 Paul's Epistle to the Romans, Ch 16, vs 10–11

27 Wilson, A N, *Paul, the Mind of the Apostle*, p 54

28 Acts, Ch 24, vs 1–27

29 Acts, Ch 8, v 9ff

30 Josephus, *Antiquities* Book XIV, Ch 8, v 3

31 Eisenman, Robert, *The Dead Sea Scrolls and the First Christians*, p 230

32 Paul's Epistle to the Philippians, Ch 4, v 18

33 Paul's Epistle to the Philippians, Ch 4, v 21

34 B. San. 81b–82b

35 Jerome, *Lives of Illustrious Men*, p 2

36 Eisenman, Robert, *The Dead Sea Scrolls and the First Christians*, p 262

37 Armstrong, Karen, *A History of Jerusalem*, p 151

38 Ranke-Heninemann, Ute, *Putting Away Childish Things*, p 173

39 Josephus, *War*, Book II, Ch XVII, v 4

40 Josephus, *War*, Book II, Ch XX, v 1

41 Johnson, Paul, A *History of Christianity*, p 43

42 Welburn, Andrew, *The Beginnings of Christianity*, p 55

43 St Paul's Epistle to the Galatians, Ch 2, v 9

44 Moore, R I, *The Formation of a Persecuting Society*, pp 12–13

45 The Revelation of St John, Ch 21, v 6

46 Baldock, John, *The Elements of Christian Symbolism*, p 29

Chapter 6

1 Johnson, Paul, *A History of Christianity*, pp 116–7

2 Ravenscroft & Wallace-Murphy, *The Mark of the Beast*, p 79

3 Johnson, Paul, *A History of Christianity*, pp 135–8

4 Ranke-Heineman, Ute, *Putting Away Childish Things*, p 278

5 Clark, Kenneth, *Civilisation*, p 17

6 Clark, Kenneth, *Civilisation*, p 24

7 Clark, Kenneth, *Civilisation*, p19

8 Baldock, John, *The Elements of Christian Symbolism*, p 32

9 Baldock, John, *The Elements of Christian Symbolism*, p ix

10 Clark, Kenneth, *Civilisation*, p 29

11 Taylor, Richard, *How to Read a Church*, p 39

12 Baldock, John, *The Elements of Christian Symbolism*, p 47

13 Taylor, Richard, *How to Read a Church*, p 24

14 Ezekiel, Ch 43, v, 2

15 Baldock, John, *The Elements of Christian Symbolism*, p 10

16 Baldock, John, *The Elements of Christian Symbolism*, p 41

17 The Gospel according to St Matthew, Ch 12, v 40

18 Baldock, John, *The Elements of Christian Symbolism*, p 51

19 Baldock, John, *The Elements of Christian Symbolism*, p 45

20 Baldock, John, *The Elements of Christian Symbolism*, p 33

21 Taylor, Richard, *How to Read a Church*, p 52

22 Taylor, Richard, *How to Read a Church*, p 27

23 Taylor, Richard, *How to Read a Church*, p 101

24 Taylor, Richard, *How to Read a Church*, p 93

25 The Gospel of St Luke, Ch 3, vs 7–9

26 The Gospel of St Luke, Ch 7, vs 24–6

27 Taylor, Richard, *How to Read a Church*, p 99

28 Taylor, Richard, *How to Read a Church*, p 97

29 Taylor, Richard, *How to Read a Church*, pp 48–9

30 Taylor, Richard, *How to Read a Church*, p 49

31 Taylor, Richard, *How to Read a Church*, p 51

32 Taylor, Richard, *How to Read a Church*, pp 13–15

33 Wallace-Murphy & Hopkins, *Rosslyn: Guardian of the Secrets of the Holy Grail*, p 90

34 Lionel, Frederic, *Mirrors of Truth*

35 Taylor, Richard, *How to Read a Church*, pp 13–15

36 Nieuwbarn, M C, *Church Symbolism*, pp 12–13

37 Taylor, Richard, *How to Read a Church*, pp 15–16

38 Taylor, Richard, *How to Read a Church*, pp 17–18

Chapter 7

1 Anderson, William, *The Rise of the Gothic*, p 9

2 Clark, Kenneth, *Civilisation*, p 9

3 Anderson, William, *The Rise of the Gothic*, p 10

4 Viollet Le Duc cited by Émile Mâle in *Notre Dame de Chartres*

5 Nieuwbarn, M C, *Church Symbolism*, pp 12–13

6 Taylor, Richard, *How to Read a Church*, p 29

7 Baldock, John, *The Elements of Christian Symbolism*, pp ix–x

8 Cited by Holt, E. Gilmore, *A Documentary History of Art*, vol 1, p 25

9 Anderson, William, *The Rise of the Gothic*, p 12

10 Charpentier, Louis, *The Mysteries of Chartres Cathedral*, p 145

11 Charpentier, Louis, *The Mysteries of Chartres Cathedral*, p 86

12 Dunlop, Ian, *The Cathedrals Crusade*, p 6

13 *La Règle de St Devoir de Dieu et de la Croissade*

14 Gettings, Fred, *The Secret Zodiac*

15 Jacques Perrier, *Notre Dame de Paris*, p 24

16 The Gospel according to St Matthew, Ch 1, vs 1–16

17 Wallace-Murphy & Hopkins, *Rosslyn: Guardian of the Secrets of the Holy Grail*, p 174

18 Perrier, Jacques, *Notre Dame de Paris*, p 1

Chapter 8

1 Wisdom of Solomon, Ch 11, v 20

2 Von Simson, O, *The Gothic Cathedral*, p 11

3 Baldock, John, *The Elements of Christian Symbolism*, p 17

4 John, James, *The Master Masons of Chartres*, p 145

5 John, James, *The Master Masons of Chartres*, p 148

6 Mâle, Émile, *The Gothic Image*, p 10

7 Baldock, John, *The Elements of Christian Symbolism*, p 35

8 Baldock, John, *The Elements of Christian Symbolism*, p 34

9 John, James, *The Master Masons of*

Chartres

10 Lesser, George, *Gothic Cathedrals and Sacred Geometry*, vol 3, plan cited by Colin Ward in *Chartres the Making of a Miracle*, p 33

11 Charpentier, Louis, *The Mysteries of Chartres Cathedral*, p 109

12 Ward, Colin, *Chartres the Making of a Miracle*, p 34

13 Anderson, William, *The Rise of the Gothic*, p 169

14 The introduction to *La Règle de St Devoir et de la Croissade* – 'The Rule of the Children of Solomon'

15 Wallace-Murphy & Hopkins, *Rosslyn: Guardian of the Secrets of the Holy Grail*, p 111

16 Anderson, William, *The Rise of the Gothic*, p39 & Bony, Jean, *French Gothic Architecture of the 12th & 13th Centuries*, p 17

17 Strachan, Gordon, *Chartres*, p 14

18 Shah, I, *The Sufis*, pp 166–193

19 Strachan, Gordon, *Chartres*, p 29

20 Ouspensky, P D, *A New Model of the Universe*, p 345

21 Fulcanelli, *Le Mystère des Cathédrales*, p 36

22 Fulcanelli, *Le Mystère des Cathédrales*, pp 39–41

23 Colfs, J F, *La filiation généalogique de toutes les Écoles Gothiques*

24 Wallace-Murphy, Tim, *The Templar Legacy and the Masonic Inheritance within Rosslyn Chapel*

25 Baldock, John, *The Elements of Christian Symbolism*, p 70

26 The Gospel of Thomas

27 Fulcanelli, *Les Mystères des Cathedrales*, p 70

28 *Les Oeuvres de Nicolas Graspony et Nicolas Valois*, Mss Bibliothè de l'Arsenale No 2516, p 176

29 Burchkart, Titus, *Alchemy*, p 189

30 Fulcanelli, *Les Mystères des Cathedrales*

31 Etteila in *Le Dernier du Pauvre* from *Sept nuances de l'oeuvre philosphique* (1786) p 57

32 Jean d'Hourey, *Nouvelle Lumière Chymique, Traite du Mercure*, 1695, Ch IX, p 41

Chapter 9

1 Kluber, Michel, 'Une Vie par Reforme L'Église', published in the journal *Bernard de Clairvaux*, par les editions de l'Argonante

2 Kluber, Michel, 'Une Vie par Reforme L'Église', published in the journal *Bernard de Clairvaux*, par les editions de l'Argonante

3 Recueil des Historians, vol 15, no 245, p 162

4 Beinhart, Haim, *Atlas of Medieval Jewry*, pp 52 & 81

5 Baigent, Leigh & Lincoln, *The Holy Blood and the Holy Grail*, p 59

6 *Bernard de Clairvaux*, par les editions de l'Argonante

7 *Liber ad milites Templi: De laude novae militiae*

8 The Copper Scroll, decoded by John Allegro

9 Hancock, Graham, *The Sign and the Seal*, p 363

10 Ravenscroft & Wallace-Murphy, *The Mark of the Beast*, p 52 and Knight & Lomas, *The Hiram Key*, p 306

11 HRH Prince Michael of Albany, *The Forgotten Monarchy of Scotland*, p 61

12 Addison, Charles, *The History of the Knights Templar*, p 5

13 Baigent, Leigh & Lincoln, *The Holy Blood and the Holy Grail*, p 61

14 Hopkins, Wallace-Murphy & Simmans, *Rex Deus*, pp 113–114

15 Hancock, Graham, *The Sign and the Seal*, pp 94 & 99, also Ravenscroft & Wallace-Murphy, *The Mark of the Beast*, p 52

16 Graham Hancock, *The Sign and the Seal*, pp 49–51

17 Ravenscroft & Wallace-Murphy, *The Mark of the Beast*, p 52

18 Robinson, John J, *Opus Cit* p 37

19 Barber, Malcolm, *The Trial of the Templars*, p 6

20 Anon, *Secret Societies of the Middle Ages*, p 195

21 Hancock, Graham, *The Sign and the Seal*, p 334

22 Anon, *Secret Societies of the Middle Ages*, p 199

23 Bruno, S T, *Templar Organization*, (Privately published) p 65

24 Bruno, S T, *Templar Organization,* (Privately published) p 165

25 Jay, Peter, *Road to Riches,* p 118

26 Consult *Les Sites Templiers de France,* published by Editions Ouest-France, for a relatively comprehensive list of most of the Templar sites definitely identified within France.

27 *Sur les Traces des Templiers dans le Var,* published by La Musée des Empreintes & Traditions Maures & Provence de Cogolin, p 2

28 *Sur les Traces des Templiers dans le Var,* published by La Musée des Empreintes & Traditions Maures & Provence de Cogolin, p 2

29 *Sur les Traces des Templiers dans le Var,* published by La Musée des Empreintes & Traditions Maures & Provence de Cogolin, pp 15–16

30 Wallace-Murphy, Tim, *The Templar Legacy and the Masonic Inheritance within Rosslyn Chapel,* p 53

31 *Sur les Traces des Templiers dans la Var,* published by La Musée des Empreintes & Traditions Maures & Provence de Cogolin, p 2

32 Written in collaboration with Marilyn Hopkins and now published by HarperCollins, Thorsens division

33 This is one of the main objectives ascribed to the Knights Templar within the pages of *The Holy Blood and the Holy Grail*

34 Wallace-Murphy & Hopkins, *Rosslyn Guardian of the Secrets of the Holy Grail,* pp 117–8

35 Eliphas, Levi, *Histoire de la Magie* (A E Waite translation)

36 Eliphas, Levi, *Histoire de la Magie* (A E Waite translation)

37 Hancock, Graham, *The Sign and the Seal,* p 333

38 J-A Durbec's article entitled, '*Les Templiers dans les Alpes Maritimes*', published by the journal *Nice Historique,* Jan/Feb 1934, pp 4–6

39 The Gospel of Thomas as written in *The Nag Hammadi Library,* James M Robinson ed, p 131

40 Guidebook to The Cathedral of Amiens, p 5

41 Fulcanelli, *Le Mystère des Cathédrales,* p 123

42 Wallace-Murphy & Hopkins, *Rosslyn: Guardian of the Secrets of the Holy Grail,* p 176

43 Quespel, G, 'Gnosticism', published in *Man, Myth and Magic,* no 40, p 115

Chapter 10

1 Gill, Eric, *Work and Property*

2 Charpentier, Louis, *The Mysteries of Chartres,* p 81

3 Caesar, *De Bello Gallico,* IV

4 Mâle, Émile, *Notre Dame de Chartres,* pp 8–9

5 Baldock, John, *The Elements of Christian Symbolism,* p 32

6 Ward, Colin, *Chartres, the Making of a Miracle,* p 7

7 Ward, Colin, *Chartres, the Making of a Miracle,* p 8

8 Clerval, *Les Écoles de Chartres au Moyen Age,* 1895

9 Ravenscroft & Wallace-Murphy, *The Mark of the Beast,* pp 73–74

10 Cited by John of Salisbury in his *Métalogique* III, 4. Patrol. Lat. Vol CXCIX, col 900

11 Ravenscroft & Wallace-Murphy, *The Mark of the Beast,* p 75

12 Anderson, William, *The Rise of the Gothic,* p 23

13 Weatherbee, Winthrop tr. *Bernardus of Chartres,* p 90

14 Ward, Colin, *Chartres the Making of a Miracle,* pp 8–9

15 Ravenscroft & Wallace-Murphy, *The Mark of the Beast,* pp 74–5

16 Ward, Colin, *Chartres, the Making of a Miracle,* p 9

17 Cited by Émile Mâle in *Notre Dame de Chartres,* p 6

18 Anderson, William, *The Rise of the Gothic,* p 67

19 Campbell, Joseph, *The Masks of God: Creative Mythology,* pp 3–9

20 The Gospel according to St Mark, Ch, 4 v 22

21 Charpentier, Louis, *The Mysteries of Chartres Cathedral,* p 81

22 Ravenscroft & Wallace-Murphy, *The Mark of the Beast,* p 73

23 Dunlop, Ian, *The Cathedrals Crusade*, pp 29–32

24 Anderson, William, *The Rise of the Gothic*, p 93

25 The Acts of the Apostles, Ch 1, v 11

26 Millar, Malcolm, *Chartres Cathedral*, p 5

27 Charpentier, Louis, *The Mysteries of Chartres Cathedral*, p 165

28 Ward, Colin, *Chartres, The Making of a Miracle*, p 63

29 Gill, Eric, *Work and Property,* Cited by Colin Ward in *Chartres, the Making of a Miracle*, p 22

30 Ward, Colin, *Chartres the Making of a Miracle*, pp 25–6, see also John James *Chartres, the Masons Who Built a Legend*

31 le Duc, Viollet, *Dictionaire Raisonné*

32 Ravenscroft & Wallace-Murphy, *The Mark of the Beast*, p 52

33 Knight & Lomas, *The Hiram Key*, pp 271–2

34 This forms the main theme for the book, *The Hiram Key,* by Knight & Lomas

35 Genesis, Ch 14, v 20

36 Millar, Malcolm, *Chartres Cathedral*, p 18

37 The Gospel according to St John Ch 3, v 14

38 Millar, Malcolm, *Chartres Cathedral*, p 20

39 Ezekiel, Ch 18, vs 17–21

40 The book of Isaiah, Ch 11, v 1

41 The Gospel of St Luke, Ch 2, v 33

42 Robert Graves in his Introduction to the first edition of Idris Shah's *The Sufis*

Chapter 11

1 Charpentier, Louis, *The Mysteries of Chartres Cathedral*, p 139

2 Charpentier, Louis, *The Mysteries of Chartres Cathedral*, p 141

3 Mertz, Blanche, *Points of Cosmic Energy*, p 105

4 Mâle, Émile, *Notre Dame de Chartres*, p 153

5 Colin Ward, *Chartres, the Making of a Miracle*, pp 33–34

6 John, James, *The Master Masons of Chartres*

7 Millar, Malcolm, *Chartres Cathedral*, p 22

8 Ward, Colin, *Chartres, the Making of a Miracle*, p 54

9 Ward, Colin, *Chartres, the Making of a Miracle*, p 55

10 Fulcanelli, *Les Demeures Philosphales*

11 Ward, Colin, *Chartres the Making of a Miracle*, p 55 see also Malcolm Millar's *Chartres*, pp 19 & 22

12 Millar, Michael, *Chartres*, p 26

13 The Revelation of St John, Ch 5, v 8

14 Wallace-Murphy & Hopkins, *Custodians of Truth*

15 Wallace-Murphy, Hopkins & Simmans, *Rex Deus*, pp 74–75

16 Gardner, Laurence, *The Bloodline of the Holy Grail*, p 116

17 I Kings, Ch 4, v 31

18 The Gospel according to St Matthew, Ch 5, v 17, cited by Malcolm Millar in *Chartres*, pp 24 & 26

19 Wallace-Murphy, Tim, *The Templar Legacy and the Masonic Inheritance within Rosslyn Chapel*, p 39

20 The Book of Isaiah, Ch 11, vs 1–2

21 Mâle, Émile, *Notre Dame de Chartres*, p 156

22 Ward, Colin, *Chartres, the Making of a Miracle*, p 54

23 Charpentier, Louis, *The Mysteries of Chartres Cathedral*, p 140

24 Mâle, Émile, *Notre Dame de Chartres*, p 157

25 Mâle, Émile, *Notre Dame de Chartres*, p 160

26 Charpentier, Louis, *The Mysteries of Chartres Cathedral*, p 25

27 Bonvin, Jacques, *Vierges Noires*, p 126

28 Mertz, Blanche, *Points of Cosmic Energy*, pp 110–111

29 Mertz, Blanche, *Points of Cosmic Energy*, p 110

30 Delaporte, Y, *Les Trois Notre Dames de Chartres*, p 11

31 Delaporte, Y, *Les Trois Notre Dames de Chartres*, p 11

32 Charpentier, Louis, *The Mysteries of Chartres Cathedral*, p 121

33 Baldock, John, *The Elements of Christian Symbolism*, p 6

34 Ward, Colin, *Chartres, the Making of a Miracle*, p 40

Chapter 12

1 Wallace-Murphy & Hopkins, *Custodians of Truth*
2 Bonvin, Jaacques, *Vierges Noires*, p 17
3 Bonvin, Jacques, *Vierges Noires*, p 18
4 Begg, Ean, *The Cult of the Black Virgin*, p 93
5 Berman, Roland, *La Vierge Noire, Vierge Initiatique*, p 19–20
6 Huynen, Jacques in *L'enigma des Vierges Noires*, 1972
7 Bonvin, Jacques, *Vierges Noires*, p 16
8 Bonvin, Jacques, *Vierges Noires*, p 21
9 Bonvin, Jacques, *Vierges Noires*, p 127–8
10 Durand-Lefèbvre, Marie, *Études Sur L'Origine des Vierges Noires*
11 Saillens, Émile, *Nos Vierges Noires, Leurs Origines*
12 Bonvin, Jacques, *Vierges Noires*, p 13
13 Begg, Ean, *The Cult of the Black Virgin*, p 73
14 Begg, Ean, *The Cult of the Black Virgin*, p 13
15 Bonvin, Jacques, *Vierges Noires*, p 101
16 Bigarne, Charles, *Considérations sur le culte d'Isis chez les Eduens*, cited by Fulcanelli in *Le Mystère des Cathédrales*, p 75
17 Begg, Ean, *The Cult of the Black Virgin*, pp 17–18
18 Olivier, Dr Paul, *L'Ancienne Statue de N D de Puy*
19 Belot, Victor, *La France des Pélérinages*
20 Begg, Ean, *The Cult of the Black Virgin*, p 19
21 Begg, Ean, *The Cult of the Black Virgin*, p xiv
22 Begg, Ean, *The Cult of the Black Virgin*, p 2
23 Jean Tourniac in the preface to Roland Berman's *La Vierge Noire, Vierge Initiatique*, p 7
24 Elkington, David, *In The Name of the Gods*, pp 105–106
25 Hancock, Grahamm, *The Sign and the Seal*, p 334
26 Wallace-Murphy & Hopkins, *Custodians of Truth*
27 Begg, Ean, *The Cult of the Black Virgin*, p 103
28 Begg, Ean, *The Cult of the Black Virgin*, p 97

29 Wallace-Murphy & Hopkins, *Rosslyn: Guardian of the Secrets of the Holy Grail*, p 105
30 Begg, Ean, *The Cult of the Black Virgin*, pp 15–16
31 Wallace-Murphy & Hopkins, *Rosslyn: Guardian of the Secrets of the Holy Grail*, p 62
32 Wallace-Murphy & Hopkins, *Rosslyn: Guardian of the Secrets of the Holy Grail*, pp 181–2
33 Begg, Ean, *The Cult of the Black Virgin*, p 13
34 Bonvin, Jacques, *Vierges Noires*, p 107
35 Begg, Ean, *The Cult of the Black Virgin*, p 26
36 Berman, Roland, *La Vierge Noire, Vierge Initiatique*, p 33
37 Graves, Robert, *Mammon and the Black Goddess*, p 162
38 cited by Roland Berman, *La Vierge Noire, Vierge Initiatique*, p 69
39 Mevlana Jalahod Rumi cited in *Dictionanaire des Symbols*.
40 Berman, Roland, *La Vierge Noire, Vierge Initiatique*, p 35
41 Begg, Ean, *The Cult of the Black Virgin*, p 137
42 Bonvin, Jacques, *Vierges Noires*, p 13
43 Bonvin, Jacques, *Vierges Noires*, pp 134–5
44 Berman, Roland, *La Vierge Noire, Vierge Initiatique*, pp 30–1
45 Berman, Roland, La Vierge Noire, Vierge Initiatique, pp 90, 95 & 96

Chapter 13

1 Ravenscroft, Trevor, *The Cup of Destiny*, p 9
2 Sinclair, Andrew, *The Discovery of the Grail*, p 77
3 Godwin, Malcolm, *The Holy Grail*, p 14
4 Godwin, Malcolm, *The Holy Grail*, p 16
5 Godwin, Malcolm, *The Holy Grail*, p 12
6 Stein, Walter Johannes, *The Ninth Century: World History in the Light of the Holy Grail*, pp 362–363
7 Godwin, Malcolm, *The Holy Grail*, p 18
8 Ravenscroft & Wallace-Murphy, *The Mark of the Beast*, p 52

9 Sinclair, Andrew, *The Discovery of the Grail*, p 27

10 Sinclair, Andrew, *The Discovery of the Grail*, pp 27–8

11 Campbell, Joseph & Moyers, Bill, *The Power of Myth*, pp 197–200

12 Published by Red Wheel/Weiser in Boston, MA, USA

13 *The Gospel of Thomas*, from the *Nag Hamadi Library*, edited by John Robinson.

14 Campbell, J, & Moyers, B *The Power of Myth*, pp 197–200

15 Campbell, J & Moyers, B *The Power of Myth*, p 199

16 Ravenscroft, Trevor, *The Cup of Destiny*, p 14

17 Campbell, J & Moyers, B *The Power of Myth*, p 163

18 Campbell, J & Moyers, B *The Power of Myth*, p 163

19 Cited by Fritjof Capra in *The Turning Point*, p 410

20 Cited by Ted Roszak in *Where the Wasteland Ends*, p 154

21 Baigent, Leigh & Lincoln, *The Holy Blood and the Holy Grail*, pp 262–268

22 Sinclair, Andrew, *The Discovery of the Grail*, p 37

23 Knight & Lomas, *The Second Messiah*, pp 114–117

24 Wolfram von Essenbach, *Parzival*, book II

25 Ravenscroft, Trevor, *The Cup of Destiny*, pp 10–11

26 Querido, René, *The Mystery of the Holy Grail*, p 3

27 Robert Graves in his Introduction to Idries Shah's *The Sufis*

28 Sinclair, Andrew, *The Discovery of the Grail*, p 75

29 Prince Michael of Albany, *The Forgotten Monarchy of Scotland*, p 118

30 Sinclair, Andrew, *The Discovery of the Grail*, p 35

31 Godwin, Malcolm, *The Holy Grail*, p 6

32 The Gospel according to St Matthew, Ch 16, v 18

33 Godwin, Malcolm, *The Holy Grail*, p 80

34 Ravenscroft & Wallace-Murphy, *The Mark of the Beast*, p 52

35 Christie-Murray, David, *A History of Heresy*, pp 104–8

36 Barber, Malcolm, *The Trial of the Templars*, p 46

37 Prince Michael of Albany, *The Forgotten Monarchy of Scotland*, pp 62–4

38 Ravenscroft & Wallace-Murphy, *The Mark of the Beast*, p 53

39 Wallace-Murphy, Tim, *The Templar Legacy and the Masonic Inheritance within Rosslyn Chapel*

40 Begg, Ean, *The Cult of the Black Virgin*, p 103

41 Robinson, John, *Born in Blood*, p 137

42 Robinson, John, *Born in Blood*, p 137

43 Robinson, John, *Born in Blood*, pp 164–166

44 Wallace-Murphy, Hopkins & Simmans, *Rex Deus*, p 148

45 Malcolm, Godwin, *The Holy Grail*, p 234

46 Hopkins, Simmans & Wallace-Murphy, *Rex Deus*, p 148

47 Cavendish, Richard, *The Tarot*, p 17

48 Wallace-Murphy, Hopkins and Simmans, *Rex Deus*, p 148

49 Starbird, Margaret, *The Tarot Trumps and the Holy Grail*, p x

50 Starbird, Margaret, *The Tarot Trumps and the Holy Grail*, p xi

51 Starbird, Margaret, *The Tarot Trumps and the Holy Grail*, p x

52 Starbird, Margaret, *The Tarot Trumps and the Holy Grail*, p 3

53 Starbird, Margaret, *The Tarot Trumps and the Holy Grail*, p 5

54 Godwin, Malcolm, *The Holy Grail*, p 236

55 Starbird, Margaret, *The Tarot Trumps and the Holy Grail*, p 45

56 Bailey, Harold, *New Light on the Renaissance*, a book which treats at length the fascinating subject of the spread of heresy at the hands of the troubadours and jongleurs of the High Middle Ages

57 Starbird, Margaret, *The Tarot Trumps and the Holy Grail*, p 25

58 Starbird, Margaret, *The Tarot Trumps and the Holy Grail*, p 27

59 Starbird, Margaret, *The Woman with the Alabaster Jar*, pp 124 & 129–131

60 1 Kings, Ch 7, vs 15–21 & 2 Chronicles, Ch 3, vs 15–17

61 Tompkins, Peter, *The Magic of Obelisks*, pp 61–62 for detailed description and illustrations of the tortures used

Chapter 14

1 Schmitt, P, *Ancient Mysteries in the Society of Their Time. Their Transformation and most Recent Echoes*
2 See Tim Wallace-Murphy & Marilyn Hopkins, *Templars in America*
3 Wallace-Murphy, Tim, *An Illustrated Guidebook to Rosslyn Chapel*
4 Gedricke –18th Century Historian of Free Masonry – cited by Wallace-Murphy in *The Templar Legacy and the Masonic Inheritance within Rosslyn Chapel*
5 Ravenscroft, Trevor, *The Spear of Destiny*, pp 1 & 2
6 Baring & Cashford, *The Myth Of The Goddess*, pp 411–412
7 Anderson, William, *The Rise of the Gothic*

Chapter 15

1 Wallace-Murphy & Hopkins, *Rosslyn: Guardian of the Secrets of the Holy Grail*, Section 3
2 Wallace-Murphy, Tim, *The Templar Legacy and the Masonic Inheritance within Rosslyn Chapel*, p 42
3 Roszak, Theodore, *The Unfinished Animal*, p 9
4 Wallace-Murphy & Hopkins, *Rosslyn: Guardian of the Secrets of the Holy Grail*, Section 3
5 Knight & Lomas, *The Second Messiah*, p 32
6 For a full description of the Egyptian Pilgrimage of initiation, see Peter Dawkins, *Arcadia*, pp 39–44 see also Wallace-Murphy & Hopkins, *Rosslyn: Guardian of the Secrets of the Holy Grail* pp 18–182
7 Ravenscroft & Wallace-Murphy, *The Mark of the Beast*, pp 69–70
8 Heselton, Philip, *Elements of Earth Mysteries*, p 78
9 Heselton, Philip, *Elements of Earth Mysteries*, p 79
10 Aviva, Elyn, *Following the Milky Way, a pilgrimage across Spain*, published by Iowa State University
11 Elyn Aviva, *Following the Milky Way, a pilgrimage across Spain*, published by Iowa State University
12 Elyn Aviva, *Following the Milky Way, a pilgrimage across Spain*, published by Iowa State University
13 Ravenscroft & Wallace-Murphy, *The Mark of the Beast*, p 51
14 *The Guidebook to Santiago de Compostela*
15 *The Guidebook to Santiago de Compostela*
16 Wallace-Murphy & Hopkins, *Rosslyn: Guardian of the Secrets of the Holy Grail*, p 142
17 Cited in *The Guidebook to Santiago de Compostela*
18 *The Guidebook to Santiago de Compostela*
19 *The Gospel of Thomas*
20 *The Guidebook to Santiago de Compostela*
21 Galatians, Ch 1, v 19; Matthew, Ch 13, v 55; Mark, Ch 6, v 3. In Acts it is assumed that James, the first 'bishop of Jerusalem' is the same James, the brother of the Lord, referred to by Paul in Galatians and by the Gospels
22 Mertz, Blanche, *Points of Cosmic Energy*, p 121
23 Ravenscroft & Wallace-Murphy, *The Mark of the Beast*, p 51
24 Wallace-Murphy & Hopkins, *Rosslyn: Guardian of the Secrets of the Holy Grail*, p 150
25 *The Gospel according to St Matthew*, Ch 6 v 22
26 Barber, Malcolm, *The Templars*
27 Wallace-Murphy & Hopkins, *Rosslyn: Guardian of the Secrets of the Holy Grail*, p 132
28 *The Guidebook to the Cathedral of Orleans*
29 Wallace-Murphy & Hopkins, *Rosslyn: Guardian of the Secrets of the Holy Grail*, p 133
30 Ravenscroft & Wallace-Murphy, *The Mark of the Beast*, p 51
31 Wallace-Murphy & Hopkins, *Rosslyn: Guardian of the Secrets of the Holy Grail*, p 135
32 Sinclair, Andrew, *The Discovery of the Grail*, p 28
33 Fulcanelli, *Le Mystère des Cathédrales*, pp 104–5

34 Wallace-Murphy & Hopkins, *Rosslyn: Guardian of the Secrets of the Holy Grail*, p 135

35 Begg, Ean, *The Cult of the Black Virgin*, p 125

36 Wallace-Murphy & Hopkins, *Rosslyn Guardian of the Secrets of the Holy Grail*, p 136

Chapter 16

1 Previte-Orton, *Outlines of Medieval History*, p 469

2 Goodwin, Godfrey, *Islamic Spain*, p vii

3 Baigent, Leigh & Lincoln, *The Holy Blood and the Holy Grail*, p 109

4 Fossier, Robert, *The Middle Ages*, vol III, p 504

5 Wright, Esmond, *Medieval and Renaissance World*, p 218

6 Fossier, Robert, *The Middle Ages*, vol III, pp 504–5

7 Wind, Edgar, *Pagan Mysteries in the Renaissance*, p22

8 Fossier, Robert, *The Middle Ages*, vol III, p 505

9 Pliny, *Natural History*, XVI xxv

10 Pater, Walter, *The Renaissance*, Leonardo da Vinci

11 Wind, Edgar, *Pagan Mysteries in the Renaissance*, p 174

12 The Gospel according to St Matthew, Ch 16, vs 21–3

Chapter 17

1 Bayard, Jean Pierrre, *Le Symbolisme Masonique des Haut Grades*

2 Robinson, John, *Born in Blood*.

3 HRH Prince Michael of Albany, *The Forgotten Monarchy of Scotland*, p 120 and Knight & Lomas, *The Hiram Key*

4 HRH Prince Michael of Albany, *The Forgotten Monarchy of Scotland*, p 120

5 Masonic Archives in Freemasons Hall, Edinburgh

6 Knight and Lomas, *The Second Messiah*, p 53

7 HRH Prince Michael of Albany, *The Forgotten Monarchy of Scotland*, pp 8–9

8 Gardner, Laurence, *The Bloodline of the Holy Grail*, p 324

9 Baigent & Leigh, *The Temple and the Lodge*, p 261

10 Baigent & Leigh, *The Temple and the Lodge*, p 262

11 Waite, A E, *A New Encyclopaedia of Freemasonry*, pp 314–315

12 Waite, A E, *A New Encyclopaedia of Freemasonry*, p 314

13 Gould, *History of Freemasonry*, Vol IV, p 88

14 Gould, *History of Freemasonry*, Vol IV, p 88

15 Wallace-Murphy, Hopkins & Simmans, *Rex Deus*, p 249

16 Baigent & Leigh, *The Temple and the Lodge*, p 263

17 Tim Wallace-Murphy, *The Templar Legacy and the Masonic Inheritance within Rosslyn Chapel*, p 31

18 Wallace-Murphy, Hopkins & Simmans, *Rex Deus*, pp 220–1

19 Knight & Lomas, *The Second Messiah*, pp 200–2

20 Wallace-Murphy, Hopkins & Simmans, *Rex Deus* p 224

21 Knight & Lomas, *The Second Messiah*, p 204

22 Wallace-Murphy, Hopkins & Simmans, *Rex Deus* pp 225–6

23 Wallace-Murphy, Hopkins & Simmans, *Rex Deus*, p 227

24 Knight &Lomas, *The Second Messiah*, p 209

25 Wallace-Murphy, Tim, *An Illustrated Guidebook to Rosslyn Chapel*

Epilogue

1 Bayley, Harold, *The Lost Language of Symbolism*, Vol I, pp 4–5 see also Library Association Record, iv. p 129

2 Starbird, Margaret, *The Tarot Trumps and the Holy Grail*, p 11

3 Bayley, Harold, *The Lost Language of Symbolism*, Vol I, p 2

4 Baigent, Leigh & Lincoln, *The Holy Blood and the Holy Grail*, p 8

5 The Lost Gospel of St Peter, v 10

Selected Bibliography

A

Addison, Charles G, *The History of the Knights Templars*, Black Books, 1995

Allegro, J M, *The Dead Sea Scrolls and the Christian Myth*, Abacus, London, 1981

Allegro, John, *The Dead Sea Scrolls*, Penguin, 1964

Allen, Grant, *The Evolution of the Idea of God*, Watts, 1931

Ambelain, Robert, *Jesus ou le Mortel Sécret des Templiers*, Robert Laffont, 1970

Anderson, William, *The Rise of the Gothic*, Hutchinson, 1985

Anon, *Secret Societies of the Middle Ages* (1848), R A Kessinger Publishing Co, 2003

Aristotle, *De Caelo II*

Armstrong, K, *A History of God*, Mandarin, 1994

Armstrong, K, *A History of Jerusalem*, HarperCollins, 1996

Ashe, Geoffrey, *The Ancient Wisdom*, Macmillan, London 1977

B

Baigent, Leigh & Lincoln, *The Holy Blood and the Grail*, Jonathan Cape, 1982

Baigent, Michael & Leigh, Richard, *The Temple and the Lodge*, Corgi, 1992

Baigent, Michael & Leigh, Richard, *The Inquisition*, Penguin, 1999

Baigent, Michael & Leigh, Richard, *The Dead Sea Scrolls Deception*, Corgi, 1992

Baldock, John, *The Elements of Christian Symbolism*, Element Books, 1997

Barber Malcolm, *The Trial of the Templars*, CUP 1994

Baring, A & Cashford, J *The Myth of the Goddess*, Penguin, 1993

Bauval, Robert & Gilbert, Adrian, *The Orion Mystery*, Heinemann, 1994

Bauval, R & Hancock, G, *Keeper of Genesis*, William Heineman, 1996

Bayley, Harold *New Light on the Renaissance*, Benjamin Blom, NY 1967 (reprint of 1904 edition)

Bayley, Harold, *The Lost Language of Symbolism*, 2 vols, Citadel Press, NY, 1990

Bayard, Jean Pierre, *Le Symbolisme Masonique des Haut Grades*, Editions du Prisme, 1975

Begg, Ean, *The Cult Of The Black Virgin*, Arkana, 1985

Beinhart, Haim, *Atlas of Medieval Jewish History,* Simon & Schuster, 1992 (English translation by Moshe Salvi) Editions Dervy, 1997

Belot, Victor, *La France des Pélérinages*, Verviers, 1976

Berman, Roland, *La Vierge Noire, Vierge Initiatique,*

Betro, M C, *Hieroglyphes, Les Mystères de L'Ecriture*, Flammarion, 1995

Bock, Emilm, *Moses*, Inner Traditions International, 1986

Bonvin, Jacques, *Vierges Noires*, Editions Dervy, 2000

Bony, Jean, *French Gothic Architecture of the 12th & 13th Centuries*, University of California Press, 1992

Bordonove, Georges, *La Vie Quotidienne des Templiers*, Hachette, 1975

Breasted, J H, *Development of Religion and Thought in Ancient Egypt*, University of Pennsylvania Press, Philadelphia, 1972

Bronowski, Jacob, *The Ascent of Man*, Little Brown, 1974

Bruno, S T, *Templar Organization*, (Privately published)

Burman, Edward, *The Templars: Knights of God*, Inner Traditions International, 1990

Burman, Edward, *The Inquisition. The Hammer of Heresy*, Aquarian Press, 1984

Bussel, F W, *Religious Thought and Heresy in the Middle Ages*, London, Robert Scott, 1918

C

Campbell, Joseph & Bill Moyers, *The Power of Myth*, Doubleday, 1990

Campbell, Joseph, *The Way of Animal Powers*, Times Books, 1984

Campbell, Joseph; *The Masks of God: Creative Mythology*, Souvenir Press, 2001

Cannon, Dolores, *Jesus and the Essenes*, Gateway Books, 1992

Cantor, Norman, *The Sacred Chain*, HarperCollins, 1995

Capra, Fritjof, *The Turning Point*, Flamingo, 1983

Cavendish, Richard, *The Tarot*, Bounty Books, 1986

Charpentier, Louis, *Les Mystères Templiers*, Laffont, 1993

Charpentier, Louis, *The Mysteries of Chartres Cathedral*, RILKO, 1993.

Christie-Murray, David, *A History of Heresy*, OUP, 1989

Clark, Kenneth, *Civilisation*, John Murray, 1980

Clerval, *Les Écoles de Chartres au Moyen Age*, 1895

Cohn-Sherbok, Dan, *A Concise Encyclopaedia of Judaism*, Oneworld, 1998

Colfs, J F, *La Filiation Généalogique de toutes les Ecoles Gothiques*, Baudry, 1884

Cotterell M, *The Tutenkhamun Prophecies*, Headline, 1999

Crossan, John Dominic, *Jesus – A Revolutionary Biography*, HarperCollins, 1994

D

D'Olivet, Fabre, *La Langue Hebraique Restituée*, L'Age d'Homme, 1990

Dafoe, Stephen & Butler, Alan, *The Warriors and the Bankers*, Templar Books, 1998

Davis, T, *The Tomb of Iouiya and Touiya*, London, 1907

Dawkins, Peter, *Arcadia*, The Francis Bacon Research Trust, 1988

De Clari, Robert, Neal, E H (trans), *The Conquest of Constantinople*, University of Toronto, 1997

Delaporte, Y, *Les Trois Notre Dames de Chartres,* E Houvet, Chartres

Desgris, Alain, *L'Ordre de Templiers et la Chevalerie Macconique Templière,* Guy Trédaniel, 1995

Devereux, Paul, *Places of Power,* Blandford, 1990

Doresse, Jean, *Les Livres Secrets des Gnostiques d'Egpte,* Librairie Plon, 1958

Dowley, Tim, Ed., *The History of Christianity,* Lion Publishing, Herts, 1977

Dubos, Rene, *A God Within,* Abacus/Sphere, 1976

Dunford, Barry, *The Holy Land of Scotland,* Sacred Connections, 1982

Dunlop, Ian, *The Cathedrals Crusade,* Hamish Hamilton, 1982

Durand-Lefèbvre, Marie, *Études sur L'origine des Vierges Noires,* Paris, 1937

E

Edwards, I E S, *The Pyramids of Egypt,* Penguin, 1986

Eisenman, Robert, *Maccabbees, Zadokites, Christians and Qumran,* E J Brill, 1983

Eisenman, Robert, *James the Brother of Jesus,* Faber and Faber, 1997

Eisenman, Robert & Wise, Michael, *The Dead Sea Scrolls Uncovered,* Element, 1992

Eisenman, Robert, *The Dead Sea Scrolls and the First Christians,* Element, 1996

Elder, Isabel Hill, *Celt, Druid & Culdee,* Covenant Publishing Co. Ltd, 1994

Eliade, Mircea, *Shamanism,* Princeton University Press, 2004

Elkington, David, *In the Name of the Gods,* Green Man Press, 2001

Eusabius, *Ecclesiastical History*

Evans, Hilary, *Alternate States of Consciousness,* The Aquarian Press, 1989

F

Faulkner, Neil, *Apocalypse – the Great Jewish Revolt against Rome, AD 66–73,* Tempus Publishing Ltd, 2002

Faulkner, R, *The Ancient Egyptian Book of the Dead,* British Museum Press, 1972

Faulkner, Robert, *The Ancient Egyptian Pyramid Texts,* Aris & Philips, 1993

Feather, R, *The Copper Scroll Decoded,* Thorsons, London, 1999

Fisher, H A L, *A History of Europe,* Edward Arnold & Co, 1936

Fortune, Dion, *Esoteric Orders and Their Work,* The Aquarian Press, 1987

Foss, Michael, *Chivalry,* Michael Joseph, 1975

Fossier, Robert (ed) *The Middle Ages,* 3 Vols. CUP, 1989

Fox, R Lane, *The Unauthorised Version: Truth and Fiction in the Bible,* Penguin, 1991

Fox, Robin Lane, *Pagans and Christians,* Penguin, 1988

Franke and Cawthorne, *The Tree of Life and the Holy Grail,* Temple Lodge Publications, 1996

Frankfort, H, *Kingship of the Gods,* Chicago, 1948

Frazer, James, *The Golden Bough*, Wordsworth Editions, 1993

Freud, S, *Moses and Monotheism*, London 1939

Fulcanelli, *Le Mystère des Cathédrales*, Neville Spearman, 1977

Fulcanelli, *Les Demeures Philosophales*, 2 vols, Jean-Jaques Pauvert, Paris, 1964

G

Gardner, Laurence, *Bloodline of the Holy Grail*, Element Books, 1995

Gardner, Laurence, *Genesis of the Grail Kings*, Bantam, 1999

Geddes & Grosset, *Ancient Egypt Myth and History*, Geddes & Grosset Ltd, New Lanark, 1997

Gettings, Fred, *The Secret Zodiac*, Routledge, Keegan & Paul, London 1987

Gimpell, Jean, *The Cathedral Builders*, Cresset, 1988

Glover, T R, *The Conflict of Religions in the Early Roman Empire* (1909), RA Kessinger Publishing Co, 2003

Godwin, Malcolm, *The Holy Grail*, Bloomsbury, 1994

Golb, Norman, *Who Wrote the Dead Sea Scrolls?* Simon & Schuster, 1996

Goodwin, Godfrey, *Islamic Spain*, Chronicle Books, 2000

Gould, Robert Freke, *History of Freemasonry, Vol IV*, RA Kessinger, 2003

Goyon, G, *Le Secret des Batisseurs des Grandes Pyramides: Kheops*, Pygmalion, 1991

Graffin, Robert, *L'Art Templier des Cathédrales*, Garnier, 1993

Graves, Robert, *Mammon and the Black Goddess*, Cassell, 1965

Graves, Robert, *The White Goddess*, Faber & Faber, 1961

Gruber, Elmer R and Kersten, Holger, *The Original Jesus*, Element, 1995

H

Halam, Elizabeth (ed.), *The Chronicles of the Crusades*, Bramley Books, 1997

Hamill, John and Gilbert R A, *World Freemasonry*, Aquarian Press, 1991

Hancock, Graham, *The Sign and the Seal*, Mandarin Paperbacks, 1993

Hassnain, Prof. Fida, *A Search for the Historical Jesus*, Gateway Books, 1994

Heselton, Philip, *Elements of Earth Mysteries*, Element Books, 1994

Holmes, George (ed.), *The Oxford Illustrated History of Medieval Europe*, OUP, 1988

Holt, E Gilmore, *A Documentary History of Art* vol 1, Princeton University Press, 1981

I

Isserlin, BSJ, *The Israelites*, Augsberg Fortress Publications, 2001

J

Jackson, J, *The Chivalry of Scotland in the Days of Robert the Bruce*

Jackson, Keith B, *Beyond the Craft*, Lewis Masonic, 1982

James, Bruno S, *St Bernard of Clairvaux*, Hodder and Stoughton, 1957

James, John, *The Master Masons of Chartres*, DS Brewer, 1991

Jaynes, Julian, *The Origins of Consciousness and the Breakdown in the Bicameral Mind*, Penguin, 1993

Jedin, Hubert (ed), *The History of the Church*, Vol 1. Burns and Oats, 1989

Jennings, Hargrave, *The Rosicrucians –Their Rites and Mysteries,* Chatto & Windus, 1879

Johnson, Kenneth Rayner, *The Fulcanelli Phenomenon*, Neville Spearman, 1980

Johnson, Paul, *A History of Christianity,* Weidenfeld and Nicolson, 1978

Johnson, Paul, *A History of the Jews,* Orion Books, London 1993

Josephus, Flavius, Whiston, W (trans), *The Antiquities of the Jews*, Nimmo, 1869

Josephus, Flavius, Whiston, W (trans), *The Wars of the Jews*, Nimmo, 1869

K

Kersten, H & Gruber, E R, *The Jesus Conspiracy,* Element, 1994

Knight, Chris & Lomas, Robert, *The Hiram Key,* Century, 1996

Knight, Chris & Lomas, Robert, *The Second Messiah,* Century, 1997

Knoup, James, T*he Genesis of Freemasonry,* Manchester University Press, 1947

Koester, Helmut, *Ancient Christian Gospels,* Philadelphia, SCM Press, 1990

L

Lacroix, P, *Military and Religious Life in the Middle Ages,* Chapman & Hall, 1874

Lea, H C, *The Inquisition in the Middle Ages,* NY, 1955

Leroy Thierry, *Hughues de Payns, Chevalier Champenois, Fondateur de L'Ordre des Templiers,* Editions de la Maison du Boulanger, 2001

Levi, Eliphas, *The Key of The Mysteries,* Rider & Co, 1969

Lionel, Frederic, *Mirrors of Truth,* Archedigm, 1991

Lizerand, Georges, *Le Dossier de l'Affaire des Templiers* (1923), Axiome, 1980

Lockhart, Douglas, *The Dark Side of God*, Element, 1999

Lost Books of the Bible, The, Gramercy Books, 1988

M

Mack, Burton L, *The Lost Gospel,* Element, 1993

Mackenzie, Kenneth, *The Royal Masonic Cyclopedia* (1877), Aquarian Press, 1987

Mâle, Émile, *Notre Dame de Chartres,* Flammarion, 1983

Mâle, Émile, *The Gothic Image*, Fontana, 1961

Malmes, *History of the Kings*, (*Cesta regum Angelorum* – c. 1127) translated by J Sharpe and published by George Bell and sons, London, 1904

Marcel, Gabriel, *The Decline of Wisdom*, Harvill, 1956

Mathews, John, *The Grail Tradition*, Element Books, 1990

Maspero, Gaston, *Recueil des Travaux Relatifs a la Philologie et l'Archaeologie Egyptiennes et Assyriennes,* III, Paris 1878

Matrasso, Pauline (trans), *The Quest of the Holy Grail*, Penguin Classics, 1977

McIntosh, Christopher, *The Rosicrucians*, Red Wheel/Weiser Books, 1987

McManners, John (ed), *The Oxford History of Christianity*, OUP, 1993

Mertz, Blanche, *Points of Cosmic Energy*, C W Daniel, 1995

HRH Prince Michael of Albany, *The Forgotten Monarchy of Scotland*, Element Books, 1998

Midrash Bereshith Rabba (Genesis Rabba), Cambridge 1902

Miller, Malcolm, *Chartres Cathedral*, Pitkin Pictorials, 1992

Mitchell, Ann, *Cathedrals of Europe*, Hamlyn, 1996

Montfull, *Les Grandes Cathédrales*, PML, 1995

Moore, L David, *The Christian Conspiracy*, Pendulum Press, 1983

Moore, R I, *The Formation of A Persecuting Society,* Basil Blackwell & Co, 1990

Murphy, Roald, *Wisdom Literature,* Grand Rapids, Michigan, 1981

Murray, David Christie, *The History of Heresy*, OUP, 1976

N

Nicholson, Helen, *The Knights Templar*, Sutton Publishing, 2004

Nieuwbarn, M C, *Church Symbolism*, Sands and Co, 1910

O

Olivier, Dr Paul, *L'Ancienne Statue de Notre Dame de Puy*, 1921

O'Shea, Stephen, *The Perfect Heresy,* Profile Books Ltd, 2000

Osman, Ahmed, *Moses, Pharaoh of Egypt*, Paladin, 1991

Osman, A, *Stranger in the Valley of the Kings*, Freethought Press, 2001

Osman A, *Out of Egypt*, Century, 1998

Ouspensky, P D, *A New Model of the Universe,* London 1931

P

Parfitt, Will, *The Living Quaballah*, Element Books, 1988

Partner, Peter, *The Knights Templar and their Myth*, Destiny Books, 1990

Pauwels, Louis & Bergier, Jacques, *The Dawn Of Magic,* Gibbs & Phillips, 1963

Perrier, Jacques, *Notre Dame de Paris*, Paris, 1996

Petrie, F, *The Religion of Ancient Egypt* (1908), R A Kessinger Publishing Company, 2003

Philips, Graham, *The Moses Legacy,* Sidgewick & Jackson, 2002

Picknett & Prince, *The Templar Revelation,* Bantam, 1997

Powell, Mark Allen, *The Jesus Debate,* Lion Publishing, 1998

Previte-Orton, C W, *Outlines of Medieval History*, Biblo & Tannen Booksellers and Publishers, 1916

Proclus Diodachus (5th century AD*) Commentaries on the Timaeus*

Q

Querido, René, *The Masters of Chartres,* Floris Books, 1987

Querido, René, *The Golden Age of Chartres,* Floris Books, 1987

Querido, René, *The Mystery of the Holy Grail,* Rudolf Steiner College, 1991

R

Ranke-Heninemann, Ute, *Putting Away Childish Things,* HarperCollins, 1995

Raschi, *Pentatuque selon Rachi, La Genese,* Samule et Odette Levy, 1993

Raschi, *Pentatuque selon Rachi l'Exode,* Samuel et Odette Levy, 1993

Ravenscroft, Trevor, *The Spear of Destiny,* Samuel Weiser, 1982

Ravenscroft, Trevor, *The Cup of Destiny,* Samuel Weiser, 1982

Ravenscroft, Trevor & Wallace-Murphy, Tim, *The Mark of The Beast,* Sphere Books London, 1990

Reymond, E A E, *Mythical Origins of the Egyptian Temple*, Barnes & Noble, 1969

Rice, M, *Egypt's Making: The Origins of Ancient Egypt 5000–2000 BC*, London, 1990

Richardson, Peter, *Herod, King of the Jews and Friend of the Romans,* University of South Carolina Press, 1996

Robertson, Roland, *Sociology of Religion,* Penguin Books, 1969

Robinson, James M, (ed.), *The Nag-Hammadi Library,* HarperCollins, 1990

Robinson, John J, *Born in Blood,* Arrow Books 1993

Robinson, John J, *Dungeon, Fire and Sword,* Brock Hampton Press, 1999

Robinson, John, *The Priority of John,* SCM Press, 1985

Rohl, David M, *A Test of Time*, Century, London, 1995

Rohl, David, *Legend – the Genesis of Civilization*, Century, London 1998

Roth, Cecil, *A Short History of the Jewish People*, East West Library, London, 1953

Runciman, Stephen, *A History of the Crusades,* 3 vols, Pelican, 1971

S

Sabbah, M & R, *Les Secrets de L'Exode,* Godefroy, 2000

Saillens, Émile, *Nos Vierges Noires, Leurs Origines,* Paris, 1945

Schmitt, P, *Ancient Mysteries in the Society of Their Time. Their Transformation and most Recent Echoes*

Schonfield, Hugh, *The Essene Odyssey,* Element, 1985

Schonfield, Hugh, *The Pentecost Revolution,* Element, 1985

Schonfield, Hugh, *The Passover Plot,* Element, 1985

Schwaller de Lubicz, R A, *Le Temple de l'Homme,* Dervy Livres, 1977

Schwaller de Lubicz, R A, *Sacred Science,* HarperCollins, 1982

Schwaller de Lubicz, R A, *Symbol and the Symbolic,* Inner Traditions, 1978

Sellin, E, *Moses and his Significance for Israelite-Jewish History* (original German publication, Leipzig, 1922)

Sepher Hajasha, Prague, 1840

Shah, Idries, *The Sufis,* Jonathan Cape & Co, 1969

Shah, Idries, *The Way of The Sufi,* Penguin Books, 1982

Sinclair, Andrew, *The Sword and the Grail,* Crown Publishers, 1992

Sinclair, Andrew, *The Discovery of the Grail,* Century, 1998

Szekely, E B, *The Teachings of the Essene from Enoch to the Dead Sea Scrolls,* C W Daniel, 1978

Smith, Morton, *The Secret Gospel,* Aquarian Press, 1985

St Clair L-A de, *Histoire Gènealogique de la Famille de St Clair,* Paris, 1905

Starbird, Margaret, *The Woman with the Alabaster Jar,* Bear & Co, 1993

Starbird, Margaret, *The Tarot Trumps and the Holy Grail,* WovenWord Press, 2000

Stein, Walter Johannes, *The Ninth Century: World History in the Light of the Holy Grail,* Temple Lodge Publishing, 1991

Stevenson, David, *The First Freemasons,* Aberdeen University Press, 1989

Stourm, *Notre Dame d'Amiens,* Hachette, 1960

Stoyanov, Yuri, *The Hidden Tradition in Europe,* Arkana, 1994

Strachan, Gordon, *Chartres,* Floris Books, 2003

Swan, James A, *The Power of Place,* Quest Books, 1991

T

Taylor, Joan E, *The Immerser, John the Baptist in Second Temple Judaism,* Wm B Eerdmans Publishing Co, 1997

Taylor, Richard, *How to Read a Church,* Rider, 2004

Thiering, Barbara, *Jesus the Man,* Corgi, 1992

Trevor-Roper, Hugh, *The Rise of Christian Europe,* Thames and Hudson, 1965

U

Upton-Ward, J M, *The Rule of The Templars*, Boydell Press, 1992

V

VandenBroeck, Andre, *Al-Kemi*, Lindisfarne Press, 1987

Vermes, Geza, *Jesus the Jew*, Augsberg Fortress Publishing, 1981

Von Simson, O, *The Gothic Cathedral*, Princeton University Press, 1988

W

Waite, A E, *The Holy Kabbalah,* Oracle, 1996

Waite, A E, *A New Encyclopaedia of Freemasonry*, Wings Books, 1994

Wakefield, Walter and Evans, Austin P, *Heresies of Middle Ages,* Columbia University Press, 1991

Wallace-Murphy, Tim, *An Illustrated Guide Book To Rosslyn Chapel,* The Friends of Rosslyn, 1993

Wallace-Murphy, Tim, *The Templar Legacy and the Masonic Inheritance Within Rosslyn Chapel*, The Friends of Rosslyn 1994

Wallace-Murphy, Tim, & Hopkins, Marilyn, *Rosslyn: Guardian of the Secrets of the Holy Grail*, Element Books, 1999

Wallace-Murphy, T, Hopkins, M; Simmans, G, *Rex Deus*, Element Books, 2000

Wallace-Murphy, Tim & Hopkins, Marilyn; *Custodians of Truth* RedWheel/Weiser, 2005

Wallace-Murphy, Tim & Hopkins, Marilyn, *Templars in America*, RedWheel/Weiser, Boston 2004

Ward, Colin, *Chartres the Making of a Miracle*, Folio Society, 1986

Ward, J S M, *Freemasonry and the Ancient Gods*, R A Kessinger & Co, 1996

Weighall, A E P, *Travels in the Upper Egyptian Desert,* London, 1909

Weighall, A E P, *The Life and Times of Akenhaten*, London, 1910 & 1923

Welburn, Andrew, *The Beginings of Chrsitianity*, Floris, 1991

West, John Anthony, *Serpent in the Sky*, HarperCollins, 1979

Wind, Edgar, *Pagan Mysteries in the Renaissance*, Faber 1958

Wilson, A N, *Jesus*, HarperCollins, 1993

Wilson, A N, *Paul, the Mind of the Apostle*, Pimlico, 1998

Wilson, Colin (Ed.), *Men of Mystery*, W H Allen, London, 1977

Wilson, Colin, *The Occult*, Grafton Books, 1979

Wilson, Colin, *From Atlantis to the Sphinx*, Virgin Books, London 1997

Winkler H, *Rock Drawings of Southern Upper Egypt*, London, 1938/9

Woods, Richard (ed), *Understanding Mysticism*, Doubleday, 1980

Wright, Esmond, *The Medieval and Renaissance World*, Hamlyn, 1979

Index